A MESSAGE FROM THE AUTHOR

You now have in your possession some unique information never made available to the public before.

PROFESSIONAL SPORTS: The Community College Connection is a milestone for junior-community colleges as a whole, and particularly their past, present, and future student-athletes and coaches, and sports history.

In addition to this being the only book of its kind, another uniqueness is that it is a yardstick by which the two-year colleges can measure one aspect of their contributions to society. It is also designed for use as another public relations resource which can be used to provide information, promote understanding, goodwill, and rapport with the community and the public at large.

We hope that you will enjoy it and it will further enlighten you about the force of the junior-community colleges.

Winmar Press
Inglewood, California

PROFESSIONAL SPORTS: THE COMMUNITY COLLEGE CONNECTION

BY MANQUE WINTERS

Copyright © 1982 by Manque Winters

All rights reserved. No part of this publication may be reproduced, stored in a retrieval system, or transmitted, in any form or by any means, electronic, mechanical, photocopying, recording, or otherwise, without the prior written permission of the author.

Order from: WINMAR PRESS
5800 West Century Blvd.
P. O. Box 91157-1157
Los Angeles, CA 90009

Library of Congress Catalog No. 84-060113
First Printing, July 1984

Cover Design and Graphic Artist:
Beverly A. Hall

References

- *Junior-Community Colleges*
  - *Athletes*
    - *Amateur Accomplishments*
    - *Professional Accomplishments*
  - *Coaches*
  - *Governing Organizations*
  - *History*
  - *Intercollegiate Athletic Programs*
    - *Championships, Records, and Results*

ISBN # 0-9613253-1-3 (soft cover)
ISBN # 0-9613253-0-5 (hard cover)

Printed in the United States of America

To Ruby Boyd Winters
— My Mom, My Teacher, My Friend —
and to the
Junior-Community Colleges Athletic Association
Directors, Athletic Directors, Coaches,
and Athletes
whose dedication, service, and performance
have proven that their skills
rank among the best.

ABOUT THE AUTHOR

Manque Winters was employed as a Specialist in Student Personnel Services for the Chancellor's Office, California Community Colleges, Sacramento, California, where his various duties included research, studies, and reports pertaining to athletics and counseling. Some of his works were "Professional Athletics and Sports as a Major Course of Study," "Major Concerns in California Community College Athletics," "Vocational - Occupational Counseling in California Community Colleges," "Revision of Requirements for the Community College Counseling Credential," "An Analysis of Counseling in the California Community Colleges," "Profiles of Community College Students," and "Drug Instruction in the California Community Colleges."

He was Head Football Coach for the Sacramento Statesmen Semiprofessional Football Team for two years. The Statesmen won one championship and one second place.

After leaving the Chancellor's Office he served on the Statewide California Community Colleges Athletic Task Force.

His Ph.D. dissertation was a research of the "Attitudes of Selected Community College Students toward Athletic Programs for Professional Development." The thesis for his Master's Degree was "A Suggested Intramural Program for Fred C. Nelles School for Boys."

During his tenure at San Bernardino Valley College he served as Dean of Students — Men, Coordinator of Student Activities, and Assistant Football Coach. While employed by the Compton High School District, Compton, California, he served at Centennial Senior High School as Vocational - Occupational Counselor, and at Compton Senior High School as Classroom Instructor, Head Football Coach, Assistant Football and Baseball Coach, and Instructor in Driver Education and Driver Training. He has also served as an education counselor for the Urban League.

At the present time he is employed in the Los Angeles Community College District.

CONTENTS

Preface and Acknowledgements i

Chapter One
Introduction 1

Chapter Two
Athletic Governance and Activities 39

Chapter Three
A Good Beginning for
the Student-Athlete 61

Chapter Four
National Junior College Athletic
Association (NJCAA) Athletes
Reported to Have Attained the
Ranks of Professional Sports 107

Chapter Five
California Association of Community
Colleges (CACC) Athletes Reported
to Have Attained the Ranks of
Professional Sports 145

Chapter Six
Postscript:
A Case for Junior-Community
College Interscholastic Athletics 191

Notes 195

Appendix A
Geographic Locations of Members in the
National Junior College Athletic Association

Appendix B
National Junior College Athletic Association
History and Champions

Appendix C
Geographic Locations of California Community Colleges

Appendix D
California Community College Champions

PREFACE AND ACKNOWLEDGEMENTS

There is enough information on the accomplishments of junior-community college athletes to write a host of books. Hopefully, this one will engrave some of their names on the athletic scrolls, and also alert inquisitors and researchers to consider the junior - community colleges as one of the more consistent constituencies that grooms the world's best athletes. Hopefully, it will make junior - community - college educational decision makers more cognizant of the career opportunities that have been provided for a large number of persons, and afford them some guidance for future planning.

This book provides a view of the junior - community colleges from an athletic perspective. It provides visibility for the colleges, the athletic association directors, the athletic directors and coaches, faculties, staffs, and communities that have nurtured the athletic programs and the athletes to an unquestionable place in the annals of professional sports. The main characters — the foot soldiers — are the athletes, and this book highlights some of them who have brought recognition, excellence, and pride to a sometimes overlooked segment of education.

There are numerous other athletes who encountered the junior - community college intercollegiate athletic experience whose names do not appear in this book but they, too, are equally representative of this segment of education. Who knows — it could have been the powerful force of peer expectations, and most definitely their contributions, that pushed the others to the pinnacle. That is very probable because, unlike the great majority of other college disciplines, the one element which must exist is the team effort — the team spirit. And somewhere in the memories of those who did attain the ranks of professional sports are remembrances of the teams, and the contests.

Behind all of these athletes is the power and influence of great teachers and leaders — their coaches and athletic directors. Junior - community colleges are teaching — and service — institutions. That will be emphasized several times throughout this book. You will witness a statement made by a highly recognized leader in a major four-year institution which will assist in better understanding the community college role "you can teach at the freshman level, you can't afford to teach at the varsity level." As community - college athletes move into the spotlights of four-year institutions and professional sports, the laboratories from which they came, and their teachers, oftentimes go unrecognized.

One recognition will be *Professional Sports: The Community College Connection.* It will be a more vivid and lasting one because the subject of junior - community college interscholastic athletics — its history, growth, development, accountability, and accomplishments — can now be placed into the archives along with other public records and historical documents that give an accounting of the times. Also, when future generations search for an understanding of the role that community - college interscholastic athletic programs served, this information will be available. It will document the intimate relationships that these programs had in the total scope of athletics, and will assist junior - community - college coaches and athletic directors in achieving the immortality they deserve.

This treatise is long overdue. It is far-reaching in its implication, urgent for use in implementation, and clear why it needs to be included in the vast pool of information about two-year colleges and athletics.

After extensive research and concluding that an in-depth, scholarly approach to this subject was nonexistent, it was the opinion of advisors and the decision of the author that objectivity be one of the major concerns for this premiere publication. A documentary approach was considered to best serve that purpose. To maintain objectivity, extensive documentation from a wide range of resources — giving the views and opinions of persons at various levels — has been used throughout the book.

The scope of information in this book elevates it above the praise of a single person, college, organization, or region of the United States or its territories. The recognition belongs collectively to the two-year colleges.

The book is not complete. There are so many things to say and so many events that are constantly occurring which relate to the subject. The book will not please everyone. The omission of some names, the style used, the manner in which some information is presented, the inclusion of a discussion, or the absence of one —

some slight occurrence — will undoubtedly evoke harsh criticism. That will be unfortunate but when working within limited parameters that has to be expected.

It took several years to collect a representative number of names and additional information on junior - community athletes who had attained the ranks of professional sports. At various stages the information had to be returned to authorities for additions, corrections, and verification. When the information could not be verified at the most likely level, it was necessary to search for any clue to continue the research.

The author stood on the shoulders of many persons, organizations, and institutions to accomplish this task. The author also avowed not to let time or conflict obscure memories and, hopefully, that has not occurred.

George E. Killian, Director, National Junior College Athletic Association (NJCAA); Wayne Unruh, Assistant Director, and other members of the NJCAA staff were always available, extremely generous, and informative. Your assistance is deeply appreciated.

Lloyd E. Messersmith, Past Director of the California Community and Junior College Association (CCJCA), and the Committee on Athletics (COA) were extremely helpful. The name of the association has been changed to the California Association of Community Colleges — Committee on Athletics, with Walter Rilliet, Director. They gave me carte blanche to the office and staff. I am grateful to both.

I am deeply indebted to Lee Samuel Vokes of Hancock Community College, Santa Maria, California. We spoke on the telephone, corresponded, and exchanged dissertations. He gave me permission to copyright any parts of his dissertation. That I did. Practically all of the history, development, and governance of the California Association of Community Colleges (CACC) which appears in Chapter Two was taken from his work. His dissertation on the subject is one of a kind.

The junior - community - college administrators made encouraging gestures.

The four-year institution athletic directors and coaches were eager to share information.

John Wiebusch, editor, NFL Properties, Inc., (*Pro Magazine*), was extremely supportive and enthusiastic.

Professional sports offices and teams reviewed their records and assisted in various ways. The Los Angeles Express office was generous. Many thanks to Joan Cordone for paving the way, and

Kathleen Parray and Kevin Ash who made research material available to me. A special thanks to Tom Fears, Bob Rose, and Bruce Dworshak.

John Curley, editor, and Nancy Walsh of *USA Today* were kind and generous.

As you will see, Fred Baer, Director, JC Athletic Bureau, San Mateo, California, shared a great deal of information.

I am deeply indebted to Ray Franks, owner, editor, and publisher of the *National Directory of College Athletics*, for granting use of information he has accumulated.

Cheryl Preston, Permissions Coordinator, *Los Angeles Times*, worked enthusiastically in instructing me about the use of articles. The depth of my appreciation would be difficult to express.

From Sacramento, California, assistance was provided by Glen Crevier, Staff Writer, *The Sacramento Union*, and Gary Voet, Staff Writer, *The Sacramento Bee*.

Mike Fleming, Staff Writer, *The Commercial Appeal*, Memphis, Tennessee, and Joanne Bliss, City of Inglewood Library, Inglewood, California, provided the information about the 1982 Liberty Bowl and Coach Paul "Bear" Bryant.

My sincere thanks to Joseph B. Iantorno, Dean of Students, College of the Desert, Palm Desert, California. When we worked together at San Bernardino Valley College, San Bernardino, California, he helped me to understand the purpose and mission of the community colleges. We have collaborated through the years and he assisted with reading and coordinating the material for this book.

My gratitude to Lloyd McCullough, Research Consultant, Sacramento, California, for planting the seed for this publication by helping me to see the need for a book of this type. He assisted with the initial planning and early direction.

Gene Mazzei, Head Football Coach, San Bernardino Valley College, San Bernardino, California, was always willing to share the information he had gathered and was equally willing to read the various drafts of the manuscript.

I would like to acknowledge the helpfulness of Clarence Mangham, Administrator of Innovative Programs, Chancellor's Office, Sacramento, California, who shared the knowledge he had gained over many years. His contributions were particularly helpful since they were an outgrowth of his experience as a community - college instructor and administrator, an adminsitrator at the state level, and also, an administrator at the national level — the American Association of Community and Junior Colleges, Washington D.C.

A multitude of tasks are involved in an effort such as this, including (but not limited to): questionnaire construction, filling and stamping envelopes, mailing, logging responses, tabulating returned information, alphabetizing names, filing, typing (over and over again), telephoning, transcribing information from taped interviews, information search, and proofreading. Acknowledgements must be made to the many persons who assisted with these efforts:

Dorris Davis Bell	Jackie Robbins
Beatrice Sumlin Blackwell	Luther Robinson
Chandra Cowans	Art, Leona, and Dale White
Countess T. Henderson	Angela Winters
Venus Jones Jordan	Pamela Winters
R. Mary Powell	Manque Winters, Jr.

There were directions from persons who had published, or had worked closely with persons who had published. These were invaluable resources:

Malachi Andrews	Mamie Hansberry Mitchell
Mae Pendleton Cowans	Paul Owens
Claudette D. Hill	Juanita Scott
Doris A. Holmes	M. Elizabeth Stallworth

My colleagues in health and physical education at Los Angeles Southwest (Community) College, Los Angeles, California, were extremely cooperative:

David Adams	Phyllis I. Keeney (Chairperson)
Danny Daniels	Benson L. Marsh
Nancy D. Easland	Wonda Power-Thorton
Frank J. Garnett	Janice Riggs
Richard Gatlin	Anthaneha "Toni" Rhodes
Leon Henry	Dorothy Strickland
Margaret Herwig (Emeriti)	Henry Washington

I was fortunate to have worked with Lawrence Jarmon, Athletic Director, Los Angeles Southwest (Community) College. His knowledge, skill, experience, and broad participation with other institutions and organizations, opened many doors.

Those persons who participated in the early stages of the search for names of junior - community - college athletes who attained the ranks of professional sports were:

Marvin Boyd	Sports enthusiast.
Lawrence Jarmon	Attended JC, and played with the Chicago Bears.
Ivan McKinney	Attended JC, and now Principal at Valley High School, Santa Ana, California.
Ron Mims	Attended JC, and was head football coach at Los Angeles Southwest (Community) College. Presently, he is assistant coach at the University of Nevada, Las Vegas.
Willard "Billy" Newton	Sports enthusiast.
Homer Post	Attended JC, and played with the New England Patriots.

Clem Brzoznowski, owner, C & C Instant Press, Inglewood, California, provided his knowledge and services, and the use of his facilities and equipment — many times during irregular hours — to assist with the lithographic needs for this book.

Jewell Hart, J.D., contributed his expertise by interpreting permission agreements and various other legal concerns.

Floye Perkins assisted with all tasks and kept things moving during the author's forced hiatus.

A very special thanks to Jessie Levine, Professional Editor, Los Angeles, California, for the final editing. We have worked together for 19 years and I am grateful for her support and friendship.

Finally, in San Bernardino, Dana Mazzei, Stacey's Book Store, introduced me to Dick and Kathy Thompson, The Book Attic Press. They, in turn, introduced me to Helen Curtis. With the assistance of all of these individuals, the book has become a reality.

M. W.

Inglewood, California

Chapter One
INTRODUCTION

Since their ignoble birth in the high school in Joliet, Illinois, in 1901, community colleges have been addressed with praise, ambivalence, and mockery. They have been called "the most democratic higher education institutions," "the people's college," "the poor man's college," "the bastard child of the educational world," and "high schools with ash trays," among others. Whatever their label, and whatever stigma imposed, they have surpassed their original expectations. They have embraced millions of students and provided them with guidance, direction, and opportunity.

Community colleges are two-year institutions. Having been referred to as junior colleges at the time of their inception, throughout the years they have also been addressed as "JCs" (jaycees), "community colleges," "city colleges," and "juco's," among other terms. The reader will notice that in this work the terms community - junior college, junior community college, junior college, community college, JC, and juco are used interchangeably. The author has chosen to use these terms throughout as each one seems to represent the mission of these institutions in carrying out their transfer, occupational preparation, and community services functions. In addition, each term appropriately represents the large number of institutions which, for one reason or another, prefers to be referred to as community college, junior college, or city college.

A popular belief is that the JCs continue to lack the "spotlight" they truly deserve. For years there has been a call for full equality and unity, and the full recognition and worth for their diversified work, as in other segments of higher education. This is not to imply that there has been a complete lack of these elements, for if there were the jaycees would never have reached their present level of development. Some unity and cooperation are demonstrated through the transfer program and other ventures. In spite of these efforts Ms. Wallace Albertson, Los Angeles Community College Board of Trustees, feels that "the community colleges have got to continue to make their visibility known. They've got to continue to let people know who they are and what they are all about."[1]

Community colleges have been an impetus in the lives of persons in various occupations. Through their portals have come persons such as:

NAME	COMMUNITY COLLEGE ATTENDED	POSITION HOLDING/HELD
Adams, Jean	Kilgore (TX)	Nationally syndicated columnist
Blumenthal, Michael W.	San Francisco City (CA)	Former Secretary of the Treasury
Donovan, Thomas	Wright (IL)	Assistant to Mayor, Chicago, IL
Duncan, Sandy	Lon Morris (TX)	Television and movie actress
Freitag, Robert F.	Jackson (MS)	Aerospace pioneer; Deputy Director, Advanced Programs, NASA
Goldberg, Arthur	Crane (now Malcolm X) (IL)	Former Supreme Court Justice and former Ambassador to U.N.
Lokas, Demetrio B.	Canal Zone (Panama)	President of Panama (1972-1978)
Norwood, Billy	Henderson (TX)	Owner, Bill Jones Oil Company and 3-N Ranches
Owens, Gary	Washtenaw (MI)	State Representative, MI (Associate Speaker Pro Tem)
Parissi, Robert	Jefferson (OH)	Member of Rock Group "Wild Cherry"
Perkins, Carl D.	Lees (KY)	Congressman
Simpson, Lee	Niagara (NY)	Legislator, Chairman of Education Committee, Niagara County

There have been innumerable others who made their initial investment in higher education at the two-year colleges. They came with — or acquired while there — a variety of desires, dreams, aspirations, objectives, and goals. Some were in pursuit of the traditional professions, occupational / vocational, or entrepreneur careers. Some pursued non-traditional kinds of careers or "human performances," and attended colleges with outstanding reputations in certain fields or where there were teachers with outstanding reputations or skills. The students came with varying

Pete Rozelle, Commissioner, National Football League (NFL), attended Compton JC (CA), in the early 1940s. While at Compton, a basketball teammate was Duke Snyder who later pitched for The Dodgers and was inducted into the Baseball Hall of Fame.   *Photo courtesy NFL.*

degrees of emotional and social intensity and, for whatever reasons, the selection of the two-year-college system and/or the teacher was the ultimate expression of belief, faith and hope.

Some desires, dreams, aspirations, objectives, and goals were to attain various levels in sports. Many accomplished that and won the top honors and awards — All-Conference, All-American, Heisman Trophy, The Athletic Congress (TAC) previously called the Amateur Athletic Union (now labeled TAC/AAU), and Olympic participants, record holders and champions.

There is much evidence to support the belief that sports/athletics is part of the heritage of the junior-community colleges. Consider this historical outlook: in 1901, Joliet, Illinois, became the first junior college. However, in 1907, California was the first state to enact legislation for the establishment of junior colleges, and in 1910 Fresno became the first junior college in the U. S. — by law. The earliest data about junior college intercollegiate athletics (discussed in more detail in Chapter Two) stated that California founded a statewide conference in 1922. Of particular interest is the fact that both two- and four-year colleges were in the conference. By 1930, California JCs were engaging in a variety of activities and were being recognized for their outstanding intercollegiate athletic programs. By 1937 they were so phenomenal in track and field it prompted them to strive for national recognition, by requesting to participate in the National Collegiate Athletic Association (NCAA) track and field championships. They were turned down by the NCAA and in 1938 the two-year colleges founded the National Junior College Athletic Association (NJCAA).

With this historical outlook in mind, one theory that proposed sports/athletics is a part of the heritage of junior colleges is the fact that they were born, created, and grew at a time in American history in which there was a great deal of emphasis on — among many other things — sports/athletics and athletes. It was during the time of:

- Walter Chauncey Camp (1859-1925) "the father of American football." During that period he introduced the forward pass, which became legal in 1906, and later he decided the names of players who had attained the highest level in football — the All American.
- Glenn Scobey "Pop" Warner (1871-1954), football coach and football pioneer.

- Knute Kenneth Rockne (1888-1931), football coach and football pioneer.
- James "Jim" Francis Thorpe (1888-1953), athlete (football, track, and baseball). Was selected football All American two consecutive years — 1911 and 1912. Participated in the 1920 Olympics (Stockholm, Sweden), winning both the pentathlon and the decathlon.
- Harold Edward "Red" Grange, "The Galloping Ghost." University of Illinois All American three consecutive years — halfback in 1923 and 24, and quarterback in 1925.

Professional sports had emerged only a few years before that period.

Sports were engulfing the established, four-year colleges, and in order to maintain some degree of control of these rampant activities, the National Collegiate Athletic Association (NCAA) was formed about 1905. Within just a few years many other sports were added to the college athletic programs.

- Football bowl games began to emerge during this period: Rose Bowl (1902), Orange Bowl (1933); Sugar Bowl (1935), and the Cotton Bowl (1937).
- The Heisman Trophy became the ultimate award for collegiate football achievement (1935).
- Boxing, somewhat as it is today — with gloves, began in 1892 and gained greatly in popularity between 1920 and 1930.
- Media began to give sports a great deal of attention. Sports broadcasting, the sports announcers, and sports commentators became popular during the 1920s.
- It was the time of Helen Wills, Jack Johnson, Jessie Owens, Bobby Jones, Ty Cobb, Babe Ruth, and Mildred "Babe" Didrikson.

Sports, athletics, athletes, health and physical education, recreation, parks and playgrounds were the height of ideas at that time. In fact, the period between 1920 and 1930 is historically referred to as the Golden Age of Sports. The four-year institutions acquired the activities that were developing during that period. The junior colleges were born into those activities. Sports/athletics was part of their heritage.

The roots of junior - community colleges are in that specific period. They grew, developed, and performed in accordance with the culture — the minds, the body of knowledge, morals, characteristics, and conditions — of that generation. That generation passed on its ideas to the next, and this book documents that the junior - community colleges were at the height of their time — more particularly, at the height of the level of ideas of their time.

Further evidence which supports the fact that junior - community colleges emerged ready to serve the nation in the area of sports / athletics can be observed from an article published by Pasadena City College. In one portion of that article, Norka Manning, Public Information Officer, wrote:[2]

PCC OLYMPIANS: PAST AND PRESENT
by Norka Manning, Public Information Officer,
Pasadena City College

For the second time this century, Los Angeles will host the modern Olympic Games. Fifty-two years have elapsed since the city first welcomed athletes from around the world in 1932.

International athletes will once again convene in the greater Los Angeles area at the 1984 XXIII Olympiad. Only a nation's best athletes are traditionally selected to participate in the world games.

Pasadena City College is privileged to have past and present Olympic competitors among its family of former students and staff. The following personal profiles have been written in honor of their singular accomplishments.

PCC salutes Olympics competitors Mack Robinson [older brother of Jackie Robinson whose accomplishments are recounted later in this chapter] *(Class of 1937), Roland Sink (business professor), Nick Martin (foreign languages associate professor), and 1984 Games participant John Siman (Class of 1972), who was coached at PCC by Martin.* [Emphasis added.]

Mack Robinson, 1936

Running, which he said came "naturally" to him, catapulted PCC alumnus Mack Robinson into the world limelight and brought him, if not acclaim, an undeniable place in sports history.

One of five children, Mack grew up in the Depression Era. His parents were separated, and the family endured hardships. In order to attend track meets, Mack said he always had to find the "ways and means to get there." Get there he did.

Faded newsreels attest to Robinson's Silver medal winning feat at the 1936 Olympic games held in Berlin, Germany. Standing on the winners' platform alongside fellow American and Gold medal winner Jesse Owens, Robinson recalls the "indescribable good feeling" he experienced when the U. S. national anthem was played during the awards.

Overshadowing the American athletes' legendary accomplishments was the notoriety given to Adolph Hitler's seeming snub of the victors.

Mack Robinson, silver medal winner in the 200 meter track event. *Photo courtesy Pasadena City College.*

Robinson, now 69 and retired, recalls little of the incident and attributes the ensuing uproar to media hype. "Hitler had nothing to do with the Olympics. The games were controlled by the International Olympic Committee," he affirms. "Hitler did his own thing. He didn't speak for all his countrymen."

Before making the Olympic team, Robinson entered the qualifying trials held in Los Angeles. There, he broke Eddie Tolan's 1932 Olympic record in the 200 meter run with a time of 21.1 seconds.

At the national trials held later that year in New York, Robinson raced against Jesse Owens of Ohio State who set a new world record running the 200 meter event in 21 seconds flat.

At Berlin, Owens won the Gold with a new record of 20.7 seconds. Robinson placed only four-tenths of a second behind Owens to win the Silver Medal. "I pushed him to set two new world records," said Robinson.

After touring Europe where American team members were hailed and treated as honored guests, Robinson recalls the sharp contrast of his homecoming. After arriving in New York to a reception by the city, the team was disbanded, and each athlete went home separately.

Robinson returned to his Pasadena home and to disappointment. There was no official recognition of his recent Olympic triumph. "It just didn't appear to be too important to the community," he reflects.

Two years after his world victory, and with three years of college behind him, Robinson found work as a sewer cleaner for the City of Pasadena. For the next four years, he swept the city streets at night. "I was never too proud to work at any job."

Describing himself as a "common laborer," Robinson held a succession of jobs over the years, including washing and polishing cars. He successfully managed to provide for his family of 10 children, the youngest of whom is now 16.

Soft-spoken and articulate, Robinson never succumbed to bitterness for what he perceived as a pervasive national prejudice. Life after the Olympics continued to be a struggle, admits Robinson, but he said, "I never gave up."

Part of this attitude was developed after Robinson's Olympic victory. While visiting at the home of an aunt, Robinson overheard two children racing around the house say, "I'm Jesse Ownes, and you're Mack Robinson."

"I realized they were emulating us. The youngsters were looking up to me. I've tried since then to be an example and live a clean and decent life," he said.

Although never having obtained formal recognition for his Olympic feat, Robinson, in later years, has been asked to speak at numerous area civic organizations.

When addressing young people, Robinson points to his own experience. "What I've achieved, I've worked for. I earned it.

"I tell young people that whatever they earn, they're willing to fight to keep. If things are given to you, you won't."

While a student at PCC in 1936 and 1937, Robinson excelled in the 100 yard dash, the 220 low hurdles, long jump and mile relay. He set a school record in the long jump of 25'5¼".

After his PCC studies, Robinson attended the University of Oregon. There, he was Pacific Coast Champion in the 200 yard low hurdles and long jump events. In 1938, he was also National AAU 200 meter Champion.

Robinson's athletic feats have won him induction into the PCC Hall of Fame, Drake University Hall of Fame (inducted at its formation in 1959), and the University of Oregon Hall of Fame.

Roland Sink, 1948

Sometimes, a little adversity works for you.

As a 22 year old, Roland Sink stood 5'7" tall and weighed a slight 137 pounds. His stature masked a formidable endurance.

A contestant at the 1948 London Olympic games, he became one of the few Americans to compete in the 1500 meter run (metric mile), an event dominated at the time by Europeans.

Rigorous conditioning won Roland Sink a place on the 1948 U. S. Olympic track team, competing in the 1500 meter run. *Photo courtesy Pasadena City College.*

Now a PCC business professor, Sink's training for the Wembley Stadium contest began years earlier. His conditioning was a result of Depression Era hardship and youthful priorities.

Sink was given 10 cents every day to use as bus fare home from school. Instead of boarding the bus, however, he would walk the two miles and pocket the money to buy candy and go to the movies. His mother soon discovered the plot because he got home late. She insisted that he hurry home on the bus to study and do homework.

Not wanting to give up his "spending money," Sink, then 12 years old, decided he'd run alongside the bus instead of riding in it.

"I noticed that the bus would stop every one or two blocks to let people on and off. I decided if I ran behind it, I could catch up at the stops," he said.

Since his own stop was two blocks from home, he had time to rest and catch his breath. He kept up this routine for two years and ran in all types of weather. The bus, estimates Sink, traveled at 30 mph. "I got to where I could tie or beat the bus to the stops."

It was this conditioning which helped him develop the tremendous stamina essential for distance running.

In high school, Sink became a mile champion. Later, he impressed USC coaches by breaking the university's record in the mile the very first time he ran the track. As a USC student, Sink was a national champion, high point winner, and captain of the track team.

During his sophomore and junior years in college, Sink was plagued with injuries sustained in training and was out for the season.

"I couldn't figure out what I was doing wrong, so I started thinking about all the times I ran home from school without getting hurt. I finally realized that I used to pace myself in order to keep up with the bus.

"When I started working out again at the track, I dressed in regular clothes and wore my tennis shoes. Each time I ran, I pretended I was racing a bus." The strategy worked.

Chosen as a member of America's track team to the first Olympic games held following the end of World War II, Sink set two goals for himself. He wanted to set a new world record by breaking the four minute mile, and he wanted to win the Olympics.

At the games, he placed fourth behind Sweden's Henri Eriksson who won the Gold. Undaunted, Sink said, "I almost made it."

Competing with athletes who were three to four years older, stronger, and more experienced, Sink distinguished himself in an event which has seldom been won by an American.

The feeling of great national pride and the impressive Olympic Opening and Closing ceremonies remain among Sink's most vivid memories. His participation in the games had a profound effect.

"It's a great cultural exchange. All the athletes lived together in the Olympic village. It gave me an understanding of people I never had before and eliminated a lot of biases," he said.

While abroad, Sink anchored the American four mile relay team in a post Olympics meet and raced against England's anchorman Dr. Roger Bannister, the first runner to crack the four minute mile. The American team won.

Four years later, Sink was a Naval coach at the Helsinki Olympics and served as an official for the U. S. track team.

While proud of his Olympics participation, Sink considers himself a "novice" athlete and concedes, "Mack Robinson is truly a champion.

. . .

The portion of this article about Nick Martin and John Siman will appear later in this chapter under "Aquatics."

There are others who became top competitors in track and field. Among them:[3]

Athlete	Community College	Olympic Year	Event
Charlie Dumas	Compton (CA)	1956	High Jump
Cornelius Johnson	Compton (CA	1936	
Earline Brown	Compton (CA)	1958	Shot Put
Ken Carpenter	Compton (CA)	1936	Discus
John Rambo	Long Beach CC (CA)	1964	High Jump

According to the JC Athletic Bureau, some athletes were National (TAC/AAU) champions while junior - community college students. San Jose City College (CA) records the following:[4]

1966 — Lee Evans (440), succeeded Ollan Casell as champion. (Evans also won in 1967, 1968, 1969, and 1982; double Olympic Gold '68 with still existing world records for 400 meters and 4x400 relay).

1976 — Millard Hampton (200) — won Olympic Silver in 200 and Gold in 4x100 relay that summer.

Other national champions produced by San Jose CC: Shot Put, Dave Laut (1979, 1981, 1983). Also 1981, NCAA 400 IH champ Andre Phillips (TAC runner-up that year).

Some other national (TAC/AAU) champions include: James Robinson, Laney, 800 — 1976, 1978, 1979, 1980, 1981, 1982); Doug Padilla, Chabot, 5000 — 1983; Francie Larrieu, De Anza, 1500 — 1972, 1973 (mile), 1976, 1977, 1979, 1980; 3000 — 1979, 1982.

Continuing, the JC Athletic Bureau also reported:[5]

PETRANOFF SYMBOLIC OF COMMUNITY COLLEGE IMPACT ON WORLD OF TRACK & FIELD

Tom Petranoff has joined Lee Evans out of San Jose City College (43.86) on the list of former junior / community college trackmen who hold world records.

Others who have held world records include discus thrower John Powell, American River (Community) College of Sacramento, and 1968 Olympic pole vault champion Bob Seagren, Mt. San Antonio (Community) College of Walnut.

While Evans and Seagren won Olympic gold medals in '68, world 100 (m) record holder Eddie Hart (Contra Costa) did so in 1972 (400 meter relay). Arnie Robinson (San Diego Mesa) improved from a long jump bronze medal in 1972 to take the Olympic gold in

1976. Also in 1976, Millard Hampton, while a student at San Jose City College (training alongside Bruce Jenner), took the Olympic silver medal in the 200 meters and won a gold on the 400 relay.

Current American shot put co-record holder Dave Laut is also out of San Jose CC, as is top-ranked U. S. 400 intermediate hurdler Andre Phillips.

James Robinson from Oakland's Laney College, is still the national JC 800 meter record holder and has been America's leading two-lap runner four times (including the present).

Current NCAA pole vault champion Dave Kenworthy of USC is from Cerritos (Community) College in Norwalk, while former world indoor record holder Dan Ripley vaulted for Cypress (Community) College and is currently an assistant coach at Mt. San Antonio.

Tyke Peacock won the World Cup title and was No. 1 ranked in the world in 1981 as a student at Modesto JC. (But Milton Goode of College of Alameda leaped 7-5¼ to beat Peacock for the 1981 California CC title and was ranked No. 3 in the USA that season, just behind Dwight Stones.)

Former national JC triple jump record holder Mike Marlow (Consumnes River) is the 1983 USA leader in that event, while Byron Criddle (Contra Costa), who took Marlow's record away with a 54-3¼ leap in the 1982 state meet, is one of the leading collegians for Houston in 1983. ... National JC javelin record holder Mark Murro (273-0) of Mesa Community College (AZ) was the first American to throw 300 feet — so the community colleges have now produced two of the only three Americans to hit that mark.

AQUATICS[6]

Junior - community colleges have made significant contributions to the Olympics in the aquatic sports — swimming, diving, and water polo. Many sources revealed that the coaches and athletes have been prominent figures in the growth, expansion, popularity, and development of specialized knowledge and skills which have made them international competitors.

Because California has a conducive climate, numerous facilities, a large number of high schools participating in these sports, and several swimming clubs, it became a leading state in the aquatic sports. Many of the early developers were from California. Among the junior - community college coaches were Bill Antilla, San Joaquin Delta (then Stockton College), who spearheaded the movement in northern California, and James "Jimmie" Smith, Fullerton College, and Urho Saari, El Camino College, his counterparts in southern California.

They perpetuated the idea, and reality, of excellence in the water sports. The torch was passed to other coaches: Art Lambert, DeAnza College; Monte Nitzkowski, Long Beach City College;

Nort Thornton, Foothill College; Ron Ballatore, Pasadena City College; Jack Flanagan, Diablo Valley College, and others.

According to Bob Horn, Water Polo Coach, University of California Los Angeles (UCLA), James R. "Jimmie" Smith is "The Father of United States Water Polo." Smith's 62 years in this sport includes 31 years at Fullerton Community College as a physical education teacher, and water polo, swimming, and diving coach. Both Horn and Smith have been inducted into the Water Polo Hall of Fame.

Smith published the first textbook in the world on water polo, *Playing and Coaching Water Polo* (1936), revised in 1948, now out of print. He originated, designed, and published the first swimming, diving, and water polo scorebook. He also coached the second Pan American Games in 1955 in Mexico City (winning a Silver Medal).

The ex-Fullerton Community College mentor, now in his late seventies and retired, has written three books that are scheduled to be published in July 1984: *World Encyclopedia of Water Polo*, *Water Polo in the Olympic Games*, and *Water Polo in the United States*.

From his publications and personal conversations, Smith has contributed a great deal of information about water polo. Thirty - five of his former Fullerton Community College students became active aquatic coaches in educational institutions. Among those presently coaching are Bob Horn (previously mentioned), Water Polo Coach, UCLA; Rick Rowland, Water Polo and Swimming Coach, Pepperdine University (CA); and Kenneth Monte Nitzkowski, Swimming and Water Polo Coach, Long Beach City College (CA).

A Few Deserved Notes About Monte Nitzkowski

Nitzkowski has been active in five Olympics: as a participant in 1952, and four times as a coach — 1968, 1972 (Bronze Medal), 1980 (the U. S. boycotted), and 1984.

He had an outstanding swimming career at Fullerton Community College for two years and after transferring to UCLA he became captain of the swimming team, and finally an All-American. He hitched up with Smith again on the Navy — Los Alamitos — water polo team and from that experience, Nitzkowski was chosen to participate in the 1952 Olympics.

During his 22 years at Long Beach City College, as water polo coach, his team has won six state championships, set four American records, and numerous community college records. If there is any truth in the belief that competition drives one to greatness, Nitzkowski's community college opponents should be given a great deal of recognition.

One needs only to review the list of Olympic Water Polo Coaches to fully appreciate the junior - community college impact upon this sport.

Year	Olympic Coach
1936	Clyde Swendsen
1948	Austin Clapp
1952	Urho Saari (El Camino College)
1956	*Neil Kohlhase
1960	Neil Kohlhase
	Urho Saari, Manager
1964	Urho Saari (El Camino College)
1968	Art Lambert (DeAnza College)
	Monte Nitzkowski, Ass't Coach
	(Long Beach City College)
1972	Monte Nitzkowski (Long Beach City College)
1976	(United States did not qualify)
1980	(United States boycotted the Olympics)
1984	Monte Nitzkowski (Long Beach City College)

*Neil Kohlhase was on James "Jimmie" Smith's 1952 National Outdoor Championship Water Polo Team (Naval Air Station - Los Alamitos).

Ken Pivernetz, Staff Writer, *Press-Telegram* (Long Beach), wrote:[7]

> Nitzkowski, the long-time Long Beach City College instructor, says the team that will go to Caracas "is within one or two players of making up the Olympic team."
>
> He says the Pan Am Games will be especially important for Gary Figueroa, John Swendsen, and Tim Shaw who were not on the FINA Cup team.
>
> ... In addition to Shaw, another Wilson High Alumnus, Jody Campbell, will represent the United States at the Pan Am Games. Terry Schroeder, Peter Campbell, Doug Burke, Joe Vargas, Kevin Robertson, John Siman and Drew McDonald are the other field players. Craig Wilson and Steve Hamann are the goalies.

Joe Vargas, mentioned in the article above, was on the intercollegiate water polo team at Mt. San Antonio Community College, Walnut, CA.

John Siman, also mentioned in the previous article, attended Pasadena City College, Pasadena, CA. Both he and Nick Martin were interviewed by Norka Manning, who shared the following:[8]

John Siman, 1984

"I couldn't live with myself if I didn't give it a shot."

The words are deliberate and spoken with the conviction derived from thorough soul - searching.

At 31, PCC alumnus John Siman, named to America's 1984 Olympic Water Polo team, is the second oldest player on the squad. His decision to try for Olympic competition was not easy and took an entire year of deliberation.

Siman had set his sights on the Olympics once before. The year was 1976, and he began training earnestly for the 1980 Moscow Olympics. A member of the national water polo team, then rated number two internationally, Siman said America's chances for winning the gold looked good.

Politics intruded into Siman's hopes and life, along with those of other Olympic athletes, when America boycotted the Moscow games.

"I basically hung it up. When it didn't happen, I felt shortchanged," said Siman, who left the country to live in Australia for six months.

After coming back home, Siman settled into a routine of working and participating in national tournament play.

As the 1984 Los Angeles Olympics drew nearer, however, Siman and other 1980 team members began to smell the gold. Disillusionment began to give place to excitement and determination.

"We've worked so hard together at being the best. We want to dominate the other teams," said Siman. A fierce competitor, he places small value in being second. "Second place is not the same. The games will determine who's best," he said.

Nine of the 13 original 1980 team members make up the 1984 team. The players' average age (including two in their early twenties) is 28. Siman plays defense and at 6'6" is the tallest player. Most water polo athletes are much smaller. Siman's height is not necessarily an advantage. "Water is an equalizer. Everyone's the same height in the water," he points out.

In international competition, the American water polo team placed sixth at a 1982 European tournament and placed fourth this year against the world's top eight teams at the FINA cup trials in Malibu. The team most recently won a Gold Medal at the Pan American Games held in August.

Siman played water polo for PCC in 1971-72 and continued the sport at Cal State Fullerton, where he earned a teaching certificate in physical education.

Like all Olympic competitors, Siman holds amateur standing and is self-supporting. To meet his expenses, Siman said, "I work as hard as I can in the fall so I can compete." He estimates he loses about $500 a week during the water polo season.

Currently a partner in a home kitchen and bathroom remodeling business, Siman said he seriously considered his options before trying out for the '84 team.

"I spent a great deal of time thinking about it. I evaluated what it would cost me, and it took me a whole year to make up my mind," he said.

Today, Siman's decision is set. "The only thing on my mind is the Gold Medal. It's everything I want. Everything else is irrelevant.

. . .

Nick Martin, 1952 and 1956

PCC water polo coach and associate professor of foreign languages Nick Martin is a study in contrast. A world class athlete and competitor in two modern Olympiads, he is also a languages scholar, member of Phi Beta Kappa, and holds a Ph.D. from prestigious Princeton University.

A naturalized American citizen, Martin became a permanent resident of the U. S. after the 1956 Hungarian Revolution.

Martin, a center / forward, was a member of Hungary's unprecedented Gold Medal winning Olympic Water Polo teams of 1952 and 1956. Unbeaten in Helsinki in '52, the team was unscored against at the Melbourne games in '56. The feat listed the team in the Guiness Book of World Records as the "winningest water polo team of all time."

Perhaps even more memorable than the team's phenomenal record in Melbourne, was the fierce water battle that erupted during the last game between the Russian and Hungarian teams. The competition took on strong political overtones as the Russians, trailing Hungary 4-0, carried the brewing national conflict into the water.

"A tremendous fight broke out. The Russian players were calling us names. Soon the water was bloodied," said Martin. One Hungarian player had his face completely cut open. Officials stopped the game. The crowd was outraged.

"It was a tremendous scandal. The public outcry was so strong, the Russians couldn't get out of the water for hours. The police were finally called to escort them out," recalls Martin.

The Hungarian team's triumphs also brought Martin personal recognition. At the 1954 European Championships held in Turin, Italy, Martin was voted Most Valuable Player. In a dazzling display, Martin scored six consecutive goals during the second half of the emotionally charged playoff game.

"It was a chain reaction. After the third shot, I didn't know what I was doing. It was a near perfect game," he said.

Martin's performance and that of his teammates was so spectacular, that the very partisan Italian spectators were completely won over and uncharacteristically cheered and applauded the Hungarian players.

As a member of the Hungarian water polo team, Nick Martin won two gold medals.
Photo courtesy Pasadena City College.

After his final Olympic competition, Martin won the first water polo scholarship awarded by USC. Collegiate play proved anticlimactic, and Martin pursued his academic studies.

He earned a B.A. degree from USC in French literature and transferred to Princeton with a Woodrow Wilson Fellowship to complete graduate work.

Martin obtained both his masters and doctorate degrees from Princeton and completed advanced studies at the Sorbonne in Paris.

Despite his academic achievements, having twice stood on the Olympic winner's platform, Martin said the experience is unequaled.

"It compares to nothing."

. . .

Further research revealed additional Olympic contenders who had participated in junior-community college intercollegiate water polo.[9]

Name	Community College	Olympic Year	Olympic Team
John Gilcrest	Fullerton	1952	Canadian
Bob Westen	Santa Ana	1956	U. S.
Gary Ilman	Foothill	1964	U. S.
Ingmar Ericcson	Foothill	1964/68	Swedish
Ralph Hutton	Foothill	1964/68/72	Canadian
Peter Feil	Foothill	1968	Swedish
Ray Rivero	West Valley	1968	U. S.
Ken Campbell	Foothill	1972	Canadian
Susy Atwood	Long Beach City	1972	U. S.
Shirley Babasholf	Foothill West	1972/76	U. S.
Bob Jackson	Foothill	1976	U. S.

Other water polo participants in the Olympic games who had backgrounds in junior-community college competition were:[10]

Name	Community College	Olympic Year
Rutledge "Bob" Bray	Fullerton	1948
Devere W. Christensen	Fullerton	1948
Monte Nitzkowski	Fullerton	1952
Marvin "Ace" D. Burns	Fullerton	1952/56/60
Bob Hughes	El Camino	1952/56
Norman Dornblaser	El Camino	1952
Bob Horn	Fullerton	1956/60
William Ross	Los Angeles City	1956
Ronald Severa	Compton	1956/60
Gordon Hall	Compton	1960
Ronald Vollmer	Compton	1960
David Ashleigh	Cerritos	1964/68
John Parker	Foothill	1968/72
James Kruse	Fullerton	1976
Joe Vargas	Mt. San Antonio	1980/84

Among the Olympic participants in aquatic sports, the following should also be mentioned:[11]

Name	Sport	Year
Mel Griffin (an official)	Rowing	1932
Pat McCormick	Diving	1952 (Gold)
		1956 (Gold)
Jim Kelsey	Water Polo	1960
Charles Bittick	Water Polo	1960
Ron Crawford	Water Polo	1960
Susie Atwood	Swimming	1968 (Silver)
		1972 (Bronze)
Ann Simmons	Swimming	1972

RODEO[12,13]

Rodeo is a popular sport in many educational institutions and, again, the junior - community colleges have made their presence known. It is one of the few sports in which two- and four-year colleges compete together. The governing agency at the college level is the National Intercollegiate Rodeo Association (NIRA).

According to Jim Corfield, General Manager, NIRA, some participating states are: Washington, Wyoming, Texas, South Dakota, Oregon, Oklahoma, North Dakota, Nebraska, Montana, Kansas, Idaho, Colorado, California, and Arizona. There are 11 rodeo regions in the United States, and about 140 member colleges. Of the 200 institutions that participate, 30% are junior - community colleges.

Students can rodeo independently as long as they are enrolled, carrying at least 12 units, maintaining a 2.0 grade point average (gpa), and in good standing at the college. However, if a college has five or more students participating they have to join the NIRA.

Among the many outstanding junior - community college participants are:

Name	Community College	Event/Year
Joe Alexander	Casper (WY)	World Champion — Bareback Four times: 1972-73-74-75;
Guy Allen	Ranger (TX)	World Champion — Steer Roping, 1982

Name	Community College	Event/Year
Bobby Berger	Lamar (CO)	World Champion — Saddle Bronc Rider, 1979
Rick Bradley	Western Texas (TX)	World Champion — Steer Wrestling, 1976
Dave Brock	Casper (WY)	World Champion — Calf Roper, 1978
Roy Cooper	Cisco (TX)	World Champion — Calf Roper Four times: 1980-81-82-83 One time — All Around Cowboy
Doyle Dellerman	Modesto (CA)	World Champion — Team Roper, 1978
Chris Lybbert	Hartnell (CA)	All Around Cowboy, 1946
Phil Lyne	Southwest Texas (TX)	World Champion — All Around Cowboy, 1971-72
Jim Roddy	Hartnell (CA)	Bulldogger, 1970-71 Holds record for the fastest tie in Salinas, California
J. C. Trujillo	Mesa (AZ)	World Champion — Bareback Rider, 1981

SOCCER[14]

In spite of the fact that soccer is a professional sport, facilities are available, and it is a low-cost sport to operate — there is not widespread participation within the two-year-college system. From the colleges that have soccer teams, however, there have come some outstanding players.

George Vizvary, professor of engineering; Ulster County Community College (NY) soccer coach; and staff coach of the U. S. Soccer Federation, discussed soccer in the two year colleges.

> We have a fine soccer program, and have produced some outstanding players. We share this with several other colleges, among them the Miami Dade (FL), Florissant Valley (MO), and the New Jersey and New York colleges.
>
> At Ulster, however, in 1983 seven out of seven of our sophomores transferred to major institutions. One of them, Chris Stanbrode an All-American, plans to attend Columbia University.
>
> In 1982, eight out of eight sophomore players transferred. Ronyl Durene, All-American, transferred to Florida International University. After one year, he went hardship and was drafted by the Minnesota Strikers.

Fernando Nasmyth, 1970 All-American was the first black player I coached at Ulster. He transferred to Cornell University, played soccer, got a law degree, and is now a corporate lawyer.

The same year, 1970, there was another All-American, Leiv Knutsen, on the Ulster team. He went on to play at the University of Rhode Island, and is now vice - president of a shipping company in New York.

There are a lot of stories to tell about the players. These are just a few that come to mind at the moment.

Twenty-three of our players went on to become professional athletes. Njego Pesa, an All-American in 1978, was drafted by the Dallas Tornados, and later played with the Tampa Bay Rowdies and Tulsa Roughnecks in the North American Soccer League (NASL). Later he was picked up by the Major Indoor Soccer League (MISL) St. Louis Steamers. When they won the Soccer Bowl in 1983, he was picked the Most Valuable Player.

In 1980, Joe Ulrich transferred to Duke University. He was the recipient of the Herman Award (comparable to football's Heisman award), and was drafted by the Chicago Sting and then the New York Arrows.

Neil Guldbjerg was on the 1978 team. He bypassed a four-year college, signed with the Detroit Express. Presently he is with the Buffalo Stallions, MISL.

ICE HOCKEY[1,5]

Canton Agricultural and Technical College, one of the two-year colleges in the State University of New York (SUNY) system, has a premiere ice hockey program. Since the inception of a national playoff in 1972, the college has won the championship 9 of the 11 years.

"The college has had numerous athletes who became outstanding NCAA players," stated Terry Martin, ice hockey coach.

Name	Four-Year Institution
Donald Vaughn	St. Lawrence University
John Dziedzic	Clarkson University
Paul Flanagan	St. Lawrence University
Rich Boprey	Clarkson University
Gary Matura	Cornell University
Bill Murray	Cornell University

Coach Martin continued:

> The list goes on and on. But one of the greatest accomplishments of our team is that in 1979, 1981 and 1983 we went to Europe and played the top (Division I) schools in Holland and West Germany. On the tour, we play four games in ten days. In 1983, out team won all four games — one in West Germany, one in Belgium, and two in Holland.

Martin added, "Several of the Canton players are now in professional ice hockey. Among them are:

Name	Four-Year Institution	Professional Team
Dick Layo	St. Lawrence Univ.	Milwaukee Admirals
Terry Sykes	Elmira College	Europe (Sweden)
Rick Gotkin	Brockport State Univ.	Europe (Holland)
Gerald Connell	Plattsburg Univ.	Europe (Holland

. . .

Large numbers of junior - community - college athletes reached other pinnacles — professional sports and/or careers closely related to professional sports. Among the many who became stylists, innovators, top personalities, world leaders, and legends, was Jackie Roosevelt Robinson.

His standards and contributions are so praiseworthy that in 1984 when the California Community Colleges started their Football Hall of Fame — selecting from thousands of junior - community - college players prior to 1965 — Jackie Robinson was the first person to be elected. The following is quoted from that announcement:[16]

> Jackie Robinson, who led Pasadena City College to an 11-0 record, scoring 17 touchdowns and 131 points in 1938 was one of the initial selectees. Known internationally as the athlete who first integrated professional baseball with the Brooklyn Dodgers, he was once named the National League's Most Valuable Player. His performance attracted tremendous crowds for Community College football games.
>
> He ran for three touchdowns and passed for three against San Bernardino. He scored two touchdowns and passed for another before a crowd of 49,000 for the Compton game. With 30,000 fans watching, he ran a 104 - yard kick - off return against Cal Tech. Besides his football and baseball exploits, he starred at all levels in

Jackie Robinson attended Pasadena City College, and then UCLA, before playing professional baseball. *Photos, courtesy Los Angeles Dodgers, are also used with the permission of Jackie's widow, Rachel Robinson (above and page 25).*

track and basketball. He long jumped 25'6" which was a National Junior College record. He participated in athletics at UCLA after PCC, where among his other accomplishments he led the Pacific Coast Conference Southern Division in scoring for two consecutive years in basketball. He was the first black ever selected to the Pasadena City College academic honor society.

In addition to those comments, Robert J. Gomperz, Director, Public Information Office, provided the following historical football information about Pasadena City College Football Lancers as it relates to Jackie Robinson. In doing so, his standards, accomplishments, and contributions can be more visibly understood.[17]

LANCERS ON RECORD
Rushing
Most Yards — Single Season

Player	Yards	Carries	Year
Reggie Brown	1549	257	1979
Albert Youngblood	1450	228	1971
Sylvester Youngblood	1441	242	1970
Elvin Momon	1194	256	1972
James DeCuir	1163	200	1977
Jackie Robinson	*1093*	*142*	*1938*
Jim Lejay	1064	137	1974
Al Napoleon	1040	156	1951
Reggie Webster	977	171	1975
Keith Bizzle	875	174	1975
Addison Hawthorne	866	140	1951
Ron Cunningham	796	96	1953
Don Roberts	779	158	1978
Don Roberts	766	136	1979
Keith Bizzle	766	109	1974
Loren Shumer	763	147	1966
Reggie Brown	723	107	1978
Jake Leicht	695		1940
Bill Busic	678	152	1937
Bob Reese	677	89	1954
Al Napoleon	658	119	1952

Most Yards — Career

Player	Yards	Years
Reggie Brown	2272	1978-79
Sylvester Youngblood	2003	1969-70
Al Napoleon	1698	1951-52
James DeCuir	1649	1977-78
Keith Bizzle	1641	1974-75
Jim Lejay	1604	1973-74
Albert Youngblood	1572	1970-71
Don Roberts	1545	1978-79
Reggie Webster	1482	1974-75
Elvin Momon	1419	1971-72
Addison Hawthorne	1419	1950-51
Jackie Robinson	*1251*	*1937-38*
Jake Leicht	1160	1939-40
Ron Cunningham	1160	1953-54
Lavell Sanders	1077	1973-74

Dodger Jackie Robinson steals home in 1955 World Series.

Scoring

Most Points — Season

- 131 — *Jackie Robinson, 1938 (11 games).* *
- 96 — Reggie Brown, 1979 (11 games).
- 85 — Michael Lansford, 1977 (12 games).
- 80 — Don Roberts, 1979 (11 games).
- 78 — Al Napoleon, 1951 (12 games); Elvin Momon, 1972 (13 games); James DeCuir, 1977 (11 games).
- 76 — Larry Ross, 1953 (11 games).
- 72 — Addison Hawthorne, 1950 (10 games); Ron Cunningham, 1953 (10 games); Albert Youngblood, 1971 (9 games); Reggie Brown, 1979 (11 games).
- 71 — Paul Gielgens, 1980 (11 games).
- 67 — Bobo Reese, 1954 (10 games).
- 66 — Duane Hill, 1970 (9 games); Reggie Webster, 1974 (10 games), and 1975 (10 games); Ellis Johnson, 1955 (10 games); Bob Ashworth, 1949.
- 62   Greg Johnson, 1971 (9 games).
- 61 — Dave Kradahglian, 1971 (9 games).
- 60 — Willie Campbell, 1966 (10 games); Loren Shumer, 1966 (10 games).

Most Touchdowns — Season

- 18 — *Jackie Robinson (1938).* *
- 16 — Reggie Brown (1979).
- 13 — Al Napoleon (1951); Elvin Momon (1972); James DeCuir (1977); Don Roberts (1979).
- 12 — Addison Hawthorne (1950); Ron Cunningham (1953); Albert Youngblood (1971).
- 11 — Duane Hill (1970); Reggie Webster (1974, 75); Ellis Johnson (1955); Bobo Reese (1954); Bob Ashworth (1949).
- 10 — Willie Campbell (1966); Loren Shumer (1966); Greg Johnson (1971); Larry Ross (1953).

Longest Plays

Longest Run from Scrimmage

- 1938 — *Jackie Robinson, 99 yards.* *
- 1979 — Don Roberts, 80 yards.

Longest Run with Intercepted Pass

- 1958 — Dave Knowles, 103 yards.
- 1979 — Vince Osby, 92 yards.
- 1980 — Mike Langston, 81 yards.

. . .

There are few sports in which junior - community college athletes are not well represented. John Hall,[18] the celebrated *Los Angeles Times* sportswriter, holds the opinion that "junior college football in California has never needed to apologize to anyone, of course, for its quality. From Hugh McElhenny to O. J. Simpson, *many of the best over the years have performed for community colleges.*" [Italics not in the original.]

In spite of the mild suppression of these institutions, either by omission or commission, they will continue to be influential. Al Carr, *Los Angeles Times* staff writer, said JC football has "steadily improved ... to a point where many experts believe good two-year college teams of today could defeat many small colleges. Though the crowds are growing smaller, the quality of the game seems assured of continued improvement."[19]

Carr, along with many experts, believes that the reason for this is "better coached teams." The judgment that Hal Sherbeck, "built the football dynasty at Fullerton College [CA]," submits is that "today, JC coaching is consistently excellent."[20]

Their excellence, considered by many to be seriously overlooked, is exemplified by several who have moved into four-year institutions, professional sports, or professional sports careers. The following information by Fred Baer, Director, JC Athletic Bureau, acquaints us with some community college coaches who made the upward transition.[21]

SUPER BOWL XVIII COACHES & COMMENTATORS ARE ALL CALIF. CC PRODUCTS

The four ex-Super Bowl head coaches in the spotlight for Super Bowl XVIII in Tampa have similar roots.

THE COACHES OF BOTH THE REDSKINS AND THE RAIDERS, PLUS THE TWO CBS-TV ANALYSTS, ARE ALL PRODUCTS OF CALIFORNIA ASSOCIATION OF COMMUNITY COLLEGES FOOTBALL PROGRAMS.

Tom Flores of the Raiders quarterbacked Fresno City College in 1954 and 1955 (including a conference championship in '54).

Joe Gibbs of Washington played for Cerritos College (Norwalk) through a pair of 8-1 regular season campaigns (1959 and 1960) and was the Falcons' most inspirational player in 1960.

The CBS duo of John Madden and Dick Vermeil played and coached at California Community Colleges.

Madden competed for College of San Mateo in the late 1950s, at Allan Hancock College (Santa Maria) in 1960 and 1961. His only head coaching position prior to tutoring the Raiders was at Hancock in 1962 and 1963 (posting respective 5-4 and 8-1 marks).

While Madden was playing at San Mateo, Vermeil was competing for Napa JC (now Napa Valley Community College). Vermeil's first college coaching position was an assistant (to Cliff Giffin) at San Mateo in 1963. He became Napa's head coach the next year and took the previously floundering Chiefs through an 8-1 season.

Los Angeles Raiders Coach Tom Flores quarterback at Fresno City College, 1954 - 1955.
Photos courtesy The Raiders.

Washington Redskins Coach Joe Gibbs played at Cerritos College, 1959 - 1960.
Photo courtesy The Redskins.

THIS IS THE FOURTH CONSECUTIVE YEAR A FORMER CALIFORNIA CC PLAYER IS A SUPER BOWL TEAM'S HEAD COACH AND THE SECOND TIME BOTH TEAM LEADERS ARE CALIFORNIA CC PRODUCTS.

In 1981 it was the Raiders' Flores (Fresno CC) downing Vermeil of the Eagles (Napa and San Mateo).

Two years ago, Bill Walsh (a former College of San Mateo player) led the 49ers to the Super Bowl crown. Walsh's first coaching job was also at a community college, as an assistant at Monterey Peninsula in 1955.

Of course Gibbs won the Super Bowl last year. (Madden took the Raiders to the title in 1977).

SO THIS WILL ALSO BE THE FOURTH CONSECUTIVE YEAR THE COMMUNITY COLLEGES HAVE PRODUCED THE WINNING SUPER BOWL COACH.

NOTES:

Cerritos College was destined to be represented in this year's Super Bowl. The Falcons also produced 49er placekicker Ray Wersching (1968-69) of the 49ers and Seattle Seahawk quarterback Jim Zorn (1971-72) — so had ex-players with three of the four squads in the NFL conference championship games.

CBS isn't the only network with a pair of former California CC players in the booth. ABC on Monday nights featured Frank Gifford

(Bakersfield College) and O. J. Simpson (City College of San Francisco).

Baer also stated that Doug Scovil "left as College of San Mateo head coach" and accepted the position as backfield coach at Navy. While at Navy, he tutored New Mexico JC transfer, Roger Staubach, to the Heisman Trophy. "Staubach," according to Baer, "was the first JC transfer to win the Heisman and was followed by O. J. Simpson and Mike Rozier."[22]

Continuing, he said:

> Current San Mateo coach Bill Dickey, who served on the same staff with Mike White at both Stanford and Cal, is also a springtime pro coach with the Oakland Invaders in the USFL. He, Tollner, and Steve Shafer of the Los Angeles Rams at one time were all on the same CSM staff (and all served as head coaches there).
>
> Meanwhile a pro player named Paul Wiggin spent his spring semesters teaching physical education at San Mateo, while still playing during the fall. But the former Modesto JC star took a job as an assistant coach with the 49ers before CSM could "tab" him; then became head man at Kansas City.

Comparatively, however, community college coaches are fairly stable. According to Killian[23] and Unruh,[24] some others that did make the upward transition are:

NAME	COMMUNITY COLLEGE	POSITION HOLDING/HELD
Anderson, Foster	East Los Angeles (CA)	California State University, Los Angeles; USC; UCLA; Los Angeles Rams
Badger, Ed	Wright (IL)	Chicago Bulls; University of Cincinnati
Beatty, Homer	Bakersfield, Santa Ana (CA)	California State University, Los Angeles
Blackman, Bob	Pasadena City (CA)	Denver, Dartmouth, Illinois, Cornell
Campora, Don	San Joaquin Delta (CA)	University of Pacific
Fitzsimmon, Cotton	Moberly (MO)	Kansas City Kings
Fowler, Ned	Tyler (TX)	Tulane
Grant, Tiny	College of So. Idaho (ID)	Fresno State
Hardin, Wayne	Porterville (CA)	Navy, Temple
Mulligan, Bill	Riverside/Saddleback (CA)	University of California, Irvine
McCutcheon, James R.	Antelope Valley (CA)	University of San Diego (Catholic)
Newman, Jim	Compton (CA)	New Mexico State; Arizona State; California State, L.A.

NAME	COMMUNITY COLLEGE	POSITION HOLDING/HELD
Richardson, Nolan	Western Texas (TX)	Tulsa
Rogers, Darryl	Fresno City (CA)	Fresno State; San Jose State; Michigan State; Arizona State
Scovil, Doug	San Mateo (CA)	University of Pacific; San Francisco 49ers; Brigham Young; San Diego State
Senmore, Enos	Bacone (OK)	University of Oklahoma
Strangland, Jim	Long Beach City (CA)	Long Beach State
Tarkanian, Jerry	Pasadena City (CA)	Long Beach State; University of Nevada, Las Vegas
Ward, Gary	Yavapi (AZ)	Oklahoma State

And there are more. Rilliet added the following information and names in a statement, "A Note Concerning California Community College Basketball Coaches:"[2][5]

> The California Community College Athletic Association is unique in that it is the only level of basketball competition in California that competes on a state-wide level.
>
> Community College basketball in California has been the proving ground for an unusually large number of successful college and university coaches. It is doubtful that any area of organization can match the current number of high quality of major college coaches that have developed in the California Community College ranks.
>
> The major reason for this high success rate is the high level of competition within the state system. One hundred colleges organized and competing on a high level prepares coaches for the college ranks. The list below is of California Community College coaches presently or formerly coaching at the college or university level:

COACH	COMMUNITY COLLEGE	COLLEGE/ UNIVERSITY
Aki Hill	Foothill College	Oregon State
Denny Crum	Pierce	UCLA and Louisville
Stu Inman	Orange Coast	San Jose State
Bob Boyd	Santa Ana	Seattle and USC
Alex Omalev	Fullerton	CSU Fullerton
Claude Rutherford	Fullerton	Idaho State
Lute Olson	Long Beach	Long Beach State/Iowa
Jim Killingsworth	Cerritos	Idaho State, Oklahoma State, TCU
Bob Dye	Cerritos/ Santa Monica	CSU Fullerton
Bill Oates	Santa Ana	St. Mary's

COACH	COMMUNITY COLLEGE	COLLEGE/ UNIVERSITY
Ron Jacobs	El Camino	Loyola
Rex Hughes	Long Beach	Nebraska, Kent State, UNLV
Mo Radovich	Fullerton	CSU Fullerton, Wyoming
John Walker	Barstow	Sonoma State
Jack Avina	San Mateo	Portland
Ed DeLacy	Santa Barbara	UC Santa Barbara
John Caine	Cerritos	Illinois Southern
Bill Berry	Consumnes River	California, Michigan State, San Jose State
Pete Mathiesen	College of the Redwoods	Chico State
Terry Layton	Los Medanos	Northwest Nazarene

One reason for junior - community college athletic prominence has been a group of highly trained, devoted, and creative athletic directors and coaches, with varying degrees of support from administration, faculty, and community. It is the athletic directors and coaches, however, who have been the cornerstone of the program.

The glamorized positions of athletic director and head coach at the community college level poses many problems. Among them are geographic location, staffing, recruiting, facilities and equipment, scheduling, traveling, benefits, and assistance for athletes.

The geographic location of the college in respect to student housing, transportation, the job producing sources, service agencies, and social activities has a direct effect upon the recruiting program.

To a great extent, recruitment for the community college coaches means taking the "rest of the best." Their four-year counterparts with scholarships, benefits, and other assistance oftentimes get the quality high school players.

The vast majority of community college athletic directors and coaches are instructors first, and coaches second. Many work with a limited or part-time staff when performing the instructional aspect of their duties. In most cases, there is even less assistance when performing the coaching aspect of their work in terms of office secretary, public relations, trainer and/or medical doctor, equipment manager, other general assistance personnel, and very often even part-time assistant coaches.

Equipment and facilities are basic to the program. However, medical supplies, projectors, the cost for filming, telephone cost, even postage can be major problems. Many colleges have minimal facilities and have to "contract" for the use of others. This adds to the problem of scheduling, increases traveling cost, affects crowd participation, and takes away the convenience of being at home, while inconveniencing the coach and the athlete.

Scheduling, which includes transportation, must be carefully considered. The costs for carrier services are an absolute but lodging and meals (in the absence of resources) must be considered.

Awards, banquets, and other symbols of recognition usually are not fully covered in the budget. Athletic directors and coaches obtain funds mostly through outside sources. For this reason, the more intercollegiate programs in which a college is involved, the more community resources that will be needed. Overall, this means that the athletic director and coaches must make and keep a lot of friends.

The biggest enemies of coaches are not always their opponents but a lack of the aforementioned resources (time, staff, money, facilities, equipment, services, care, and concern). An inside look at one coach's predicament was seen by Glen Crevier, Press Writer, *The Sacramento Union*.[26]

> Frankly, Jerry Sullivan would prefer to be sitting in a dark room, his projector reeling, his mind mapping strategy for Saturday's Bay Bowl at Hughes Stadium.
>
> But there are too many distractions. Reporters are picking his brain this week, and he's feeling uneasy, catapulting from anonymity into the limelight so suddenly.
>
> "You're the fourth newspaper guy this week that wants to talk to me," he says.
>
> College recruiters are bugging him, too. A table in his office is littered with business cards deposited by assistant coaches who have stopped off at Sac City College the past two months.
>
> Sullivan gets up from his desk, walks to the other side of his office, and grabs a handful of business cards. Some flutter to the floor.
>
> "Look at this," he says, as he flips each one back onto the table. "Tennessee. Illinois. Brigham Young. Kansas. UCLA. Pacific." He counts off a few more schools before dumping the cards back on the table. "They've all been here."
>
> He estimates that recruiters from 50 schools have paid a visit in recent weeks, looking over five or six players who have the potential to go big-time.

"It's been absolutely crazy These guys are all over creation. I try to be cordial, but cripes, I don't have time for them all. I just tell them to come watch practice."

Pamphlets from Idaho, North Texas State and Purdue cover the coffee table. Many more rest on the bookshelves. And Sullivan's daily mail, consisting mostly of inquiries to his senior players, is still untouched and stands a foot tall.

As we talk, a recruiter from Kansas is in the next room, watching films, and one from Minnesota has just knocked on the door, asking to borrow another projector.

There are none available, Sullivan informs him. "We've gone through three already this season. The only one still working is the one I'm using to watch San Francisco."

He means the City College of San Francisco — Saturday's opponent — not the 49ers.

The guy from Minnestoa leaves, disappointed, and Sullivan says, "Hell, I'm trying to get ready for a big game."

But distractions keep getting in the way.

Sullivan seems a little edgy, but he understands: It's the price you pay for success.

His program may be the best in the nation when it comes to junior colleges.

In four years, Sullivan's teams have won 42 of 45 games, two mythical national titles, two Bay Bowls and four Camino Norte Conference championships.

By his recollection, 24 players have graduated to major-college programs, including Greg Murphy, Minnesota's starting quarterback this season, and Dave Kilson, who went to Nevada-Reno and now plays for the Buffalo Bills.

"He's the first one who made it to the pros," Sullivan says produly. "Mark Bonner (who went to Oregon State) was signed but later cut by the Raiders."

When Sullivan inherited the program four seasons ago, the team had lost 22 straight games and recruiters were as foreign on campus soil as Martians.

"The situation then was not very pleasant, to say the least," says Dick Pierucci, Sac City's athletic director. "But the bottom line now is that Jerry is committed to having an outstanding program."

The Panthers are 9-1 this year, despite losing their starting quarterback, highly touted Mark Murphy — Greg's brother — to a knee injury in the fourth game.

That misfortune hasn't hindered progress. Sac City averages more than 40 points a game, and its defense should be nicknamed the "Iron Curtain," allowing opponents only two touchdowns in the last six games.

"This program is the talk of the junior colleges," says Lawrence Cooley, the guy from Minnesota, while waiting around for a projector. "The coach has a fine reputation for recruiting good athletes and good people."

Sullivan is disappointed his program isn't the talk of the town, too.

The Panthers, it seems, has all the mass appeal of a bad movie. Crowds at Hughes Stadium are often small enough to count during timeouts.

"I guess with Sac State and Davis, people around here just don't realize the talent we have on the football field," Sullivan says. "They get most of the publicity. But, heck, in four years, we haven't lost a home game. We visit places like Pasadena, Fresno, Merced, and the people there really support the program."

In jest, Sullivan says, "Maybe we ought to join the Far West Conference (he means the Northern California Athletic Conference) and play Sac State and Davis. We could have our own Causeway Classic."

He doesn't laugh, though.

There's nothing funny about being a stranger in your own back yard.

But it is not all coaching. The fact that many players attend college solely for the athletic experience forces athletic directors and coaches to assume other roles. The coach becomes a tutor and facilitator — a combination of parent, counselor, friend, confidant, psychologist, social worker, and agent. It sums up to services, but the broad range of services is far more inclusive than the college traditional guidance, pupil - personnel, or student - personnel services. They include "hand to hand" guidance, being continuously accessible, personal sharing, and providing a wide range of resources.

When athletes reflect casual attitudes and behavior regarding eligibility, transfer, and/or degree of completion of educational objective, it may become necessary to "piggyback" them as they take the giant step into higher education. It can be a full time and strenuous task to struggle with them during this stage of adjustment, social growth, and development.

With time, teaching, and experience, the coaches strive to assist each athlete in seeing things as they really are, knowing themselves as individuals, and then dealing with all of this in relationship to the outcomes each one personally desires. The degree to which they can instill discipline, which is a combination of seriousness of purpose, direction, poise, and character (conduct, attitude, and behavior), the more positive outcomes for the coaches and players. These, not just physical skills alone, are what the juco coaches refer to as the basics.

Before Pasadena City College (PCC) head football coach Al Luginbill retired after the 1977 season (that season PCC won the Metropolitan Conference and the state and national football titles) he emphasized that:[27]

> ... we do as much coaching and probably more than the four year schools.
>
> We recruit the best high school athletes we can find. We concentrate on those who can better benefit from starting out in a two-year college. But they all have something. Then we are committed to excellence and dedicated to sending as many as we can into four-year schools on scholarships.

His statement "but they all have something" was extended by many community college athletic directors and coaches throughout this study. They were eager to discuss, but yet had some compassion for, the athletes who "didn't quite make it." They reflected sadness about those who terminated their college experience prematurely, were extremely delighted for those who attained the ranks of professional sports, and were boastful of those who succeeded in other endeavors. They expressed gratitude for the camaraderie, the fellowship, and the athletic experience. It is apparent that the attitudes they were reflecting are consistent with the attitudes of the community colleges.

Again, reiterating Coach Luginbill, "then we are committed to excellence and dedicated to sending as many as we can into four-year schools on scholarships."[28] To single out all of the two-year college athletes, past and present, who attended four-year institutions on athletic scholarships would be an interminable task. A cursory enlightenment of the numbers can be realized by analyzing one interscholastic sport that terminates into professionalism, in one college. Let us remain with the Pasadena City College football team.[29]

PCC has documented data that over the past 13 years (1969-1982) approximately 280 of their football players have received athletic scholarship aid to four-year institutions. This averages close to 20 football players per year.

The college has estimated that, at a minimum monetary value of $3,000 per year, for a two and one-half year scholarship, the football program has generated about $1,600,000 in student athletic aid at four-year institutions over this period.

The diversity, vast geographical range, and athletic divisions of the four-year institutions into which juco athletes transfer are impressive.

During the regular juco season, playoffs, and championships, four-year institution coaches are afforded the opportunity to recruit from the greatest source available for instant quality products. Case in point: during the 1980 California State Community College Championship Basketball Tournament, at floor level, there were almost as many four-year institution coaches and recruiters as spectators. A brief moment with them revealed that they were highly organized in their recruitment efforts. The wealth of information which they could spout about the hundreds of individual players in the community colleges, and their respective teams and coaches, was highly accurate and astounding. From among this group of recruitment experts one could obtain specific information relating to players' backgrounds, speed, size, strengths, grade point average, attitude, conduct, behaivor, coachability, and various other concerns.

"Recruitment of junior college athletes by four-year institutions continues to grow in intensity each year," said Director of NJCAA George E. Killian, in *In the Sports Spotlight*. Continuing, he wrote:[30]

> As the nation's senior colleges face the ever growing problems of finance more and more turn to the junior college athlete to buttress their teams. The following statements show why:
> 1. Scholarship need only be given for two years instead of the traditional four.
> 2. No one is recruited unless they have actually proven their ability under game conditions.
> 3. More actual playing time is available to the junior college player than to a regular senior college freshman or sophomore; this giving the juco (junior college) athlete a better chance to develop his skills.
> 4. Not only are junior college athletes seasoned athletic veterans but they have been found to be academically sound by fulfilling the requirements for graduation from the junior college level.

"Despite controversy, put-downs, and perhaps lack of recognition," said Killian, "junior and community colleges have earned an important place in the national sports picture."[31] A more lengthy discussion of the importance of the junior - community - college athlete will be presented in Chapter Three.

Messersmith, Rilliet, and Killian agree to the prolificacy of the jucos. Messersmith[32] feels that the two-year colleges have been significant in the educational and developmental lives of many professional athletes. "In addition to being recruiting havens for college coaches," he said, "professional scouts have identified many potential professionals at this level." Rilliet[33] declared that "unquestionably, community colleges are 'blue chip' institutions." According to Killian,[34] "many of the athletic stars at the big universities and on the professional gridirons can trace their training back to two-year colleges."

This is a plus for the two-year colleges' athletic programs. The general public, many involved in education (including the JCs), and even the sports public are unaware of their vast contributions. It is understandable that, even though it lacks thoroughness and justice because the last known residence of the athlete is the four-year institution attended, the JC becomes anonymous.

But beyond the JCs, its administrators, athletic directors, coaches, and players are the low-profiled governing organizations. In order to put into full perspective the athletic program of the JCs, the next chapter presents a rarely publicized profile of these governing organizations.

Chapter Two
ATHLETIC GOVERNANCE AND ACTIVITIES

Another reason for athletic prominence in the junior and community colleges must be credited to the knowledgeable, aggressive, and steadfast leadership at the top levels of governance. These levels are the National Junior College Athletic Association (NJCAA), which includes Mississippi and some independents; the California Association of Community Colleges — Committee on Athletics (CACC-COA); and the Athletic Association of Community Colleges, which includes the state of Washington and some other colleges in the Northwest. Mississippi and Washington — as well as California — were original members of NJCAA, but reorganized in recent years. This chapter — in part — will give a bird's-eye view of both perspectives. Only the two larger associations, NJCAA and CACC-COA, will be presented.

Before entering into further discussion about the bifurcated governance of community colleges, the issue of the division of NJCAA and the CACC-COA should be discussed. As occurs in many human situations, a lack of attention or recognition, communications, and resources; distance; an absence of rules and regulations that are comfortable for parties involved; and the feeling of not being sufficiently in control of decision-making can create internal conflicts which are not easily resolved. Differences in perception of style, image, physical and social conditions, and also demeanor are often factors which may weigh heavily upon organization. When elements of individual success and strength are added to those conditions, a perfect formula for independence exists. This could have been the case in the parting of the ways between NJCAA and CACC-COA.

In-depth research indicates there is little evidence that the physical health of the community colleges was impaired. There is an absence of malice which is noted in the following article:[1]

STATE OF UNION IN JCs STILL DIVIDED
by Susan Fornoff *USA Today*

Commissioner Walter Rilliet wishes that the winner of his California Association of Community Colleges basketball tournament March 11-13 could go on to the nationals.

And executive director George Killian wishes that his National Junior College Athletic Association's national championship March 15-19 in Hutchinson, Kan., included California.

But, as far as the USA's junior colleges are concerned, the state of the union remains divided. Once again, as in every other sport, there'll be a California champion and a national champion.

"I don't see why they don't join," Killian said. "And that's a big question right now, because it really does nothing but hurt the athletic programs of their schools."

Said Rilliet: "The problem is when we've talked about it, I've gotten the feeling that: 'You guys pay your dues, use our rule book and come on in.' Well, we don't want to do that. It's nothing against their rule book. I think people like to paint a picture of California sitting back and thumbing our nose at the rest of the country. If we could work it out logistically so we could have a national champion, I think it would be great."

California teams have proved to be no better and no worse than the rest of the nation when they have met teams outside of the state. In the last national junior college football championship, Henderson (Texas) beat Pasadena 40-13 in front of 40,000 in the Rose Bowl. That was in 1966.

In the last national championship any California junior college participated in, 1978, Golden West in Huntington Beach, Calif., won the women's softball champtionship.

"Every year they had to sell cupcakes and wash cars just to justify going to wherever the championship was," Rilliet said. "It meant a lot of traveling, a lot of time away from campus. Finally, the cost became so prohibitive to go out of state that we had to say that would be the last."

The financial struggle in the community colleges has cost many athletic programs. Last year there were 16 women's gymnastics programs in California. This year five remain.

So the trend has been to avoid expensive and time-consuming trips. Of course, every time a really outstanding team comes along, especially in baseball, the question comes up again: why can't this team, which might indeed be a national champion, prove it?

"If we let men's basketball go and not women's basketball, then we're bad," Rilliet said. "If we let the football team go and not the soccer team, we're in trouble. We have to look for some balance."

Of the 107 community colleges in California, 96 have some kind of athletic program.

Killian's NJCAA has 510 men's basketball teams and 423 women's teams, so California could increase its membership by 20 percent.

All organizations have close alliance with the high schools, which reflects that they have not strayed from their roots. Of equal concern, however, is articulation with the four-year institutions. They are obligated by contract (also conscience, promises, etc.) to direct full attention to developing measures which will serve a multisituational multiclientele. In sports this refers to students entering directly from high school, intercommunity college transfers (in and out of district), and transfers from four-year institutions as well as transfers to four-year institutions.

In order to hold policies, rules, regulations, etc., to a minimum, to prevent the abundance of "red tape" which is prevalent in higher education institutions, but mainly to make higher education "accessible," their responses to problems, issues, and concerns are both simple and practical. Cases in point are the eligibility and transfer rules. Their posture often places them in precarious positions, which leaves them open to severe criticisms. But, those are the hazards that are built into that system.

The national organization governing athletics for junior and community colleges is the National Junior College Athletic Association. It is located in Hutchinson, Kansas, and is under the leadership of George E. Killian. Following is a summary of its history (development, organization, governance, and activities):

HISTORY OF THE NATIONAL JUNIOR COLLEGE ATHLETIC ASSOCIATION[2]

The idea for the NJCAA was conceived in 1937 in Fresno, California. A handful of junior college representatives met to organize an association that would promote and supervise a national program of junior colleges sports and activities consistent with the educational objectives of junior colleges.

The constitution presented at the charter meeting in Fresno on May 14, 1938, was accepted, and the National Junior College Athletic Association became a functioning organization.

Colleges represented at the charter meeting were Bakersfield, Chaffey, Compton, Fullerton, Glendale, Los Angeles, Pasadena, Riverside, Sacramento, San Bernardino, San Mateo, Santa Monica and Visalia.

The initial activity sponsored by the NJCAA was track and field. Sacramento played host to the first National Junior College Track and Field Meet in 1939, which started a series of annual meets, unbroken except for three years during World War II. While the first meet drew only California schools, the second, in Modesto, in 1940, assumed a wider scope with participants from Phoenix, Arizona, and Trinidad, Colorado, in addition to the Californians.

While founded by California men, there was no intention for the NJCAA to be just a "West Coast Organization." This became apparent when Trinidad College's invitation to sponsor the 1941 track meet at Denver, Colorado, was accepted.

The NJCAA was fast gaining national recognition. At the 1941 meet in Denver, teams representing colleges from east of the Mississippi joined southern and west coast members.

After Pearl Harbor, only one more meet was held during the war years. This was staged at Visalia, California, and was the last sponsored activity by the NJCAA until the spring of 1946, when the fifth National Junior College Track and Field Meet was held at Phoenix, Arizona.

In 1945, the NJCAA, weakened by the war and not yet ready to renew activities, had given its blessings to an individual basketball tournament at Compton. The tournament mushroomed into a national activity by 1947, with teams participating from as far away as Washington and Louisiana. Other schools from the Great Lakes area, the middle west, and the east coast clamored for invitations that could not be provided. Clearly, a nationwide basketball program, sponsored by the NJCAA, was a necessity.

Compton invited the NJCAA to call a special meeting in connection with its 1947 tournament, to consider a national basketball program, from which grew the present regional and national tourney plan.

Attempts were made to carry on this extensive program of national competition, but lack of entries and financial hardships caused the curtailment of golf, tennis, boxing, gymnastics, and swimming after a three-year trial. However, these events could be conducted at any time in the future when requests from five or more regions were filed.

In 1949 the NJCAA was reorganized by dividing the nation into sixteen regions. The officers of the association were the president, vice president, secretary, treasurer, public relations director, and the sixteen regional vice presidents. The *NJCAA Bulletin* was authorized and published as the official organ of the association. Among other official acts, policies for conducting regional and national events were written, the constitution was revised, the organization was incorporated as a nonprofit corporation, and the first *NJCAA Handbook* was published. This booklet gave status and stability to the organization that it had lacked in previous years.

Hutchinson, Kansas, became the site for the NJCAA Championship Basketball Tournament. Cosponsors, the Lisle Rishel Post, American Legion, and the Hutchinson Junior College hosted this event in 1949.

The growth of the organization and the work of the committees outmoded the 1950 handbook, necessitating a second edition in 1952.

The NJCAA, working with the American Association of Junior Colleges Subcommittee on Athletics, wrote and adopted the "Statement of Guiding Principles for Conducting Junior College Athletics" in 1953. In 1954 it expanded its scope to include individual and team scores of all member colleges.

Steps were taken to obtain low-cost and reliable insurance for the NJCAA members. The Insurance Committee was responsible for obtaining the NJCAA Insurance Plan from the Associated Agencies. The plan, as adopted, covered major and catastrophic accidents with a minimum cost to each member school.

The NJCAA obtained representation on various national rules committees during 1954. Also, the name, *NJCAA Bulletin*, was changed to the *JUCO REVIEW.*

The Statistics Bureau became the Service Bureau in 1955 and began to compile and release weekly ratings of member college basketball teams. For the first time, the official All-American Junior College Basketball Teams were selected by the Bureau. Previous to this time, the All-Region and All-NJCAA tournament teams were considered to be the All-American Teams.

The important contributions to the NJCAA program in 1956 included the addition of football statistics and rankings to the Service Bureau program. The adoption of policies for conducting the National Football Championship and awarding the contract to the West Hollywood Kiwanis Club, was culminated in the initial game, played at the Los Angeles Coliseum. Coffeyville, Kansas, defeated Grand Rapids, Michigan, for this first NJCAA Football Championship.

In 1957 another important step was taken by the NJCAA. An affiliation with the National Federation of State High School Athletic Associations (NFSHSAA), and the National Association of Intercollegiate Athletics (NAIA) was formed to work together on many common interests. The primary emphasis, in the initial state, was placed on jointly producing playing rules in football, six-man football, soccer and baseball, and the continued use of common codes in basketball, track and other major sports. This affiliation was christened the National Alliance.

By 1958, the scope of the NJCAA had been recognized by other national organizations and the association was asked to participate in various national projects. These included (1) the People to People Sports Committee, a foundation to promote international good will through sports, (2) President Eisenhower's Physical Fitness Commission, (3) a study on equipment and supplies for physical education, athletics and recreation, sponsored by the Athletic Institute and the American Association for Health, Physical Education and Recreation, and (4) the publication for the first edition of the *Blue Book of Junior College Athletics* by McNitt, Inc.

Baseball entered the national program during this year when the NJCAA Invitational Tournament, with the Grand Junction Chamber of Commerce and Mesa College of Grand Junction, Colorado, as the first cosponsors of the event. Authorization was also granted to conduct National Invitational Tournaments in golf, tennis, wrestling and cross-country. Odessa, Texas; Rochester, Minnesota; Farmingdale, New York; and Alfred, New York, were chosen as the sites for these events.

National Invitational Meets in swimming and rifle were sanctioned in 1960. These and other recent additions to the national program pointed to a need for a revised handbook. Money was allocated for its printing in 1961.

In addition to the printing and distribution of the new handbook in 1961, the *JUCO REVIEW* publication site was changed from Ogden, Utah, to Buffalo, New York. A newspaper known as "Junior College Sports" was published in Grand Junction, Colorado, and the NJCAA played an important supporting role in this new venture. The year 1961 was also the first NJCAA Invitational Soccer Tournament in Middletown, New York.

All-American awards in soccer were approved by the 1962 legislative assembly. This year marked the entrance of the NJCAA into the Basketball Federation of the United States of America, the United States Gymnastics Federation and the United States Track and Field Federation.

In 1963, the NJCAA became a member of the United States Olympic Committee and was granted ten (10) votes on the committee and one representative on the forty-six (46) member Board of Directors. Representation on the NCAA Rules Committee in Track and Field, Wrestling, and Basketball was obtained during this period.

An agreement was reached with the Alee Shrine Temple of Savannah, Georgia, to bring the NJCAA Championship Football Game back into the national program in 1964 after a lapse of four years. This game was named the NJCAA Shrine Bowl.

The Chamber of Commerce and Mesa College of Grand Junction, Colorado, were awarded a new five-year contract in 1965 to conduct the NJCAA Championship Baseball Tournament. Also, in 1965, the NJCAA was given a voice on various U.S. Olympic Games Committees and our representatives were active in formulating plans for their sports in the overall Olympic program.

The rapid growth of wrestling in the junior colleges and the resulting increase in the number of teams coming to the National Invitational Wrestling Tournament warranted the establishment of a national championship event in this sport in 1966. Once again revisions were made in the *NJCAA Constitution and By-Laws*, and the *Handbook* was brought up to date in preparation for printing a fourth edition in 1966.

Negotiations were completed for two post-season football games. One sponsored by the Southwest Grid Classic, Inc., was called the Wool Bowl, and was played at Roswell, New Mexico. The second, named the Silver Bowl, was sponsored by Sterling College and the Sterling Rotary Club in Sterling, Kansas. Both bowl games were played for the first time in the fall of 1966. This same year a new 10-year contract was closed with the Lysle Rishel Post 68, American Legion, and Hutchinson Community Junior College of Hutchinson, Kansas, to continue to conduct the NJCAA Basketball Tournament at its present site.

The American Medical Association Committee on the Medical Aspects of Sports invited the organization to participate in their activities in this field. Also a liaison committee between the AAJC and the NJCAA was formed.

The year 1967-68 was one of many changes in the NJCAA. Membership stood at 391 colleges. The 1967 legislative assembly approved a grant-in-aid to Michael Mould, Keystone Junior College, LaPlume, Pennsylvania, to write a complete history of the NJCAA to fulfill a requirement for the completion of his doctorate degree at Springfield College, Springfield, Massachusetts.

In 1968 the legislative assembly reorganized the administrative structure from the 16 regions, established in 1949, to 19 regions. This was accomplished by dividing Region VIII, Region I, and Region XV to form three new regions. Membership had now reached 419 colleges.

The NJCAA, for the first time, conducted its own Olympic Trials in basketball. A squad of ten players competed in the final trials in Albuquerque, New Mexico. Athletes of member colleges also competed in Olympic Trials for wrestling and track and field.

A third post-season football game, sponsored by the El Toro Foundation of Yuma, Arizona, was added to the football program. Called the El Toro Bowl, its first competiton came in 1968.

Membership in the United States Collegiate Sports Council, the United States Baseball Federation, and the United States Wrestling Federation were accepted by the NJCAA in 1968, and a National Invitational Gymnastics Meet was added to the program.

In 1969 the appointment of George E. Killian as full-time Executive Director was approved by the legislative assembly, and the new office was officially opened August 1, 1969, in the Hilton Inn, Hutchinson, Kansas.

At the time of the 1970 legislative assembly, membership had increased to 476 colleges. A National Invitational Bowling Tournament was added to the program. Also, a Scholarship and Grant-In-Aid Committee was established to study existing practices and to make recommendations for future appropriate actions.

Two post-season football games, the Mid-American JUCU Bowl and the Green Country Shrine Bowl were added in 1971, along with National Invitational Championships in Ice Hockey and Judo. The membership reached an all-time high of 501 members.

The year 1972 saw the addition of decathlon, fencing, and indoor track to the growing Invitational Championship scene. The Championship football game was moved to Yuma, Arizona, from Savannah, Georgia, and became known as the Sunkist El Toro Bowl. The membership climbed to 513 for the 1971-1972 college year.

In 1973 the legislative assembly reorganized the administrative structure from 19 regions, established in 1968, to 21 regions. This was accomplished by dividing Region III and Region XIX to form two new regions. Membership reached a record 533.

1974 saw the addition of three invitational championships in volleyball, basketball, and tennis for women. The NJCAA "amateur rule" was completely rewritten by the Board of Directors. Membership climbed to a record high of 544.

A major change in the structure of the NJCAA occurred in 1975 when the Board of Directors approved a Women's Division. National Championships for women were approved in volleyball, basketball and tennis. National Invitational Championships for women were slated in field hockey, skiing, gymnastics, track and field, softball, and swimming and diving. Membership climbed to a record 568.

The year 1976 saw the membership of the NJCAA reach 296 for its Women's Division, and 586 for its Men's Division. The Board of Directors reorganized the administrative structure from 21 regions to 22 regions by dividing Region XVII.

In 1976-77 the Women's Division sponsored four championship tournaments and eight invitational championships, while its membership grew to 345, twenty-one sporting events were offered to the 580 members of the Men's Division, including the revival of the Junior Rose Bowl. The Board of Directors approved the concept of divisional play in the sports of cross-country, tennis and golf for the 1978-79 college year.

In 1977-78 the membership in the Women's Division reached 471 while the Men's Division dropped back to 574. The Rodeo Bowl was added to the men's football program. The women's championship basketball and volleyball teams went to Mexico City for competition with the Mexican National Institute of Sport.

The year 1979 saw the addition of the Eastern Bowl to the list of sponsored NJCAA football bowl games, as well as the first invitational Fall Golf Championship. The Women's Indoor Track and Field Championship moved from an invitational status to national championship status.

The year 1980-81 saw the Women's Division membership reach 490 members. Extensive changes were made in the Handbook and Casebook to bring about a more uniform interpretation of NJCAA policy for the membership.

The year 1982-83 saw the advent of a reorganization as the Board of Directors voted to increase the number of regions from twenty-two to twenty-four. Region IV (Illinois) was divided into Region IV and Region XXIV. Kentucky and Tennessee became the new Region XXIV. Authorization was also granted to employ a new Administrative Assistant with primary responsibilities in the women's division.

NJCAA WOMEN'S DIVISION[3]
Philosophy

It is the basic belief of the Women's Division of the NJCAA that the athletic program for the women complements the existing programs offered by the NJCAA. The Women's Program is an integral part of the total educational process, which fosters sound educational goals concurrent with those of the member institution.

Because of the uniqueness of the Community/Junior College, it is important to provide an organization which provides equal representation through the twenty-two elected regional directors for each division. The Women's Division of the NJCAA provides programs which afford opportunities for the participation of all community college students. Through the existing structure of the NJCAA, representatives of both the Men's and Women's Divisions work together to develop and maintain eligibility rules, which will be applied equally to all athletes, both male and female.

For those Community Colleges seeking an affiliation for their women's athletic program, the NJCAA offers an organization that can meet the individual needs of all students because it provides national competition for all eligible member schools through regional affiliation.

It is important to emphasize that the Women's Division is dedicated to meeting the needs of all women athletes, providing them with the highest caliber of national competition in a wide range of sports.

NJCAA POSITION PAPER:
LEADERSHIP ROLES OF WOMEN
IN TWO-YEAR COLLEGE ATHLETICS[4]

From its inception, the Women's Division of the National Junior College Athletic Association has fostered among its goals the encouragement, promotion and advancement of all Women's Athletic Programs in the junior college. In order to insure progress in meeting these objectives and goals, women of competency and experience, as well as those whose backgrounds have been limited, should not be excluded from leadership roles. As a group, we are strongly opposed to any and all measures which would remove or exclude capable, qualified and/or interested women from assuming those leadership positions relating to Women's Athletics. It is a specific concern that the Women's Regional Directors position be held by a woman.

We would strongly urge all regions of the NJCAA to provide for access to an input from women within their respective regions at each regional meeting relating to the business and conduct of the Women's Division. In those regions where few women currently serve in any leadership capacity, we would urge that a conscientious, active and ongoing effort be made to identify, attract and develop the leadership potential of women throughout that region.

> It is through these efforts that we hope to expand leadership opportunities, promote conscientious awareness, stimulate further interest on the part of women in the NJCAA, and to recognize the significant contributions women can make in the leadership and administration of women's athletics.

The Appendices contain information on the following: Geographic Regions of NJCAA, Membership in NJCAA (Men's Division), Recognized Sports Participated in by Member Colleges (Men), Membership in NJCAA (Women's Division), Recognized Sports Participated in by Member Colleges (Women), and NJCAA: History, Record, and Results of Activities.

California community colleges are governed by the California Association of Community Colleges (CACC). Noteworthy, as was mentioned earlier in this chapter, is that it is an independent organization. Located in Sacramento, California, under the leadership of Walt Rilliet, Commissioner of Athletics, problem solving and decision making are handled in conjunction with a geographical representation of an appointed Committee on Athletics (COA). Prior to late 1981 this organization operated under the name of California Community and Junior College Association - Committee on Athletics (CCJCA-COA) under the leadership of Lloyd E. Messersmith, who served as the director from 1967 to 1981.

Although the general public may be acquainted only vicariously with the total athletic activities of the CACC-COA, the absence of formal information makes them less aware of the history, development, and governance of the organization. The most complete, comprehensive, and reliable information has been compiled by Lee Samuel Vokes.

Before presenting a more detailed, formal accounting of the history, development, and governance of CACC-COA, Vokes expressed the difficulty he encountered in assembling the information:[5]

> Of all the time and energy spent in gathering data for this study, the most difficult procedure was obtaining knowledge of the existence of the specific athletic conferences before 1946. In fact, the first mention of specific schools belonging to specific conferences does not appear in the SAC [State Athletic Committee] meeting notes until 1949. Records have been lost, thrown away as being meaningless or not kept in a specific place for future historical use. Many of those individuals who were in a position to know are deceased or cannot remember sufficiently to be considered a primary or secondary source from a historical viewpoint. Nevertheless, some vestige of what occurred is available.

The following was taken from his work:[6]

The earliest California state-wide interscholastic conference involving junior colleges that can be documented at this time was the California Coast Conference, founded in 1922. Of the eight original members, four were junior colleges and four were four-year institutions. Prior to 1932 six additional teams were added, of which four were junior colleges. Continuing, Vokes added:[7] In 1932 the four-year colleges withdrew, and the junior colleges began to form their own conferences.

Documentation revealing the specifics of how the conferences were organized has not been obtained. It is suspect, however, that in those early beginnings a single conference was developed in each of the three regions. Athletic associations were being organized. As more junior colleges were added in a respective region, it became necessary to add more conferences. The purpose of the associations was to organize, promote, and supervise athletes in their respective areas.

The Southern California Junior College Association was formed in 1925, the Northern Junior College Athletic Association in 1928, and the Central California Athletic Association in 1929. In order to establish unity, efficiency, and control it was necessary to bring these associations under one body. This was accomplished by establishing the California Junior College Federation, in 1929, to develop state-wide rules and policies.[8]

All of the associations were primarily composed of administrative personnel with the exception of the central association, which included other faculty members and some students.

By 1930 intercollegiate athletic competition in a variety of activities was engaged in by California junior colleges. Their accomplishments in athletics had been so phenomenal that:

> ... the initial thrust for a national organization to recognize junior college athletics came about as the result of a specific sport and, largely, a specific individual. The sport was track and field, and its early leadership was furnished by Dr. Oliver E. Byrd, who, at its inception, was coach of track and field at San Mateo Junior College in Belmont, California.[9]

Documentation of the accomplishment of the junior colleges in track and field reveals that, of all the interscholastic activities:

> ... none within the state was better organized or more widespread than track and field. During the 1930's conference track

49

and field championships were held in northern and southern California, and by 1934, the quality of the state's junior college program in this activity had developed to the point where all national junior college track and field records with the exception of the 100-yard dash were held by athletes representing California.[10]

To implement a means of obtaining national recognition of junior college athletes, a meeting was held "in conjunction with 1937 West Coast Relays (sometimes known as the Fresno Relays) in Fresno, California."[11] A committee was established whose purpose "was to consider possible national organization of and participation in the [National Collegiate Athletic Association] NCAA track and field championships."[12] The NCAA turned down the committee's request, "probably because of the NCAA's feeling that their championships should be limited to four - year institutions."[13]

The following year (1938) "a second meeting was held . . . coinciding again with the West Coast Relays track and field meet."[14] The result of this meeting was the acceptance of a constitution for an organization to be known as the National Junior College Athletic Association. "The real reason for the formation of the NJCAA was a recognition of those track and field records which were close to national caliber."[15]

In 1941, for the first time since its inception, the national track and field meet along with the NJCAA meeting was taken out of California (West Coast Relays in Fresno). It was held in Denver, Colorado, hosted by Trinidad (Colorado) Junior College.[16]

World War II intervened in December 1941, and all activities were suspended until 1946.

1946

World War II had ended. Junior colleges multiplied rapidly across the nation. The needs of individuals, the needs of business and industry, and the G.I. Bill triggered a population explosion which was significant to their growth. More junior colleges were established in California during the period 1946 to 1950 than ever before in its history, until the years 1966 to 1970.

NJCAA scheduled the fifth track and field meet and the annual meeting, the first after the war (1946), in Phoenix, Arizona. A significant historical point which came into effect at that meeting was a decision to expand the activities to all sports engaged in by junior colleges at that point in time. Also, at this meeting, the nation's JCs were divided into eight separate districts.[17]

California expressed some concerns. The majority of the schools were from the California area. Many of the top contenders were from California. The fact that national championships were pitting California teams against each other, but were traveling across country to engage in the contest, caused a great deal of concern to California colleges. Along the same line, with the number of colleges which California had that were participating in athletics, the organization, control, management, rules and regulations, and scheduling within the state became a primary concern. This prompted the California Junior College Federation to take a position against post-season competition for their colleges when participating outside of California.

However, that action was not immediately enforced. Some factors which occurred to cause the delay were: the lines of communication between NJCAA and California were open; California had not then changed, but was thinking of changing from a federation to the California Junior College Association; and most significant during that year, 1946, both entities sanctioned the Little Rose Bowl (later to become the Junior Rose Bowl). That bowl was originally suggested by the Pasadena Chamber of Commerce. After considerable energies were spent working out the details of management and control, that game continued for 21 years.

1947

NJCAA had a special meeting in Compton, California, to consider the first annual basketball championship. In addition, plans were made for the first annual golf and tennis championships to be held in Lexington, Missouri, with Wentworth Military Academy as the host school.[18]

The NJCAA regular meeting was held in Phoenix, Arizona, in conjunction with the Sixth Annual Track and Field Meet.[19]

During this same year the Athletic Committee of the California Junior College Federation underwent reorganization and was reconstituted as a subcommittee of the California Junior College Association - State Athletic Committee (CJCA-SAC). Many of its members were desirous of establishing a state junior college association to regulate and control its approximately 41 junior colleges.[20]

The CJCA-SAC became the governing body for junior college athletics in California. It was to serve as a unit which would formulate general rules and regulations, supervise management of intersectional athletics and championships on the state level, and set the machinery by which policy revisions could be brought to vote by the association.

Even with all of the activity that was taking place in California, that state remained a member of NJCAA. Discontent, however, was continuing to mount between CJCA-SAC and the NJCAA. It was a devastating blow to the relationship when, during this year, the new committee adopted the provision that, in case of any conflict between the two organizations, California junior colleges would have to abide by the CJCA-SAC rules.

1948

NJCAA had divided the United States into 16 regions, and the total membership had increased to 122 schools.

The NJCAA annual meeting was held in conjunction with the first national basketball tournament, which took place at Southwest Missouri State Teachers College.[21]

California's Marin College, winner of the contest, was not reimbursed for expenses because the tournament was not a financial success. This distressed the CJCA-SAC, along with the fact that it was highly possible two of its member colleges could travel across country and meet in the national tournament.

1949

The NJCAA annual meeting was held in Hutchinson, Kansas, in March, along with the national basketball tournament.[22] At that time "the institutional membership had increased to 191 members,"[23] with California having approximately 47 participating colleges and the other 144 being from the other states.

The California Junior College Association - State Athletic Committee (previously mentioned that it was established in 1947) became the mechanism by which athletics could be better organized and controlled.

1950

California's discontent persisted. The idea to break away from NJCAA was again seriously discussed, and statements to that effect were developed in May 1950. "The final breaking point between NJCAA and the California SAC was initiated during the fall meeting of the SAC held at the Hotel Durant in Berkeley on October 6-7, 1950."[24]

An accounting of the action at that meeting follows:

> First order of business was the letter written May, 1950, by Secretary Leo Wadsworth upon the recommendation of the committee, to Mr. Reed Swenson, President of the National Junior College Athletic Association, concerning its undemocratic form of organization. Mr. Wadsworth received no reply to his letter to date.
> Considerable discussion followed concerning participation of the California Junior Colleges in national competition. The committee arrived on agreement of the following resolution to be submitted to the California Junior College Association, at the November meeting, for its consideration and approval.
> For some years the members of the Committee and many of the Junior College Administrators and coaches have been concerned:
> (a) because of the heavy expense involved in sending athletes to the so-called national events of the National Junior College Athletic Association;
> (b) and because these events are participated in to only a small degree by athletes representing Junior Colleges outside California;
> (c) and because these events are, in the main, simply additional contests between Junior Colleges in California, which in most instances have already met one or more times during the season of the sport;
> (d) and finally because of the completely undemocratic form of organization of the National Junior College Athletic Association.
> The State Athletic Committee recommends to the California State Junior College Association that, under the present conditions, California Junior Colleges discontinue participation in events of the National Junior College Athletic Association.
> On motion of Mr. Jamison and seconded by Mr. Chastain, the above recommendation was approved and the motion was carried.[25]

The result was:

> The presentation was made to the parent body, CACC, at its November meeting in Yosemite and the resolution was passed. It was at this point that the break between the organizations became complete, and beginning on September 1, 1951, California Junior Colleges could no longer participate in NJCAA national events.[26]

Between the years 1946-1950 the new committee had been aggressive in its efforts to respond to the state needs, interests, and concerns. The committee continued to sanction the Junior Rose Bowl game and, in addition, sanctioned the following for its state junior colleges. Quoting Vokes:

> The Gold Dust Bowl made its first appearance on December 11, 1948 ... and its first participants were San Francisco City College and Chaffey College.
>
> The Potato Bowl received its first sanction ... for December 3, 1949 ... participants ... were Boise Junior College, Boise, Idaho, and Taft College of California. In the previous year, 1948, the game had been between two four-year schools (Santa Barbara College and Willamette University). The game, like the Junior Rose Bowl, continued until 1966, when the state playoff system took over for football. The Potato Bowl was conducted under management procedures similar to those utilized in the Junior Rose Bowl.
>
> The Olive Bowl made its appearance in 1949 ... at the same meeting that sanctioned the first Potato Bowl ... and was traditionally played on Thanksgiving Day in central California.[27]

Continuing, Vokes added:

> The SAC did not sponsor or sanction any state meets or tournaments in any sport for the year 1947-48 [excluding bowl games]. However, many other events did receive sanction during the period between 1946-1950. A generalized list is as follows:
>
> 1. A post-season football game, sponsored by the Veterans of Foreign Wars to be played December 18, 1948.
> 2. A sanction for Fresno Junior College to play a freelance football schedule since they were not associated with a conference. Phoenix College had the same privilege.
> 3. A preseason basketball tournament at Chaffey College.
> 4. An annual sanction for the Modesto basketball tournament usually held in December or January.
> 5. NJCAA events in basketball, swimming, boxing, gymnastics, golf, track, tennis, and baseball.
> 6. The Compton Relays in track and field.
> 7. The Southern California Junior College baseball tournament held at Citrus College.
> 8. A Christmas vacation basketball tournament to be held at Hartnell College.
> 9. The approval of a Boxing Conference patterned after the Pacific Coast Conference. Participants were to be Compton, Bakersfield, Muir, Pasadena, and Sequoia.[28]

During the period from 1950 to 1955, several football bowl games came into existence. California schools could only participate in those events controlled by the State Athletic

Committee (SAC) even though sponsored by outside organizations,[29] as shown in the following listing:

BOWL	SPONSOR	SITE
Junior Rose Bowl	Pasadena Junior Chamber of Commerce	Pasadena
Potato Bowl	Shriners Organization	Bakersfield
Olive Bowl	Lions Club	Lindsay
Optimists Bowl	Optimists Club	San Diego
Gold Dust Bowl	Vallejo 20-30	Vallejo
Desert Bowl	Palo Verde College	Blythe
Fish Bowl	Harbor College	San Pedro
Orange Show Bowl	San Bernardino 20-30 Club	San Bernardino
Alfalfa Bowl	Optimists Club of Lancaster	Lancaster
Sequoia Bowl	Sanger Hospital Guild	Visalia
Santa Rosa Elks Benefit	Santa Rosa Elks	Santa Rosa

State meets and tournaments in interscholastic sports, other than football,[30] were:

SPORT	YEAR SANCTIONED	SITE
Baseball	October 1951	--
Basketball	Spring 1951-52	College of Sequoias Visalia, CA
Golf	May 21, 1951	Stanford University Palo Alto, CA
Swimming	May 10-11-12, 1951	California State Polytechnic College San Luis Obispo, CA
Track	May 25, 1951	East Los Angeles Junior Cellege Los Angeles, CA
Water Polo	December 3-4, 1954	--

The Appendix contains information about California Association of Community Colleges (CACC) state championships.

In those sports where there is no accounting for championships beyond a certain year, the statistics were still being sought at the time of this publication.

The community college associations develop provisions concerning athletic conferences, playing rules, eligibility, residence, recruiting, penalties, seasons of sports, and rules for play-offs and tournaments. They also establish rules, regulations, and policies for problems, issues, and concerns. The associations are obligated to only their member colleges.

Presently California community colleges, as a whole, do not subscribe to NJCAA. Of the 107 colleges within the state, approximately 96 have some kind of intercollegiate athletic programs. These 96 colleges are in 12 conferences; five have memberships in both organizations (CACC and NJCAA). The CACC membership covers them for state recognition, while membership in NJCAA allows them national recognition in selected sports. The CACC colleges which are members of both organizations are assigned to the states of Arizona, Nevada, Utah, and Colorado. Respectfully, CACC — the "twilight zone" or "lost region" — does not dictate or regulate the efforts of any of its colleges to become bona fide members of NJCAA.

Community colleges that are not members of NJCAA are not considered for national competition, *i.e.*, play-offs and tournaments. Also, athletic team members are not considered for invitational, regional, national, and international competition. One exception, however, was the Junior Rose Bowl (sponsored by the Pasadena Junior Chamber of Commerce) which was played in Pasadena, California, to determine the "mythical national championship of community college" football. According to the *California Community and Junior College Association News* (CCJCA) [*NOTE:* The organization is now the California Association of Community Colleges (CACC)]:

> ... The Junior Rose Bowl was first started in 1946, when Compton College played Kilgore, Texas, and it continued until 1967, when CCJCA switched to a [state] play-off system.[31]

During that period, close to 950,000 fans watched the top California JC football team play against "the most outstanding rival from out of state,"[32] which included teams from[33] "Texas ... eight times; Oklahoma, seven; Mississippi, twice; ... Minnesota, Arkansas, Idaho and Washington, once each."

In 1976:

> ... the *Los Angeles Times* in conjunction with the California Community and Junior College Association ... led the way in reviving the Junior Rose Bowl game ... Nearly 30,000 fans witnessed ... when the California entry, Bakersfield College Renegades, captured a 29-14 victory over Ellsworth, Iowa,[34]

After the 1977 contest, in which 15,000 fans witnessed Pasadena City College (Pasadena, CA) defeat Jones County Junior

(Mississippi) 38-9, the Junior Rose Bowl was again discontinued and California returned to a state play-off system.

A summary of the Junior Rose Bowl games may be found in the Appendix.

Let us deviate for a moment to discuss some of the concepts of the Junior Rose Bowl.

During the revival of the Junior Rose Bowl game in 1976-1977, its committee was enthusiastic that it would again rise to prominence. They envisioned the benefits it would serve the athletic program by keeping it, as Killian said, "in the sports spotlight," and that it would also enhance the total efforts of the junior - community colleges.

> "The Junior Rose Bowl game is excellent for all community college athletics," said Dr. Robert A. Lombardi, chairman of the Committee on Athletics of the California Community and Junior College Association. "It definitely promotes interest and calls attention to the community college programs."
>
> Dr. Lombardi, along with Dr. Lloyd E. Messersmith, CJCA executive director, serves on the Junior Rose Bowl Selection election committee.
>
> "The California community colleges compete in a full range of men's and women's sports," said Dr. Messersmith, "and the Junior Rose Bowl helps to emphasize the quality of our athletic programs. We are happy to be a part of the effort to reestablish this traditional game."
>
> At the national level, support for continuing the Junior Rose Bowl was expressed by Cecil Perkins, president of the National Junior College Athletic Association's Football Coaches Association and head coach at Potomac State in Keyser, West Virginia. "It's the best thing that can happen to junior college football. If every team in the country thinks they have a shot at the Junior Rose Bowl, it's terrific for all of us," he said.[35]

The Junior Rose Bowl was one of the most unique developments that ever occurred in the history of the two-year colleges. With regard to athletics, it was unequaled. Disregarding logistics, external and internal to the JC's, that mystical national championship was the highest level of visibility. By having the two major organizations involved, it served as both a buffer and a bond. Within the JC's it was one of three unifying national athletic events in the major sports.

Bear in mind that a national championship was being conducted in track and field and in basketball until the latter part of 1950. The national championship in those two events was before a definite division between the governing organizations. The significance of the Junior Rose Bowl was that it was the only unifying athletic event that continued after the division between NJCAA and CJCA-SAC. Of importance was the fact that, in order for it to be successful, it forced both organizations to relax tensions and set aside differences, if any, to bring together the best of the system.

Even though most of the advantages may have greatly served the JCs internally, externally they provided a climate for coaches and players (JCs, four-year institutions, and high schools) to become personally acquainted when ordinarily they probably would never have done so. They also provided an opportunity to share new ideas, techniques, and innovations, and created better communication and understanding that would enhance the JCs, the coaches, and the players.

The hope for the continuance of the Junior Rose Bowl extended far beyond that of being *merely* an athletic contest, but more as a means of building a monument to the two-year colleges in the same manner and style as the bowl games served the four-year institutions. It was a challenge — a quest to revive "El Dorado." It was a legacy to a new generation. It was an acknowledgment to the community, a memento to its sons and daughters, and a trophy to all of the athletes who dared to chance to "catch the golden ring." Measuring this foresight against today's conditions, perhaps that committee and those sponsoring entities were avant - garde in their efforts.

. . .

In conclusion, there is considerable evidence that the development and growth of activities in the junior - community colleges have been in direct proportion to what the individual colleges could handle. Releaguing, rescheduling, and the inclusion of activities are areas which have been observed. The commendable quality is that when growth and development occur they are planned and controlled by the individual colleges and conferences, and not as a result of persuasion from the governing organizations.

Another commendable quality has been that the sometimes devastating influences of politics, attitudes, and competition, or the need for power, have not pressured any of the junior college organizations to the extent that the philosophy and goals of athletics have been seriously hampered. In many systems the organizations, and those who govern them, stifle the efforts of their constituents. The bureaucracy stifles what should and needs to be done.

Also, in many instances, the basic needs, interests, and concerns of the individuals become secondary to the motives of their leaders. As much as budgets will permit, the colleges have continued to provide support services to assist students in accomplishing their goals and objectives. Counseling and guidance, speech and reading laboratories, learning and child care centers, peer counselors, tutors, and job finding assistance are integral parts of the educational program.

Finally, judging the JCs against the reasons for their existence (teaching, service, accessibility, open door policy, a less stressful environment) and their educational philosophy (providing experiences which will assist them in obtaining employment, transferring, becoming responsible family members and citizens, and career planning), they deserve the highest commendation. From an athletic perspective they have been ultraimpressive, if significant advances toward expected outcomes (transfers to four-year institutions and athletic careers) are barometers.

Because of these reasons, and more, we shall see in the following chapter that the JCs can be a good beginning for the student athlete.

Chapter Three
A GOOD BEGINNING FOR THE STUDENT-ATHLETE

Iantorno,[1] Mazzei,[2] and McCullough[3] observed that it is not the development of physical skills alone which makes the two-year college athlete a bona fide talent. They theorized that the two-year college environment enhances mental and emotional growth, while providing a unique opportunity for a gradual adjustment in conduct, attitude, and behavior. (Shock and stress related to the higher education experience will be discussed at greater length later in this chapter.) The result manifests itself in social growth and character development. As Iantorno stated, "There can be some profoundness when coaches say we didn't win this year but we developed a lot of character."

Their observations are consistent with several theories of social growth and character formation:[4]

> While it has been stated in many different ways — by educators, philosophers, social scientists, psychologists, politicians, and others — it is generally agreed that the total function of education includes not only the teaching of subject matter but the development of character as well.
> ... One aspect of character development ... is moral development.
> But character, in inclusive concept, means more than simply one's moral outlook. It includes the individual's self-perceptions, attitudes about self — self-concept in general. Self-concept is not easy to define, but we know from many years of study that the individual's self-concept plays a vital role in all of the mental processes, including learning. The way a person treats others, the way he responds to the environment, the way he challenges the obstacles that confront him at every point in living, are all related, directly or indirectly, to the person's self-concept.

Richard L. Moore, President of Santa Monica Community College, said:[5]

> I started out as a critic of athletics, but I've come to learn that athletics really changed the lives of a lot of people. A lot of people give a great deal of time. Coaches give their lives.
>
> I came out of a "pure" academic system and that was my orientation — that was my interest, books and other pure academics. Through this, I developed character, integrity, and confidence.
>
> Some people start out with athletics and through this they build integrity, character, and confidence. One purpose of educational institutions and other basic systems in society (family, church, community) is to provide wholesome experiences... to open doors. If you don't have athletics, you close a whole door.
>
> Some people only come because of athletics. Fine. Now they are in my mouse trap and I can try to open up doors for them.

Freddie Goss thinks the community college experience for the athlete is extremely beneficial. Before resigning as head basketball coach at the University of California, Riverside, he related some specific advantages:[6]

> Great players come from many sources — high schools, community junior colleges, military, and even playgrounds — but considering the traditional sources of recruitment, the odds are against finding the great instant player in the high schools.
>
> When you get players out of high schools who have limited experiences in traveling, have not been away from home overnight, have not socialized with people in the major college environment, and have not been exposed to the major college experiences, and when you combine this with the fact that they may not be from a strong and stable family and educational background, to say the least, you may be recruiting players who are emotionally and socially handicapped. All of these factors play an important part in the performance of young players.
>
> On the other hand, the community college players have been exposed to many of the disciplines and experiences which are demanded by the four-year colleges. For these reasons I think, in most cases, the community colleges may be the best overall route young players should take. It puts a lot of pressure on them to travel clear across the country and be expected to perform against the best — at their best. A number of coaches even though they have freshmen who are eligible to play right out of high school are recommending that they go to a community college which will help them to develop that social I.Q.
>
> It's tough to make a lot of mistakes and survive at the four-year college level. At the community college level, players have the same high - level experiences but at the slower process which enhances

their adjustment to the college curriculum, environment, and routine. The competition is also at a high level and in that environment they can make a few mistakes while preparing themselves for entry into the major college universe.

Gene Wellman, Chabot College athletic director, submitted to an interview pertaining to examining the athletic success, and the benefits for, the student-athlete attending a community college. His views were of his particular community college, but they reflect broad sentiments. Here are portions of that interview:[7]

SPECTATOR: Is the Golden Gate Conference competitive enough?

WELLMAN: Our league has always been very competitive, and with the addition of DeAnza, West Valley, and Foothill, it's just unbelievable.

I look at the baseball situation where we have three players drafted and everybody thinks, my god, you're going to have a super team. But San Mateo had five players drafted, and West Valley seven. That's just for openers — I don't know what the others had.

SPECTATOR: What kind of program can you sell high school athletes to have them come to Chabot, rather than a four-year school?

WELLMAN: I think our program for the first two years is better than anybody's, and sometimes, people laugh when you say that.

I tell them our program is better the first two years than USC or Santa Clara, and they think I'm kidding. When you're a freshman or sophomore there, you're not getting what the varsity is getting. You're getting hand-down equipment; you're not the number-one team; nobody cares about the frosh or JV's at the university level.

SPECTATOR: Then it's better to go Chabot? Why?

WELLMAN: Three reasons. One, better teachers — there are better teachers at the community college. No question about it. I think they're more interested in the students.

Two, financial reasons — athletic scholarships help, but it is still very expensive to live away from home. Actually, only a few do get scholarship help. By attending a community college, they can save anywhere from $400 to $4,000 in a two-year period.

Three, a better chance to play. Usually a player knows who he has to compete with to make the team. At a state college, or university, many top players never get past their freshman year. There is just too much competition.

SPECTATOR: What kind of fringe benefits can you offer prospective athletes?

WELLMAN: We can't offer them anything but an opportunity to get a good education and a chance to play on a solid team.

It's a fact that most high school players don't know what they want to do after high school. Chabot is a transition period and when they leave here they usually know at what level of competition they can compete, and that's very important. The most important thing for an athlete is his education and an opportunity to play.

SPECTATOR: Don't most prospects look beyond community colleges?

WELLMAN: Many outstanding athletes contacted out of high school have no real idea how difficult it is to make any college program, including ours. There is a lot of social pressure to attend the four-year school. Most high school athletes don't really know their athletic abilities.

Many student-athletes who could have gone to four-year schools without scholarship help come here, and then end up getting a full scholarship to Cal, UCLA, etc. We had two baseball players who went to Cal from last year's team, Mark Sill and Larry Kowalishen. We have football players and wrestlers at UCLA and Cal, basketball players throughout the state.

SPECTATOR: Do most top high school players think they are "super - super - athletes?"

WELLMAN: Yes, because they are at that level. Most have received many awards in high school, and their high school coaches and the community believe in them.

Reflecting on and scrutinizing the variety of experiences they have had, years later many former junior - community college athletes praised, not only the intercollegiate athletic aspect, but the overall junior college experience and program. Paul McCarthy, *Tribune* (Oakland, CA) Staff Writer, reported as follows:[8]

COMMUNITY COLLEGES WORTHWHILE FOR MANY ATHLETES
By Paul McCarthy
Tribune Staff Writer

Sports careers, like footballs, take strange bounces.

Norm Thompson couldn't help but reflect on the truth of that statement in recent weeks as first the high school athletic stars signed letters of intent and later their big brothers in college sweated out the National Football League draft.

Even though Thompson never really agonized over letters or the draft, he has some definite ideas about *pressures young athletes endure* today.

"I see a lot of high school ball players being catered to by prospective coaches and alumni," said Thompson, until recently as assistant football coach at Laney College. "I think a kid would be wise to sit down and evaluate the people he's talking to — not so much as an athlete, but as an individual and as a student.

"He should look at what the school has to offer in a chosen field, keeping in mind what the future holds after college and, possibly, pro ball."

Lots of young people have no real career goals at 17 and 18, and should consider community colleges, he said. Two-year schools today offer a lot of opportunities for maturity.

"We used to look at JCs as 'high schools with ash trays,'" Thompson laughed. "But that's not the case anymore. The California community college system is ideal for many young adults trying to make a decision about their future."

High school kids in 1983 are exposed to pressures previously reserved for the college athletes of Thompson's day. No wonder so many wind up without a degree or any career skills once their playing days are over.

Thompson, now 39 and a part-time trainee with a major bank, looked back on nine seasons as a defensive back with the St. Louis Cardinals and the Baltimore Colts after All-American honors with Utah.

His football career at San Francisco's Galileo High really didn't hold much promise at first.

"I was all-city in track and basketball, but in football, I got hurt and didn't play all that much," he recalled.

Even though he measured just 6-foot-1, Thompson had talent that his hurdles ability and a high jump best of 6 feet, 10 inches earned him a track scholarship from San Jose State.

There was just one complication.

"I got married in my senior year of high school, and when my wife got pregnant, I took a job instead of going to college.

"I worked as a ship painter and sand blaster at Bethlehem Steel in San Francisco. It was hard work, so football came easy after that," Thompson added with a smile.

He had no trouble, either, after high school in realizing that there should be more to life than chipping paint.

So Thompson enrolled at Laney College — even while working at Bethlehem and playing football. His idea was to learn the machinist's trade.

"I had always played a lot of sandlot football, and when I saw the kids at Laney, I figured I could do that well," he explained.

How well he did is written in the Utah and NCAA Division I archives.

Thompson still holds the NCAA record for best average return per interception, 50.6 yards, in 1969 as a junior. And he shares, with 1945 Army All-American "Doc" Blanchard and nine others, the NCAA record for most TD interceptions in a season at three, also that junior year.

"I was a receiver turned defensive back," Norm said with relish, "so I knew what to do with the ball when I caught it. Even in the pros, I think I averaged about 20 yards per interception."

As an All-American cornerback, Thompson really didn't have to sweat out the 1968 NFL draft.

At 25, though, he nearly challenged MacArthur Lane of Oakland and Utah State as the oldest St. Louis rookie. Lane, like Thompson, was a Cards first-round pick in 1968 — when he was 26.

The ex-Laney star wrote a little football law, too, when he played out his option with the Cards and signed as a free agent with Baltimore on April 1, 1977.

"The word free agent doesn't really mean much in the NFL any more. I am the only one who ever moved from one team to another (as a free agent) and the old team was guaranteed compensation. I'm a walking legend," Thompson said.

"I had a lawyer, Richard Bennett in D.C., that was really working for me. We put a renegotiation clause in there and it made me a six-figure player. I hated to leave St. Louis, because the players were really close. I enjoyed those years with Terry Metcalfe, Mel Gray and that offensive line..."

"It was a championship team and the guys on defense did a lot of things off the field together. We and our wives and girlfriends really enjoyed ouselves getting together after the games."

Neck and back injuries shortened his career. The alternative would have been surgery, but Thompson passed on that, feeling the risk was too great. He never had surgery to repair a busted cheekbone, either.

"I lost about three - quarters of an inch (in height), and I still have a lot of pain, even now," he said.

Because he had a taste of the working world before college, Thompson was able to adjust when his NFL career ended in 1979.

To repay some of his debt, he serves on the board of directors for National Sports Career Management, a group headed by ex-49er Delvin Williams.

The NSCM program aims at assisting players and their families to contend with the pressures associated with a pro athlete's life and make the transition to other careers when he is finished with pro sports.

Thompson said players have to realize many new - found friends hang around only when an athlete is riding high. The need to begin planning for an alternative career must start early — not when a player is on his last legs.

It's working within the United States Football League better than in the established NFL. Officials in the new league seem to be more aware of potential problems such as drugs, injuries and fly - by - night influences that threaten pro careers, Thompson said.

[Emphasis added.]

In all probability, one of the "pressures young athletes endure" today, mentioned early in the article, experienced by many students, not only athletes, is the overall pressure of the various higher education environments.

Alvin Toffler[9] "coined the term 'future shock' to describe the shattering stress and disorientation that we induce in individuals by subjecting them to too much change in too short a time." Perhaps nowhere is this concept experienced more than in one's encounter with higher education institutions, and particularly four-year institutions.

According to Proctor, in *Survival on Campus*, when the student:[10]

> ...leaves the safe harbor of his parents' home and enters the rough waters of the university ... each faction competes for the loyalty of the new freshman, and sometimes this rivalry borders on an open warfare in which the ... student may become a casualty unless he is careful.

Continuing, Proctor said:[11]

> A new experience is never what we expect it to be, and the arrival of a freshman at college is no exception to this rule. No matter how many pictures a university catalog displays, no matter how vivid or accurate the descriptions of the campus, the incoming student will always face a cultural shock as he tries to adjust to his new surroundings.

He also added:[12]

> ...A war, subtle but devastating, is being waged on American college campuses. This conflict does not involve bombings or violent political protests or setting fire to buildings. The battle, instead, is being fought by both students and instructors at university dining halls, dormitory rooms, and social events. The weapons are questions: What do you believe? Why do you believe it? If you believe that way, why do you behave in the way that you do?
>
> The ultimate prize in this war is the student's mind, his basic orientation toward life, his allegiance to one world view or another. These are critical, formative years, when the young person must make decisions about life largely on his own, with little opportunity to consult with the folks back home. He must decide what values to live by, what career to follow, and what kind of person to choose for a marital mate.

Dintiman and Greenberg elaborated on some of the concepts, facts, and trends associated with stress which may be encountered in the college experience:[13]

> College life is an experience that is, for most, both enjoyable and fondly remembered, but it can be very stressful. Many of the stressors affecting college students are bacteria or viruses. The close living quarters shared by students residing in dormitories or apartments foster the rapid spread of communicable diseases ... Of course, other stressors such as lack of sleep, examinations, and inadequate nutrition all contribute to the spread of such diseases. Even students who live at home and commute to the campus are in close proximity to fellow students in classes and are susceptible, though perhaps not to the same degree, to the same illnesses.

Other stressors associated with college life have to do with changes and decisions, which are normal and part of the maturing process. The existence of these stressors should be acknowledged. For students living away from home for the first time, the need to care for themselves, independent of the family, can be a trying experience ... The strain of not seeing people who have been seen every day of one's whole life can be troublesome as well and, for some, homesickness is an intense stressor.

Of course, there are substitutes for the people one misses. Friends of the same and opposite sex often temporarily replace the absent family members. This process in itself may be stressing, though. The need to make friends and to date bring with them the fears of being unsuccessful at these tasks.

... The decisions college students are required to make are often very important. Your decision regarding what to do and become for the rest of your life may be very stressing to you. And there are many other decisions as well.

They go on and on. Whereas all of life involves decision making, college life is somewhat different. It may be the first time that a student is required to make decisions relatively independent — decisions of real importance, that is.

According to Insel and Roth, the effects of these stressors are that "approximately 1,000 college students take their own lives each year, and this figure is twice as high for college students as for people the same age but not in college."[14] Dintiman and Greenberg said: "Interestingly, the reason for these suicides is not difficulty with schoolwork but rather the feeling of isolation that results from not being able to establish close personal relationships."[15] Expounding on this concept, they added:[16]

College students experience alienation due to a budding independence and increased social isolation, questions of self-worth resulting from having to make new friends and the fear of failing at this task, and confusion regarding important decisions that must be made. Add to this the need to do well in courses and on examinations and the effect that failure here might have upon self-esteem, and the stresses of college life might appear overwhelming. The "grin - and - bear - it" attitude professed by some to meet these stresses is just not successful.

The degree of shock varies, depending on the student's apperceptives. Among the many encounters to which the students must adjust are, first, the college process — registration, lines of people, bookstores, definitive schedules, and time lines.

Second, there is a degree of shock in the change of environment. This includes being in a different location, an expanded campus, increased classrooms, larger class sizes, new faces, competition with students of various academic levels, and, most of all, the loss of personal identity in classroom settings and in the student service areas.

Third, during the academic process the student encounters professors he does not know (some who are world renowned); various and rigid teaching styles and techniques; numerous assignments to be completed in a limited amount of time ("semipaper chase"); and extensive, detailed, and curved graded exams. If a student's financial or social status depends on academic standings, in addition to shock, the student experiences stress.

If, after a day of academics, a student has to take part in intercollegiate athletics and compete with upperclassmen who are, in part, competing for all-league, conference, division, or maybe Heisman awards, or only trying to assure their scholarships, but most of all trying to achieve professional status, that becomes additional shock combined with a high degree of stress.

The reality of the position of these educators is addressed by Stanford University's football coach, Bill Walsh. After playing six of 11 games in 1978, Stanford's record was 3-3, with their last game being a 34-31 loss to the Washington Huskies. Coach Walsh said:[17]

> "It's almost unforgiveable for Stanford to play like that, and that includes everybody concerned, the players, the assistants, the head coach.
> "We have a lot of sophs and freshmen; I suppose that that's the problem.
> *"They are young men under a lot of stress* [italics not in the original] and doing their best."

The "shock/stress" produced by these kinds of situations will cause players to react in various ways. Drugs, alcohol, and other socially unacceptable behavior have been noted. Some drop out and become entangled in the social webs of society, and circumstances cause them never to return. Some just drop out.

Dan Sewell wrote this about San Francisco's running back, Delvin Williams, who was traded to the Miami Dolphins to assist the 49ers in acquiring O. J. Simpson:[18]

> Williams, oldest of three brothers and a retarded sister, credits high school coach Tom Hendrickson with motivating him into college at the University of Kansas. Williams nearly did the same thing many other collegians from his neighborhood had done — dropped out.

"John Novotny (the man in charge of the scholarship program) got behind me then (after a 1.8 first semester average). He said I had to go to class, that was 50% of it. He said he was going to see me graduate."

Williams was almost clipped by a chemistry course but he eventually pushed his average up to 2.7, a C-plus. He graduated on time in what he says may be his proudest accomplishment.

"Others from my neighborhood got in college but I was the first one to follow it through," he said. "A lot of guys had excellent atheltic ability, but they didn't exploit it."

Others return years later and are faced with extending themselves to vie with younger players, but many immediately transfer to a two-year college.

Like many other JCs, Los Angeles Southwest College — winner of the Southern California conference basketball title in 1978 — experienced the results of players transferring from four-year institutions. Their 15-man roster included six players from out of state but more significant, when related to the present topic of discussion, three of those 15 players transferred from four-year institutions. All three were starters during the 1979 season. Coach Leon Henry commented:[19]

Sometimes the four-year system is too big for them. They get lost in the shuffle.

It isn't embarrassing for a player to return to a J.C. In fact, it's smart. It takes a degree of intelligence for a student to recognize immediately that he's in fast company and he has to make some changes.

Several other colleges in the area reported similar activity. Lloyd Messersmith,[20] past director of athletics of California Community and Junior Colleges (CCJCA), reported that this "back and forth" transferring is found up and down the state. If a high school graduate attends a major four-year institution and ends up "red shirting," then he might stay and take the red shirt. If it looks like the class of ball playing is going to be too heavy for him, he will come back and play the community college and then return to a four-year institution which plays the class of ball he can handle. (Note: in most cases a player will not return to the same four-year institution.)

It's not just peculiar to California. Roy Sommers, Athletic Director, Niagara County Community College, the 1978 NJCAA basketball champions, reported that they are getting a fair amount of transfers from four-year colleges:[21]

It seems that since the NCAA has relaxed their requirements — freshman eligibility — some of the students who should be coming to two-year colleges are going to four-year colleges. I noticed that our recruiting is becoming more difficult, but then it seems like some of the students are becoming more dissatisfied and are coming back.

Many of the high school players, especially in our area, think in four-year college terms before they think in two-year college terms, and if they can get into a four-year college, they prefer to do it. In a lot of the cases, high school coaches push them in that direction. I don't know their reasoning for this — whether it gives them prestige or not — but the players seem to follow their advice. Along the line many of the players get disillusioned, some drop out, and some filter back into a junior college.

Wayne Unruh, Assistant Director, NJCAA, summarized the national trend for players in four-year institutions transferring back to two-year colleges by responding:[22]

We see that pretty much in every state throughout the United States. We see a large number of players do that but I don't know their reasons exactly.

Many of these players are leaving the four-year colleges in good academic standing to transfer to a two-year institution and be immediately eligible. So in a way our rules do not discourage the transfer.

Unruh's concluding statement, *"so in a way our rules do not discourage the transfer,"* and the fact that such rules do exist for the community colleges, reflects the recommendations pertaining to "Open Access" as outlined by the Carnegie Commission of Higher Education. In part, they expressed:[23]

Among the reasons for the rapid advance of community colleges are their open-admissions policies, their geographic distribution across the country, and their usually low tuition policies. They also offer more varied programs for a greater variety of students than any other segment of higher education, provide a chance for post-secondary education for many who are not fully committed to a four-year college career, and appeal to students who are undecided about their future career and unprepared to choose a field of specialization. In addition, they provide an opportunity for working adults to upgrade their skills and training. There are now over 1,000 two-year colleges in the United States and there is no doubt that community college enrollment will continue to grow rapidly in the 1970s. As growth continues, there will be unsettled issues and problems relating to community colleges. Satisfactory resolution of these unsettled issues and problems is of importance and urgency for the future of higher education in the United States.

> *The Commission believes that there should be an opportunity within the total system of higher education in each state for each high school graduate or otherwise qualified person to enter higher education* [italics not in the original]. This does not mean that every young person should attend college — many will not want to attend and there will be others who would not benefit sufficiently to justify the time and expense involved. *Community colleges should follow an open - enrollment policy* [italics not in the original], while access to four-year institutions should generally be more selective. Thus, community colleges will play a crucial role in the provision of universal access.

Transferring is not only peculiar to the community colleges. Lateral transfers, especially in basketball, are common at the four-year institutional level. A difference is, however, the four-year colleges (NCAA) transfer rule requires players to remain in residence at the new institution one year before they can resume competition.

According to a *Los Angeles Times* article,[24] some basketball players that have made lateral transfers in past years are the following:

Cresenta High School (La Cresenta, CA) All-American Greg Goorjian, who attended Arizona State University (ASU) immediately after high school, after one year transferred to Nevada, Las Vegas, and ended up at Loyola Marymount;

Clift Pruitt, Verbum Dei High (Los Angeles, CA) All-American, to University of California at Los Angeles (UCLA), and later the University of Alabama, Birmingham;

Leonel Marquetti, High School All-American, Verbum Dei (Los Angeles, CA), attended the University of Southern California (USC) and later Hampton Institute;

Dwight Anderson, Roth High School (Dayton, Ohio), Kentucky first and USC second;

Kyle Macy, Peru High School (Peru, IND), to Purdue and eventually Kentucky; and

Todd May, Virgie High School (Virgie, KY), from high school to Kentucky and later transferred to Wake Forest.

The article stated that between 40 and 60 players have made lateral transfers in each of the last three years. "The thing is," the article continued, "while the player almost always helps the program, the program doesn't always help the player."[25] Goorjian's father, also basketball coach at Loyola Marymount, said his son "was emotionally destroyed by his experience at ASU."[26]

With the previous information as a background, the role that the two-year colleges serve by having the "open - enrollment" policy can be better understood. They not only serve the needs of student - athletes, they provide the same "universal access" for all qualified persons. Continuing to focus on the student - athlete, however, the subject of transfer will conclude with this commentary:[27]

> Stan Morrison has lost an unusually high number of transfers at USC, three this year alone. To him, it's no mystery. Everybody comes to him a star is the problem.
> "Young people, all heavily recruited, all been stars," he says of his incoming freshmen. "But only five of these stars can ever be on the court at the same time."
> Morrison leans back at his desk and says his recruits are so ill-equipped for anything but stardom he actually finds it necessary to teach his players how to sit.
> "A week before our first game," he says, "we rehearse sitting on the bench. It's not something any of them have ever done."
> Morrison understands the players' high expectations. A coach who recruits players who know how to sit well will not coach for long. A coach needs players with high expectations. Still, all these expectations clattering around on the same team can cause problems.
> Morrison's had two of those problems in Ken Johnson and Gerry Wright, two of his three transfers this year (the third, John Korfas, was not a problem; he was simply at the wrong level and recognized it). Johnson and Wright both had expectations of starring roles. Those expectations apparently unfilled, they left.
> To Morrison, the answer is to bring back the rule prohibiting freshmen from playing varsity basketball. He cites all the traditional arguments — transition from high school to college campus, the academic and social adjustments required, etc. But he also cites the ego argument.
> "I look around the country and there's no doubt there are freshmen who can contribute mightily," he says. "But all freshmen? That's naive, unrealistic and unreasonable. And yet they all expect to."
> If there was freshman basketball, "They could all be starters, get lots of minutes and not have the pressure of a varsity outcome. Playing for the varsity is out of their hands, it's a rule. They can't be unhappy over it. The other advantage is *you can teach at the freshman level. You can't afford to teach at the varsity level.* [Italics not in the original.]
> "This would make a lot of difference to some players. I think back to a player like Gus Williams. What would have happened if he didn't have the opportunity to play freshman ball. He would have been a disaster, that's what."

With freshman basketball, a player couldn't complain about playing time until he was a sophomore. At that point, he wouldn't be so inclined to leave, having already invested two years.

That would effectively end wide - spread transferring. As for the cost of having freshman basketball, Morrison says it's really an economy.

"Look at the cost of losing a kid you recruited, all that investment," he says. "Then look at the cost of him going to another university where he'll sit on scholarship, for a year."

Morrison has since decided he won't contribute to the trend by accepting any more transfers. Although he helped the team by accepting Dwight Anderson out of Kentucky three years ago, he has now decided the risks of accepting an unhappy player are not worth it.

"The odds are against you," he says.

There are not a lot of coaches lining up behind Morrison, though. Jerry Tarkanian, whose son was displaced by the domino effect of transferring, will continue to accept transfers. Why not, he asked. "Their cars are all paid for."

On a less flip day, Tarkanian says, "If basketball is important to a kid, he may have to transfer." Maybe even to Nevada, Las Vegas.

The community college system assists another important group — the foreign student athlete. The créme de la créme world class performers, especially in track and field, have been endemic to the four-year institutions. More recently, however, large numbers of foreign aspirants are coming to the United States and enrolling in community colleges because that system can more readily absorb them. The magnitude of one issue prompted major newspaper coverage in an article, *"JC Track Coaches Voicing Concern on Foreign Affairs."*[2,8]

Ron Allice, head track coach, has led Long Beach City College to the best record in California Community Colleges' track and field history, and out - measured his opponents in 1983 to win the fourth consecutive Southern California and state men's track and field champions. (See Appendix D: Track — California Community College Champions, 1951 - 1983.) Since moving to Long Beach City College (1979) from Compton High School (CA), his team has never lost a dual meet.

Because of the large numbers of world class foreign student - athletes on his 1983 team, opposing coaches were concerned. Some voiced the opinion that the concentration of these athletes in a limited number of community colleges might become a trend which would limit the less fortunate colleges' chances of ever winning.

In response to inquiries regarding the composition of his team, Allice said:[29]

> ... What happened this year may never happen again. A lot of this has to do with the Olympics being here ... I have never cut an athlete, no matter how limited their skills, in all my years of coaching ... I'm not going to turn them away.

Those elements which characterize the community colleges (accessibility, open - enrollment, diversity, services, and the like), even to those within the system, like democracy, constantly test the state of mind, attitude, conduct, and behavior of those that govern, administer, and implement the system.

Another relevant but disregarded fact is that JC athletic expenditures are monies well spent considering the large number of athletes that transfer to four-year institutions, and keep in mind that transfer is one of the college's functions. These individuals, especially those from deprived backgrounds, are afforded opportunities which far exceed their counterparts. The scholarships and grant - in - aid received through expenditures for interscholastic athletics far exceed the total scholarship and grant - in - aid available to the remainder of the student body.

Gene Mazzei, head football coach at San Bernardino Valley College and winner of the 1982 Inland Empire Lions Bowl, explained it in this manner:[30]

> Let's say a two-year college interscholastic athletic program costs a college $50,000. Quoting Pasadena City College figures — at the minimum value of $3,000 per year for two and a half years, totaling $7,500 — if ten community college athletes receive scholarships to four-year institutions, that's the college investment. Now that's accountability.
> This is not suggesting that interscholastic athletics are the most viable program in the college. It's only pointing out that there is a direct and identifiable return on every dollar spent, plus more. That's good business.

Further emphasis is the following. A study of the expenditures for interscholastic athletics in comparison to the number of athletes that received direct and immediate financial benefits (in addition to the invaluable social benefits) and the total amount of money the program generated in scholarships and grant - in - aid was conducted in Los Angeles, the nation's largest community college district.[31]

According to the Athletic Director's Research Committee, it disclosed that the college year 1981-1982 interscholastic athletic expenditure was an estimated $1,467,000. During that period approximately 210 athletes received scholarships or grant - in - aid to four-year institutions. Contrary to Pasadena City College valuation of the minimum worth of a scholarship to be $3,000 per year, the research committee estimated the minimum worth of a scholarship during that period had risen, due to an increase in the basic educational cost, to an average of $4,500 yearly. Based on these figures, athletic scholarships or grant - in - aid to four-year institutions, based on a two-year stay at the four-year institution, totaled approximately $1,800,000. A two - and - one - half - year stay at the four-year institution reflected that the district procured an estimated $2,225,000. Significant, also, is the fact that approximately 25 athletes transferred to four-year institutions without scholarships or grant - in - aid.

Another reason why the two-year colleges are a good beginning for the student athlete is that coaches at four-year institutions have positive feelings about community college athletes. It provides them with seasoned, quality, systematized, and low - cost products. Community college transfers have had additional time for physical, mental, emotional, and social growth in a far less stressful environment, an opportunity to upgrade their athletic skills and understanding of the higher education process, and, it is more economical to carry a student for two years than for four years. In short, the community colleges are nurturing environments whose products are instant performers.

John McKay, former head coach at USC and now head mentor with the Tampa Bay Buccaneers, on occasion recruited back - to - back "superstars" from the community colleges — first, O. J. Simpson from San Francisco, and the year after O. J. left (1969), Clarence Davis from East Los Angeles Community College.

McKay gave this testimony to the dexterity and skill of the community college athlete:[32]

> Stanford was next, and they began the game with a new formation for them, the power-I. But we should have recognized it. We had invented it. But we couldn't even line up right against our own formation. They outgained us by 140 yards in the first half and had us down 17-0 before we knew what hit us. We lost, 33-18. It was a sad joke. Stanford dominated us by running our own formation against us.
> Since we had also lost our opener to Alabama, our record was now 2-4. What the hell had happened? Had the game passed me by?

Had we gotten fat and lazy? People were all excited about the wishbone formation that season, but Nebraska was still using our I-formation and was on its way to a second straight national championship. What was the matter with us?

The morning of the Notre Dame game, seven days after Stanford, I finally realized what had gone wrong. I called a meeting of our coaches.

"The reason we haven't been winning," I said, "is that we are playing the wrong people. And our biggest weakness is that we don't have anybody else to play. We're playing people who do not run fast enough to play this game — and we're the slowest on defense. Any time we play a team with real good speed, we get outrun. And offensively, all the backs we have fumble too much."

I realized we had not been selective enough in our recruiting. We began to think, heck, we've been winning like crazy, and we're just going to keep winning, and that's all there is to it. When you assume you're always going to win, you ease up in your recruiting without even knowing that you're doing it. We'd think, "Ah, this player's all right. He can play. He's a lot like old Joe who played here when we had O. J."

Only we didn't have O. J. now. And all of a sudden a coach gets six or eight of these marginal players, and if he gives only 20 scholarships a year, like we do, he's in trouble. You can't give 20 scholarships and make eight mistakes.

I made up my mind that we weren't going to play defense anymore with players who weren't exceptionally fast — particularly on the outside. Most college offenses are option - oriented, and with the success of Oklahoma in 1971, we felt more and more teams would be going to the wishbone. I decided that if anyone was going to beat us, they weren't going to outrun us.

The solution was to recruit a large group of freshmen and junior college transfers who could fly. [Italics not in the original.]

I had actually begun to realize we were too slow in 1970, when our defense yielded 21 points a game, far and away the most of my career. So we recruited a brilliant group of freshmen, which included defensive players like All - American Richard Wood, Charles Phillips, Dale Mitchell, Ed Powell and Marvin Cobb, and offensive players like Anthony David, Allen Carter, Pat Haden, and my son Johnny. But 1971 was the last year freshmen were not eligible, so they couldn't help us yet.

We thought we had improved the varsity too, but we hadn't. We had not recruited enough good people from junior college who could play right away, and we had not made enough defensive changes among the people we had. We were too stubborn. We continued to think that some of the players who couldn't perform in 1970 could do it in 1971 — and they couldn't.

So that day at Notre Dame, besides alternating our quarterbacks, we went back to our old defensive alignment — three down linemen and four linebackers — made a couple of personnel changes and upset the Irish. We finished with four wins and a tie in our last five games.

But we still needed vast improvements so we not only recruited more quick freshmen *but also nabbed some top JC transfers like offensive lineman Booker Brown, a future All - American, and linebackers Jimmy Sims and Ray Rodriguez.*

And our 1972 defense was the fastest I had ever seen. The longest run those kids allowed in 12 games was 29 yards, and seven of the starters were new. The defense has been fast ever since. [All above italics are not in the original.]

Don Coryell, presently the coach of the San Diego Chargers, was the head mentor at San Diego State when that university became nationally conspicuous in football. He accomplished that with a fistful of "instant ready, willing and able" players — JC transfers.

This has not been a single strategy. Joseph Durso gave this commentary:[33]

> Long Beach State was one of those pretty, anonymous colleges that were part of the mushrooming California University system. It had almost 30,000 students by the late 1960s. But the average age of the students was twenty-four. Half of them were married. Clearly, there was not a rah-rah spirit around, not when people had to worry about going to a job or taking care of a family.
>
> Where do we want to go? Dr. Fred Miller asked school officials in 1966 when he took over as athletic director. They said they wanted to make a name for themselves. The problem was that there were comparatively few alumni (the schoool had opened in 1949) and only limited financial backing.
>
> "If you can catch fire with an athletic program, the effect on the school spirit is tremendous,' says Dr. Miller. 'Take City College of New York, a commuter school. Remember when they won the basketball Grand Slam in 1950? Spirit is what holds a school together — it's not going to be a poetry book.'
>
> Enter Tarkanian, and a supporting actor, Jim Stangeland, football coach.
>
> "Who cared? I cared," says Tarkanian. "They gave me a recruiting budget for my first year of $100. The community of Long Beach didn't care."
>
> Tarkanian came up from the ranks of the junior colleges, where he had established himself as the best in the West. His teams won J. C. championships every year. And that is how he began to build Long Beach State — on junior college transfers.
>
> "Football is a long haul in building a reputation," he (Dr. Miller) explains, "but in basketball you need only one or two standouts."
>
> By 1972, even after Long Beach had made it to the top four in national ranking and had come within one point of upsetting

U.C.L.A. in the national championship tournament, the college's recruiting budget was under $3,000. It was going to be raised to $7,500 in 1973, but Tarkanian quit and switched to an unknown — the University of Nevada at Las Vegas.

Jim Stangeland also came from the ranks of the junior colleges.[3,4] He was head coach at Long Beach City College and later assistant to John McKay at USC before becoming head coach at Long Beach State University. With a strategy similar to Tarkanian, he skillfully recruited the JC players who assisted in establishing Long Beach State University as a football power also. Among them were Leon Burns (Laney, California); Terry Metcalf (Everett, Washington); the Youngblood brothers, Sylvester and Albert (Pasadena, California); and Homer Post (Los Angeles City, California); along with a host of others.

More recently the University of Illinois used a similar strategy. For 16 consecutive years they had one of the worst teams in the nation. Their reputation as a fierce competitor depreciated beyond respectability while compiling a 6-24-3 record from 1977-79.

In 1980 the university hired Mike White as football coach. Four years later, 1983, the "Fightin' Illini" had risen from the cellar to win the Big Ten Conference Championship and the right to represent the conference in the Rose Bowl. But the team's accomplishments within those four years aroused public emotions ranging from extreme trauma to sheer ecstasy. Coach Mike White was honored by being named the "Walter Camp Football Foundation Coach of the Year."

Before continuing, a summary of the University of Illinois' accomplishments is provided in order to maintain a historical perspective of dates and events:

Year	Won	Lost	Tie
1980	3	7	1
1981	7	4	
1982*	7	4	
1983**	10	1	

*Received Liberty Bowl bid.
**Won Big Ten Conference Championship, and the right to represent the conference in the Rose Bowl.

The 1982 Liberty Bowl brought Coach Mike White against the legendary Coach Paul "Bear" Bryant.[3,5] The historical significance was that coach Bryant had publicly announced that he would retire following that game. In the December 29, 1982, Liberty Bowl (played in Memphis, Tennessee, the home of the Liberty Bowl) the University of Alabama defeated the University of Illinois 21-15. It was truly his last game. Coach Bryant died approximately one month later, January 26, 1983, age 69, after a brilliant 38-year career. He left behind the best record in collegiate football history — 323 wins, 85 losses, 17 ties.

In the Rose Bowl, January 2, 1984, Pasadena, California, UCLA defeated the University of Illinois 45-9.

With this perspective, here is the "rest of the story" about the University of Illinois and their use of JC athletes.

The University of Illinois' situation was unusual and multifaceted. There were some external forces that had mixed emotions about the Univeristy of Illinois' extensive use of JC athletes. Throughout the years, the many persons contacted and the vast amount of material researched for information garnered for this book, the JC athlete was never depreciated. When a hint of this appeared, it proved to be interesting and informative. The objective approach would be to share these attitudes. In doing so, to limit personal feelings only excerpts from articles by persons who had direct access to the information will be used. Even though the articles present much of the same information, all of them are used in an attempt to validate the objectivity, fairness, and accuracy of each person that presented the information.

Mark Heisler, ". . . But Look Who's in the Rose Bowl," said:[3,6]

> . . . In 1980 a new athletic director, Neale Stoner, was hired out of Cal State Fullerton. Stoner put the entire athletic department on notice, right down to the sports information director, that their performances were being reviewed. He then fired the football coach, Gary Moeller, without benefit of further review, and paid off the last two years of his contract.
>
> Moeller's records were 3-8, 1-8-2 and 2-8-1. There had been one winning record (6-4-1) since the slush fund scandal of 1966. One of the students' flipcard sections was disbanded due to lack of interest.
>
> White was hired and began moving his family to Champaign. When opportunity knocks, a man has to answer, doesn't he?
>
> "I was about to kill him," says his son Chris, now the Illinois placekicker, laughing. "It took a little while to get us all there."
>
> White brought in only four junior college transfers in his first season. "Two of them are making $4 million in the pros now," he says. They were Dave Wilson and Tony Eason. Eason was redshirted. Wilson passed for 621 yards in a loss at Ohio State. Illinois went 3-7-1.

The next year, White brought in 22 junior college players. Michigan's Bo Schembechler made plain his distaste, as did Illinois high school coaches. Most of the jucos were backs and receivers; Illinois writers asked if an Illinois - born player would ever carry the football again for the state university.

"There's a definite split in the conference on junior college players," said Michigan Athletic Director Don Canham, from Ann Arbor. "Bo has spoken out a number of times at national meetings about using JC kids to build the backbone of your team . . .

"You do tend to wonder why a great athlete went to a junior college in the first place, instead of going right to a major university. Maybe the kids who go to a junior college in California have made all A's and they just want to play right away. In the Midwest, there's the assumption that the average junior college kid was deficient in high school in one way or other. If there is a stigma, that's it. But we just run our own program. Bo has never said anything to me privately about Mike White or Illinois."

Illinois went 7-4 in White's second year, and the tide of protest subsided. A year later, the Illini went 7-4 again and got a Liberty Bowl bid. Now in Illinois, there was some acknowledgment that, for throwers and catchers, it was the warm weather ports of California, Texas and Florida.

"We figured that out right away," White says. "If we didn't want to be on the Greyhound out ourselves in three - four years, we had to get them.

"We couldn't get the blue,- chip high school players. Now we could be good Ol' boys, please everbody and recruit the people who couldn't get into Michigan or Notre Dame. And four years later, they'd be sticking another sign in front of my door" . . .

In an article entitled "It Took the Illini 20 Years to Fight Back," Mark Heisler wrote:[3][7]

. . . Along the way, there was a disappointment or two, and here is how some of it went, as viewed by a close observer, Bob Auler, a Champaign, Ill., lawyer.

Auler is an Illinois alumnus and a booster. Under Gary Moeller, he was even enlisted to take still photos of game action from the press box, as the school's budget wouldn't stretch far enough to hire a professional. This gave him a chance to monitor the disappointment up close and personal.

"In 1974," Auler said from Champaign, "I decided to get involved with the Illinois football network. I hired Dick Butkus to do color commentary. Butkus was recently retired and he thought it'd be neat to come back to the old school . . .

Pete Elliott, who coached the 1964 Rose Bowl team, had records of 6-3, 6-4, 4-6 with his next three teams and was fired after a slush fund was discovered and the NCAA moved in.

The Illini went on probation and hired Jim Valek. He was a jocular man, but less so after going 4-6, 1-9, 0-10, 3-7 and getting fired.

Bob Blackman, who'd built Dartmouth into the perennial Ivy League kingpin, was retained. He went 5-6, 3-8, 5-6, 6-4-1 (the only winning season between Pete Elliott and Mike White), 5-6 and 5-6. Then he was fired.

Since it was obvious that no Big Ten outsider would do, the Illini turned to Gary Moeller, an assistant to Bo Schembechler's staff at Michigan. Moeller went 3-7-1, 1-8-2, 2-8-1 and he was fired ...

This led, finally, to the hiring of Mike White as coach, and, four seasons later, to this year's 10-1 record and the long - awaited return to the Rose Bowl ...

Schembechler ripped the Illini for failing to respect Moeller's contract and rehired him. Schembechler has also groused about White's use of junior college transfers. Michigan players were among the first to accuse Illinois players of late hitting, the "Biting Illini" allegation. Until this season, Illinois hadn't beaten Michigan since 1966 (or Ohio State since 1967). In Champaign, the ending of those losing streaks was treated as if it were V-E Day.

"Did you see 'The Big Chill'?" Auler asked. "The scene where they show a Michigan game with Schembechler on the sideline? When they showed that in theaters in Champaign, the audiences just erupted with booing and hissing. People were making obscene gestures at the screen.

"When we had the trouble about Dave Wilson (the wrong high school transcript was submitted, resulting in conference disciplinary action and Wilson hiring a lawyer — Auler — to fight it), Schlembechler picked an argument with Wilson on the field after the game.

"The lowest moment we had might have been two years ago. We went up there (Ann Arbor, Mich.) and took the lead, 21-zip on 'em. They came back and turned it into a rout. It was 50-21 and that s.o.b. was still passing. They beat us 70-21." ...

Continuing, Auler said:[3][8]

... "We were always the nice guys with the good academics. High school coaches kept sending us their third - best player. The best would go to Notre Dame, the second best to Michigan. If the third best wanted to be an accountant or a lawyer, they'd send him to us. 'He might start in his senior year.' That's what we used to hear all the time.

"The opening game of the 1978 season, we played Northwestern. *Sports Illustrated* analyzed the game this way: 'Can either team win?' You know what the score was? Zero zero. I saw people sitting at the 50-yard line, fanning a handful of season tickets, trying to give them away.

"Illinois-Northwestern was generally the last game of the season, at Dyche Stadium in Evanston, Ohio State and Michigan would be playing on TV. I can remember, under Moeller, I had four tickets and I couldn't give them away. I went up alone and got there about a quarter before 12. The first thing I thought was I had the wrong day or the wrong place. I got out of the car and there was one tailgate party going on. I thought they'd called the game.

"This year, we sold out Dyche Stadium. Almost 70% were Illinois fans. We stole their stadium. After the game, Illinois fans tore down the goal posts. The Northwestern people knew it was going to happen. They'd even asked us to pay for the goal posts."

What had gone around had come around. The rest of the conference might have been muttering about junior college transfers. At Illinois, all they knew was it was a long time between goal posts.

Gary Voet, under the headline "Illini's Return: Fluke or White's Genius?," talks about the Illinois turnaround:[39]

...What could a coach from California, whose recruiting techniques were unheard of among Big Ten coaches, do to turn around a faltering football team? Not only what could he do, but how? And when?

"To be perfectly honest," said White, "I really didn't expect to get this far this soon. What you try to do when you take over a program is to establish two things, and in this order. You try to become competitive and then you try to win. The first step is usually a 3-to-4-year program. But a year ago, when we got close to Ohio State, we knew something was happening.

"We got an invitation to the Liberty Bowl last year with a 7-5 record. At best we were an average team. But we had the opportunity to get bowl experience and good work habits.

"This year we started beating teams like Ohio State and Michigan. That sort of shocked us. To get to the winning point that fast, I mean."

How Illinois went from 6-24-3 in '77-'79 to 27-16-1 under White's guidance is open to speculation. Some say it was White's recruiting, with heavy emphasis on junior college transfers from the West Coast, a technique frowned upon by most Big Ten coaches. While White was bringing in the "California Connection," as he calls his transfers, the rest of the Big Ten coaches were sticking to their annual recruiting game plan — tapping the endless supply of Midwestern players.

Some say the turnaround is the result of White's ability to bring enthusiasm back into the Illini football program...

In an article entitled "Illinois Feels Right at Home in Pasadena," Mark Heisler spoke about the "California Connection."[40]

Proving that you can go home again, Illinois' football team has arrived in Pasadena. If it was true that you really can't go home again, they'd have had to play this Rose Bowl game in Wichita.

The Illini have 21 players who live in California, or attended high school or junior college here. Five come from one school alone, Pasadena City College.

This is going to produce a Rose Bowl like never before. It is going to be less of the usual West Coast - Midwest, cultures - in - collision than a civil war, the War Between the State ...

Illini Coming Home
THE CALIFORNIA CONNECTION

Pasadena City College Quintet

Player	Pos.	Ht.	Wt.	California School
Mo Bias	LB	6-1	220	Pasadena CC
Tim Brewster	TE	6-4	230	Pasadena CC
Curtis Clarke	DE	6-4	250	Pasadena CC
Vince Osby	LB	5-11	210	Pasadena CC
Archie Carter	LB	6-2	220	Pasadena CC

From Other California JCs

Dave Aina	TE	6-5	250	CCSF
Larry Ashley	RB	5-11	195	Sierra JC
John Ayres	DB	6-1	190	Contra Costa JC
Dwight Beverly	HB	6-0	200	Long Beach CC
Ken Cruz	QB	6-1	190	CCSF
Harry Gosier	DB	6-3	195	College of Redwoods
Randy Grant	WR	5-10	185	Chabot JC
Clint Haynes	LB	6-3	220	El Camino JC
Shane Lamb	QB	6-3	210	Mira Costa JC
Bob Sebring	LB	6-1	220	Saddleback CC
Mark Taggart	LB	6-4	225	San Jose CC
Mike Weingrad	LB	6-2	240	Hartnell JC
David Williams	WR	6-3	195	Harbor JC

From California High Schools

Mike Giddings	WR	5-11	180	Newport Harbor
Jack Trudeau	QB	5-4	190	Livermore Granada
Darryl Usher	DB	5-10	170	San Mateo

Notes:
• *Placekicker Chris White was born in Lafayette, Calif. He attended high school in the Bay Area until his father, Mike, moved to Illinois.*
• *Coach Mike White was born in Berkeley, played and coached at Cal.*
• *Assistant head coach Max McCartney played at Whittier and was an assistant at Stanford and Cal.*
• *Quarterback coach Bob Gambold was an assistant at Stanford.*

It would be enlightening to analyze the experiences of each player who was a member of the "California Connection," or of JC players who transfer and utilize the information to assist persons who will be making similar choices. In the absence of a collection of opinions, the experience of one player can be examined.[4,1]

... Brewster is one of the rarities, born not in California, but in ... a tough New Jersey town, Phillipsburg, who had to call Pasadena CC before he was invited West. He was a wide receiver there, and had to contact Illinois to arrange for a chance to make it as a tight end. He takes pride in his street - fighter, up - from - the - alley image ... "Champaign (home of the University of Illinois) was a cultural shock. Cultural shock, I'm telling you. Coming from New Jersey, out to California and back to Illinois, it was traumatic at first.

"It's Champaign and then there's *nothing*. Champaign - Urbana, the University of Illinois and that's it. You drive 4-5 miles in any direction and you're in *corn*. Chicago was 2½-3 hours away. Kam's (a Champaign beer hall) gets old after a while. It definitely took some getting used to."

They definitely took some getting used to, for Champaign, too. Brewster went to Illinois in 1981, a member of Mike White's first big class of California JC players. They arrived amid great alarm, on the part of other Big Ten coaches, Illinois high school coaches, and any Illinois high school player who still dreamed of carrying the ball for the U of I. Not that there were a lot of the latter left.

"It wasn't so much the people at Illinois," Brewster said. "It was just the Big Ten people who were making a big fuss. There was a lot of flak about it, but it was handled well. The guys on the team from Illinois, the Don Thorps, they were great.

"There was a lot of kidding. They'd talk about the sunshine guys, the party guys from California. We'd call the guys from the Midwest country boys, hillbillies, that stuff. People thought I was from California, because I was from Pasadena CC. I always made sure to say I was from New Jersey, to get out of that California - Illinois stuff."

Three years passed. Brewster redshirted and was awarded a scholarship. In his varsity season, he started out with the second string, won the job early in the season, caught 46 passes and wound up in the Liberty Bowl.

This season, he caught 59 more, which makes him the No. 3 Illini receiver all-time, after a two - year career. The Illini are in the Rose Bowl and Californians have become *de rigueur* at all the best parties in Champaign.

..."When I was in high school," Brewster says, "I was a year ahead of a kid named Jim Clymer. He was the other wide receiver. I had better stats. I thought I was a better player, but he got all the attention.

"His senior year, he was recruited by about every school in the country. He ended up going to Stanford. This was his senior year and he finally played. We played Stanford this year and we went out there and there was my buddy, Jim Clymer.

"After the Michigan game this year, Bo Schembechler came up to me and said, 'I missed on you, right? I recruited your buddy but I missed on you.' That made me feel pretty good."

Jim Newman, "Diamond Jim,"[4,2] was appointed as head basketball coach of California State University, Los Angeles, in June 1983,[4,3] after serving as assistant coach at New Mexico State and Arizona State Universities. He, too, like the aforementioned, had dwelled in the arena where many future stars and superstars are born. He had been a class basketball player at Harbor

Community College (Los Angeles, CA) before gaining national attention as a player at Arizona State University. Later, as head mentor at Compton Community College, he not only reestablished it as a basketball power but also rewrote pages of history by his accomplishments with JC players.

Newman labels the JC player as an "instant quality" product. In isolated cases he, too, feels that these players can probably match skills with many in small four - year institutions. Case in point: Compton Community College, in 1975, was invited to participate in the United Negro College Fund Basketball Classic against such colleges as Tuskegee, Moorehouse, and Xavier University. Xavier was rated one of the top ten teams in the National Association of Intercollegiate Athletics (NAIA) — Division II — and they were undefeated at the time. Compton won that classic, defeating Xavier by 20 points. Newman's coaching ability and the skill of his players were well utilized.

Here's how Newman assessed that victory:[44]

> It's no question that Xavier has better players and more depth. They had talent equivalent to any major university in the country, even UCLA, that particular year. Xavier unveiled a team with some players who had ability equal to "Slick Watts," who had graduated from that college a year before, and some team members measuring approximately: two 6'9" forwards, two 6'8" forwards, two 6'10" post men, and three guards 6'3" and above.

Competitive coaching and skilled players have placed and kept the community colleges "downstage - center." Their players can fit into any aspect of a four - year institution program, that's why they are a utopia for recruiting. Newman elaborated:[45]

> Let's say that a college selected some great high school players to replace some upperclassmen. Two to three years hence the upperclassmen are leaving and those high school players may not be performing near expectation. You can see the position that college is in if they have to maintain a high level of competition.
>
> An instant group of high school seniors, in most cases, can't provide the needs. At that point the college is forced to go the JC route.
>
> I think, in most cases, the four - year institutions would like to bring their players in as early as possible and carry them through their program and perhaps by-pass the JCs. That may be good strategy. There isn't necessarily anything wrong with that and there's lots of high school talent — I mean good high school talent.

The high schools are a stronghold for talent. The abundance, accomplishments, and prolificacy of high school athletes are highly publicized. In many instances their talents, their desire to leave their immediate community, their willingness to await an opportunity to become a regular team member, a willingness to chance the possibility of injury and academic success in a more intense environment, and a desire to reap immediately the attractive benefits including the publicity and prestige, cause them to chance the four - year institutions. Upon entry some of them, too, become "superstars" en route to professional sports as a career.

Haskell Cohen gives an accounting of this by focusing on former players who were selected to *Parade's* high school All - American teams. In basketball:[46]

> Kareem Abdul-Jabbar of the Los Angeles Lakers; Pete Maravich of the New Orleans Jazz; Spencer Haywood and Bill Bradley of the New York Knicks; Artis Gilmore of the Kentucky Colonels; George McGinnis of the Philadelphia 76ers; Ralph Simpson of the Denver Nuggets; and Bill Walton of the Portland Trailblazers.

Of this group two did attend a community college — Spencer Haywood and Artis Gilmore.

Parade's 1976 team listed 40 players (four teams) who were selected by coaches, recruiters, and newspapermen covering high school athletics. Twenty states were represented and New York led with six players, followed by California with five. Cohen made these comments:[47]

> Two pertinent and significant points highlight the selection of this year's *Parade* All - American High School Basketball Team. One: for the first time ever five or six of the best high school players in the nation will be invited to try out for the Olympic basketball team to represent the United States in Montreal this summer. Two: some professional teams, notably the Philadelphia 76ers, have been scouting high school performers, and a few of the boys on *Parade's* 20th All - American squad may skip college to try their luck in the money ranks.

Whereas high schools have been recruiting havens for professional baseball teams dating back several years, about 1976 they began to emerge as a posture for professional basketball teams.[48]

> Last year Bill Willoughby of Dwight Morrow High School in Englewood, N.J., and Daryle Dawkins of Evans High School,

Orlando, Florida, cast their lot with National Basketball Association teams, while two years ago the highly heralded Moses Malone made the jump from Petersburg High in Virginia to Utah in the American Basketball Association. Malone currently is a member of the Spirits of St. Louis of the ABA.

The performances of Daryle Dawkins and Moses Malone added a new dimension to the potential prowess of the high school athlete. As infrequent in occurrence this might be for high schoolers, the accomplishments of these two players, in that sport is a brilliant history. Dawkins' performance assisted the 76ers to three National Basketball Association (NBA) title playoffs in the last six years, losing to Portland in 1977 and the Los Angeles Lakers in 1980 and 1982. After the 1982 season the 76ers replaced Dawkins, signing Malone to the highest salary contract in professional basketball history, $13 million for six years. The 76ers won the 1983 NBA championship title by beating the same Laker team, 115-108.

Prior to the first game for the championship title, the Moses Malone vs Abdul - Jabbar statistics revealed that "in 26 games against each other since Malone entered the NBA in 1976, he [Malone] has averaged 27.2 points and 16.7 rebounds to 25.4 points and 10.3 rebounds for Abdul-Jabbar."[49]

After downing the Lakers in four consecutive games, a *Los Angeles Times* news article gave this praise to Malone:[50]

> But after their latest disappointment last season, the 76ers signed center Moses Malone to a $13 million, six-year contract. Anyone who wondered if he was worth it only had to watch this series. If Erving is the doctor, Malone is the undertaker. He buried the Lakers.

In cooperation with the United States Tennis Association, *Parade's*[51] top ten boys included Walter Redondo, a 16 - year - old from St. Augustine High School, San Diego, who "heads the list of those likely to replace Jimmy Connors ... and other Kingpins of men's tennis." Also, Van Winitsky and Larry Gottfried, both of Piper High School, Lauderhill, Florida; and John McEnroe, Jr., of Trinity High School, New York City, New York; and Jim Hodges of Landon High in Bethesda, Maryland. The top ten girls highlight Barbara Hallquist, Arcadia High in Arcadia, California; Rebecca Sadoff, Coral Gables High School, Coral Gables, Florida; and Sherry Acker, Kalamazoo High School in Kalamazoo, Michigan.

Cohen's report on past members of *Parade's* All-American High School Football Team[52] selection, now in the pros, included Calvin Hill of the Cleveland Browns, Mike Reid of the Cincinnati Bengals, Joe Ferguson of the Buffalo Bills, Jim McAlister of the New England Patriots, Tony Dorsett of the Dallas Cowboys, and Joe Washington of the Baltimore Colts.

In February 1977 a *Los Angeles Times* survey revealed the early recruiting results of some of the nation's high schools and some of the California JC football players into four-year institutions, as shown in the following listing:[53]

	Preps Recruited	JCs Recruited
UCLA	16	4
USC	12	11
Stanford	21	8
California	9	2
Washington	19	
Washington State	17	4
Oregon	17	5
Oregon State	3	
Fresno State		23
San Diego State		25
Cal State Fullerton		13
Cal Poly Pomona	21	5
Long Beach State		13
Arizona	12	3
Arizona State	16	8
Colorado	17	5
Colorado State		1

Among the JC recruits were two top California athletes — Eddie Walker (Antelope Valley), one of the nation's best running backs; and an all-state defensive back, Willie Crawford (College of San Francisco).

As mentioned previously, the chart reflects the early recruiting efforts. USC is listed for only six JC players; however, before the 1977 season they had signed a total of 11 JC players.

The following data are also the results of a *Los Angeles Times* survey which was published February 1983, the morning after the first day that high school players could sign a national letter of intent:[54]

PAC 10	Top Preps Recruited (From Nation's High Schools)	JCs Recruited (Mainly California JCs)
USC	15	6
UCLA	17	1
Arizona	22	7
Arizona State	9	3
California	17	9
Oregon	11	3
Oregon State	8	3
Stanford	20	
Washington	25	2
Washington State	4	3
PCAA*		
Cal State Fullerton	15	6
Cal State Long Beach	6	18
Nevada Las Vegas	3	
Utah State	12	8
Pacific	8	16
San Jose State	3	19
Southland		
Cal State Northridge	6	3
San Diego State	21	
Others		
Air Force	2	
Alabama	16	
Auburn	22	
Boise State	4	
BYU	2	
Colorado	19	2
Colorado State	3	4
Florida	13	
Georgia	19	
Illinois	19	2
Iowa State	1	1
Kansas	1	3
Kansas State	1	
LSU	13	
Michigan	2	
Michigan State	28	4
Minnesota		2
Mississippi State	8	
Nebraska	22	
Northern Arizona	1	
Notre Dame	18	
North Carolina	1	
North Carolina State	1	
Northwestern	1	
Ohio State	16	
Oklahoma	18	1
Penn State	2	
SMU	2	
Southern Mississippi	1	
Tennessee		1
Tulane	1	
Utah	4	
Weber State	1	
Wyoming	2	1

*Pacific Coast Athletic Association

And these are the early signers of letters of intent. Whereas the previous survey reported high school students from across the nation, all, except approximately ten of the JC players, were from California. When the 1983 football season began, a multitude of two - year college athletes from across the nation took residence in four - year institutions.

The incoming head football coach at USC, Ted Tollner, has carried on the tradition of recruiting JC football players. It was an important part of the recruiting efforts of his predecessors — John McKay and John Robinson — who presently are head coaches with the professional football Tampa Bay Buccaneers and the Los Angeles Rams, respectively.

To replace the 25 players who might possibly be lost for the 1983 season, of which 12 would be starters, Coach Tollner announced that "JC players would have high priority in his recruiting plans. He wanted to bring in about eight or nine JC transfers to provide immediate help"[5 5] if the team is to remain in top contention. A degree of certainty that was utilized in order to assure that some of these JC transfers would be available to the team is best demonstrated by the fact that ". . . the Trojans have signed six JC players to letters of intent including three All - Americans, and they're already enrolled."

In addition to the previous remarks by Goss, the following comments by Newman will give some additional insight into the differences between the high school and the JC players:[5 6]

> It's tough to overlook the JCs because some of the players are better than those they have brought through their program for two or three years. So you find even though they are labeled JC — the players are better than what they have.
>
> Again, if a college is trying to break into the Division I ranks, they have to seek the top - notch athlete who can deal with that level of competition. If resources are of concern, their problem is aggravated. In either of these situations, especially the latter, they can't select from the high school — they have to go to the JC and get those players that they know can compete against anyone. They can get the level of skill they need regardless of whether it's a regular, spot, or special palyer.
>
> Bear in mind, a high school player is recruited strictly on potential, whereas they may never reach that potential or display the skills to play at that level.
>
> A JC player is recruited on what they know he can do, otherwise they wouldn't recruit him. The bottom line is good JC players are like polished diamonds — they are quality, they appeal to many, and they are valuable.

Their quality, appeal, and value persist to enable them to become highly conspicuous in professional sports. It is questionable whether any representation in professional sports exceeds that which comes via the JCs. This information is known within the media and professional and college sports circles. The public, however, has only a slight knowledge of the numerous professional athletes who are products of the JCs. Professional sports announcers and other information sources often neglect, either by omission or commission, to emphasize the fact that an athlete attended a two - year college. It has been noted that when an athlete moves from a JC into a four - year institution, the emphasis for publicity is the athlete's four - year institution, and may even emphasize the high school, but completely omit the JC. It has also been noted that the same practice exists when JC alumni are recognized for their talents, skills, and accomplishments in other occupations. Many persons believe this is a disservice and that it has hampered the visibility, recognition, and accomplishments of the JCs. The JCs realize more than ever before that modesty is a luxury they can no longer afford. Modesty during periods of affluence may be a virtue, but it can hurt when a crisis occurs.

A rare article giving visibility, recognition, accomplishments, and praise to the JCs, their athletic programs, and their athletes was published in 1977 by *PRO!*, the magazine of the National Football League. Following is that article in its entirety:[5][7]

JUNIOR COMES OF AGE

By John Horgan

The community college is no longer a mere holding tank, as more than a few NFL players and coaches will attest.

The junior college. You remember it? That was the shoestring operation down there in the rented building next to the Greyhound depot, the place with the undistinguished student body, the wafer - thin budget, and about as much local stature as the neighborhood flasher.

The junior college was an academic court of last resort a generation ago. It was the unwanted stepchild, the runt of the educational litter in the eyes of skeptics. The four - year colleges treated the JC with calcualted disdain.

But in the last 20 years, things have changed.

In America today, there are junior colleges in all 50 states. In all, there are upwards of 1,200 junior colleges in operation, about three - quarters of them public.

So grown up has the system become that these schools don't like to be called "junior" any more. Almost all of them are now known as community colleges.

During the mid-1960s, it seemed a new community college was being opened every week. The growth was remarkable. Enrollments rose from one million to more than three million students in a single decade. Today, about half the post - secondary schools in America are community colleges. They enroll more than 3.5 million students. An estimated 38 percent of all freshmen enrollments are at two - year institutions.

Even with this expansion, even with clear acceptance by both the public at large and by the students themselves, the community colleges are still something of an unknown quantity.

However, that doesn't hold true among athletes, especially football players.

Perhaps the case of O. J. Simpson makes the point. Simpson, as a college football player, was known for his play at USC in 1967 and 1968. Simpson's two seasons with USC were superlative, culminating in the Heisman trophy in his senior year. In two years, he scored 36 touchdowns and rushed for 3,423 yards on 674 carries.

But where was he in 1965 and 1966, his freshman and sophomore years? He was at City College of San Francisco. It was there that Simpson actually had his finest hour as an amateur athlete. In one game against San Jose City College in 1965, O. J. scored six touchdowns, carried the ball 17 times for 304 yards, and averaged nearly 18 yards per carry.

In two years, Simpson scored 54 touchdowns, 46 of them by rushing. He carried the ball only 281 times for 2,552 yards, an average of 9 yards per carry. His team won 18 straight games in those two seasons and Simpson's future was set.

Interestingly, Simpson's JC marks were broken by another young man destined for USC and the professional game, Clarence Davis of East Los Angeles College. David capped his own 1976 pro year with Oakland by running for 137 yards against Minnesota in the Super Bowl.

Simpson and Davis, however, are just two of the more than 200 former community college football players now earning a living in the NFL. *At the outset of last season [1976], the league's 28 press guides and veteran rosters showed 219 community college alumni on NFL clubs. Of those, 109 came from California's system.*

Three schools topped the list of contributors to the NFL in 1976. Northeastern Oklahoma A & M College of Miami, Oklahoma, had eight players on NFL rosters. Arizona Western College of Yuma, Arizona, had seven, and City College of San Francisco had six.

Four old-line NFL teams each had 13 JC products: Detroit, San Diego, San Francisco, and Los Angeles. The two new entries into the

League, Tampa Bay and Seattle, totalled 29 between them, with Seattle fielding 23.

Besides Simpson, some of the names and two-year colleges of other NFL standouts include:

Roger Staubach of New Mexico Military Institute, Roswell, New Mexico; *Billy Kilmer*, Citrus Community College, Azusa, California; *Fred Dryer*, El Camino College, Torrance, California; *Terry Metcalf*, Everett Community College, Everett, Washington; *Mel Gray*, Fort Scott Community College, Fort Scott, Kansas; *Larry Brown*, Dodge City Community College, Dodge City, Kansas; *Ron Jessie*, Imperial Valley College, Imperial, California; *MacArthur Lane*, Laney College, Oakland, California.

Ron Yary, Cerritos Community College, Norwalk, California; *Claudie Minor*, Mt. San Antonio College, Walnut, California; *Rick Upchurch*, Indian Hills Community College, Centerville, Iowa; *Haven Moses*, Los Angeles Harbor College, Wilmington, California; *Altie Taylor*, Diablo Valley College, Pleasant Hill, California; *Jerrel Wilson*, Pearl River Junior College, Poplarville, Mississippi; *John Matuzak*, Iowa Central Community College, Fort Dodge, Iowa; *Skip Thomas*, Arizona Western College; *Bob Lee*, City College of San Francisco.

There is at least one NFL player who went only to a community college. Placekicker Tom Dempsey attended Palomar Community College of San Marcos, California, and did not continue at a four-year school.

Dempsey is following in some large footsteps. Joe Perry, one of the NFL's greatest running backs, went to Compton, California, Community College and bypassed the four-year institutions.

Compton has produced a number of NFL notables. Besides Perry, Hugh McElhenny went there. So did the league's commissioner, Pete Rozelle.

The list of JC alumni is even larger, but you get the idea: *Community colleges have made their mark in the NFL. Their influence figures to remain undiminished in the future. The two-year schools provide many high school graduates with a second chance, a form of academic, athletic, and social breathing room.*

Students attend community colleges for a variety of reasons, not the least of which are a desire to remain near home, a lack of adequate grades to enter a university, a lack of funds, a lack of a clear picture of what to do after college, and a desire to take certain vocational or technical courses which only the JC can provide.

For a football player coming out of high school, the two-year school can be a boon to his development, both as a person and as an athlete.

"When O. J. Simpson was in high school in San Francisco, he was an all-city back," says Dutch Elston, Simpson's coach at City College of San Francisco. "But the big schools were not really interested in him at that point. His linemen were not very good and he didn't glitter as he should have."

"In our situation, we try to put these kids in a showcase so they can get scholarships to four - year schools," he says. "We also try to win. We want to do both. We want our players to display their talents, to look good on film."

Yearly, about 25 percent of the athletes on Pacific 8 Conference rosters have at least one year of JC experience. Some schools on the West Coast have even more JC athletes. In 1975, for example, San Diego State's 67-man roster contained 53 players who had come to the school from a community college.

USC traditionally seeks JC transfers. In 1975, the Trojans had 24 former JC players out of 72. In 1976, they had 21 out of 58. Another 18 were freshmen.

USC coach John Robinson, a former assistant with Oakland Raiders, believes he needs to recruit "about six or eight good JC players a year."

"This is a very important part of our program," says Robinson. "A JC is good for a kid who might be a late developer. Or he might not have the type of offer he wanted out of high school. Or he may have done poorly in the classroom. The JC is a good place to begin your college education."

Dick Vermeil agrees. Vermeil, the head coach of the Philadelphia Eagles, played for and coached at Napa Junior College in Napa, California. He is also a former head coach at UCLA.

"The junior college is super, especially for a kid who hasn't displayed the talent necessary for a major school," he says. "The JC is a place where kids with comparable skills can compete against one another and improve as they do so."

Vermeil contends that the competition at the community college level can be very good. "It used to be that just a few schools in California would dominate because there were fewer schools. But now there are a lot more. So many new ones have been added that the competition is spread out."

Vermeil says the only way he could have continued with his education out of high school was at a community college. "I just wasn't ready for a big school, either in the classroom or outside it," he says.

"The JC gave me a chance to grow up. How many high school seniors do you know who know what they want to do with their lives? Not many. I wish there were more JCs in the East. They are an invaluable resource for young people."

Several NFL players echo that view. *Matt Blair* of Minnesota says by going to Northeastern Oklahoma A & M he got the opportunity to "open up as a person."

Blair, one of the five Vikings to have attended a two - year school, feels strongly about his JC experience. "I'd really suggest that a young person attend a JC. The teachers there take a personal look at you, a closer look, I think, than you get at a major university. Coming right out of high school to a big school, you can get lost."

Blair's days at Northeastern were an eyeopener for him because he had not originally intended to continue with his education after high school. "I thought I would just finish high school and get a job," he says. "But I got an offer to play football and get an education and it paid off."

Willie Hall, one of eight Raiders listed as JC alumni last season, says he had no intentions of continuing with his schooling after his senior year in high school.

"I wasn't planning on anything after high school except working," he says.

Instead of working, he went to Arizona Western College. "There were eight kids in my family and I was planning on getting a job. But the opportunity to play in Arizona presented itself and I took the offer."

One of Hall's teammates on the Super Bowl champion Raiders, *Clifford Branch*, had a different reason for going to Wharton County Junior College in Wharton, Texas. Branch says he was so overwhelmed by scholarship offers out of high school that he decided to spend some time at Wharton.

"I didn't have any goals in mind at that time," Branch says. "The JC gave me time to consider some things. I got in ten games as a freshman. At that time, freshmen weren't eligible for the varsity. I guess what the JC gave me most of all was time to think."

Former San Francisco 49er *Jimmy Johnson* says his one year at Santa Monica College was the best of his academic career.

"It was a special year for me," he says. "I will always look back on that year as something special in my life."

"At Santa Monica I got into the flow of my studies. I learned to use my time better. I wanted to play sports, too. And the Santa Monica athletic program was probably better than most frosh programs at that time. At Santa Monica I learned what studies were all about. I can't say enough good things about it. I can say without qualification that the JC enabled me to get into professional football."

What Johnson liked about Santa Monica was that he sensed a close feeling of community there. "The step from high school to a major school would have been more drastic than going to the JC first. You knew just about everyone there. It can get pretty isolated at some of those large schools, you know."

He adds that he had no intention of pursuing his football career after high school. He wanted to play basketball. But at Santa Monica his coaches convinced him to play football, as well as basketball. He also ran on the track team.

"I wanted to spend two years at Santa Monica," he recalls. "But UCLA wanted me, too. In the end, I transferred to UCLA."

Four-year schools are becoming increasingly aware of the value of pipelines into the community colleges.

"You find JC players in the Big Eight and SEC where you didn't find them before," says Ron Wolf, director of player personnel for Tampa Bay. "It used to be that these players were pretty much confined to the West Coast schools. But now we're seeing them on a national basis."

The community colleges themselves are not organized on a national basis, however. There has long been a split between the California schools and most of the remaining schools.

The National Junior College Athletic Association was formed in 1937 in Fresno, California, to promote and supervise junior college sports. California dominated national championship competition to such an extent that, by 1950-51, the schism was complete. California, which had won 22 or 23 national JC titles in five sports up to that time, was severed from the parent body, and went its own way.

Today, the NJCAA represents about 600 schools. There are three other associations as well: one in California, one in Mississippi and one for schools in the Pacific Northwest.

Still, football does provide all of the country's two - year institutions with some common ground. In spite of the differences which exist between the various regions, there is one thing they can agree on: the Junior Rose Bowl.

The Junior Rose Bowl, played in the mammoth Pasadena facility that also hosted the 1977 Super Bowl, has been played for 22 years, beginning in 1946. There was no game between 1966 and 1975 for a variety of reasons, the most important of which was the fact that California schools wanted to try an intrastate playoff system instead.

But the state playoffs didn't draw well and a movement was begun to resurrect the Junior Rose Bowl, pitting the best teams in the nation against one another. After a 10-year hiatus, Bakersfield College of California beat Ellsworth Community College of Iowa Falls, Iowa, 29-14 in 1976.

The game was typical of how the series has gone in the past. California schools have won 15 times, lost six, and tied one. Compton and Bakersfield each have won three games, more than any other school. In 1976, Bakersfield finished the season with an 11-1 record and the nation's top ranking.

Last year's game also exemplified the contrast that can exist in community college football.

Bakersfield is a large school, with an enrollment of nearly 10,000 full - time and part - time students. It has a fully equipped, 150-acre campus that bristles with modern facilities. It is basically a commuter college in a city of over 70,000 people. Its football team's 85-man roster showed only three out - of - state athletes in 1976.

Ellsworth, on the other hand, is quite different. The school has just 825 students. The college is located on a five - acre campus in a small farming community of about 7,000 persons. Its programs, while ambitious, are necessarily limited. However, its football team listed 26 out - of - state players on its 58-man roster last season. One of those out - of - state athletes was from Nigeria.

Ellsworth's coach, Vern Thomsen, says, "The four-year schools in the Big Eight, Missouri Valley, and Big Ten like our program, our winning record and they place some fine young men with us for two years." For Ellsworth, the loss in the Junior Rose Bowl was its only one of the season. The school finished the year with a 9-1 mark, averaging 43 points a game.

The Junior Rose Bowl has provided many future professional football players with a stage for their talent.

Adrian Burk, the former Philadelphia Eagle, played for Kilgore College of Texas in the first Junior Rose Bowl in 1946. *Hugh McElhenny* ran for 114 yards and two touchdowns for Compton in the 1948 game. Ex-Chicago Cardinal *Keever Jankovich* played for Santa Ana College of California in the 1949 game.

In 1954, *Earl Leggett*, the former Chicago Bear, played for Hinds Junior College of Raymond, Mississippi. *Margene Adkins* of Henderson County Junior College of Texas participated in two Junior Rose Bowl games, in 1965 and 1966, catching five touchdown passes. Adkins went directly into pro football after his two JC seasons.

"Look at some of those names," says Dick Mansperger, director of player personnel for the Seattle Seahawks. "You can see what junior college experience can do. It gives kids a chance to play ten full games as freshmen and sophomores. In terms of playing time, there's no comparison to a four-year school, especially for the player who hasn't matured, the kid who might be tall enough and big enough, but who hasn't put it together yet as an athlete."

Mansperger, whose quarterback in Seattle, *Jim Zorn*, attended Cerritos Community College in Southern California, says the Seattle franchise is seeking the young athlete who shows potential. "We want a player to be able to progress; to get better every year," says Mansperger. "When you get a kid like that you have something more than just a number."

"Take Zorn. He's probably a good example. Dallas had to let him go. They already had enough quarterbacks. They hated to do it because they saw his potential. We can afford to go with Jim. He has improved tremendously already. And he is going to be better."

Mansperger, who played and coached football at Palo Verde College in Blythe, California, says football at the two-year level is often geared to recruiting and to offensive and defensive design (strategy) rather than individual techniques (tactics).

"We didn't have the staff at Palo Verde necessary to teach techniques," he says. "We were less concerned about how a defensive back used his feet on a particular play than about whether he knew who he was supposed to be covering in that situation. We didn't have the time to get too far into fundamentals. There was no spring football. We had the players, at the most, for two years."

Naturally, that is one of the great imponderables about community college athletics. You never know from one year to the next precisely which players will be in uniform for you.

In spite of some cases of outright recruiting, the community colleges, along with their athletic programs, retain their sense of broad - based interest for any and all students.

Begun originally in 1901 in Joliet, Illinois, the two - year idea has proven itself to be a major benefit for just about all who have come in contact with it.

The need for community colleges is going to continue to be felt, according to most education experts.

Dr. Clark Kerr, chairman of the Carnegie Council on Policy Studies in Higher Education, says that public community colleges can be expected to increase at an accelerated rate over the next 10 to 20 years.

A major reason, according to Kerr, is that the community colleges traditionally serve older students, part - time students, low - income persons and individuals who are seeking only certain specialized courses which don't lead to a degree. As American society ages, due to declining birth rate and improved medical techniques, the number of these students will increase.

Kerr adds, "Community colleges must keep the doors open to persons of all ages who will come for varying lengths of time, to achieve a variety of educational goals and at intervals throughout their lives."

Those doors are open even in football. At City College of San Francisco, a 63-year-old San Francisco businessman turned out for football in the fall of 1975.

The coach, Dutch Elston, wasn't really sure what to do. The gentleman was taking courses at the school, had passed the required physical examination, and was eligible for play. There was no rule that would bar him from the same program that had produced O. J. Simpson.

"He wanted to be a running back," says Elston. "He lasted about fourteen practices. He found that he had a hard time recovering from all those bumps and bruises. The other players liked the guy a lot. But he quit."

The system let him make his own decision. [Italics are mine.]

Giving objective consideration to the various avenues into the four - year institutions, and then, perhaps, professional sports as a career, the JC is not the only viable alternative, but its high level of productivity, accessibility, broad offerings, services, and less threatening environment have opened and reopened doors. A positive measure of the validity of the junior - community colleges to move persons toward careers in professional sports is the numbers they have already assisted into professional sports careers.

Perceptively expressive of this validity is, to some degree, the following publication:[5][8]

CALIFORNIA CCs GROOM 7 BREWERS FOR A WORLD SERIES FEATURING 13 EX-JC/CC PLAYERS

SAN MATEO, CALIF. — Seven former California Community College baseball players are members of Milwaukee's 1982 World Series team. In fact, 11 players on the Brewers' 25-man Series roster played JC baseball — three in the National JC Athletic Association, one (Don Sutton) in the Mississippi JC Association, and seven for the California Association of Community Colleges.

St. Louis features outfielder Willie McGee of Diablo Valley College, Calif. (who hit .296 this year) and third baseman Ken Oberkfell (.289) of Belleville Area CC, Ill. (Also, Card first baseman Keith Hernandez attended College of San Mateo but did not play for the Bulldogs.)

Milwaukee World Series relief act Bob McClure did play for San Mateo, leading the Bulldogs through a pair of 18-3 Golden Gate Conference championship seasons (1972-73) with a 15-1 league record those years, after which he signed a pro contract. The two-time GGC pitcher beat out future Oakland A's Mike Norris of CC San Francisco and his Bulldog teammate Bob Souza for GGC pitcher of the year and All-America honors in 1973.

Three of the 1982 World Series players competed for teams in the same community college conference, the Golden Gate — McGee, McClure, and Brewer catcher Ned Yost (Chabot).

Rollie Fingers (ex-Chaffey) had 29 saves and a 2.60 ERA for Milwaukee this season.

HERE'S THE LIST OF MILWAUKEE'S FORMER CALIFORNIA CC PLAYERS

P — Rollie Fingers (Chaffey College, Alta Loma); Jim Slaton (Antelope Valley College, Lancaster).

C — Ned Yost (Chabot College, Hayward).

SS — Rob Picciolo (Santa Monica College).

OF — Mark Brouhard (Los Angeles Pierce College); Marshall Edwards (Los Angeles CC).

The other players include: P — Don Sutton (Mississippi Gulf Coast JC); Moose Haas (Catonsville CC, Md.). 1B — Cecil Cooper (Blinn JC, Tex.). OF — Charlie Moore (Mesa CC, Ariz.).

THE CALIFORNIA COMMUNITY COLLEGES ALSO CONTRIBUTED SIX ADDITIONAL PLAYERS TO THE TWO OTHER DIVISION CHAMPIONS.

CALIFORNIA ANGELS: SS — Rick Burleson (Cerritos College, Norwalk); 3B — Doug DeCinces (Los Angeles Pierce College) who hit .301 with 30 homers in '82; OF — Bobby Clark (Riverside CC) and Brian Downing (Cypress College) who hit .281 with 28 home runs.

ATLANTA BRAVES: 1B — Bob Watson (Los Angeles Harbor College) and Chris Chambliss (Mira Costa College, Oceanside) who hit .270, 20 HR, 86 RBI in 1982.

106 OF 301 FORMER COLLEGE PLAYERS IN MAJORS ARE FROM JCs (54 FROM CALIFORNIA CCs)

Earlier this year Collegiate Baseball published a list of the 301 "college baseball products" who were on major league rosters at the start of the 1981 season.

Of that group, more than one third (106) played JC/CC ball — the majority (54) in California!

The totals:
California Association of Community Colleges 54
National JC Athletic Association 48
    (Mississippi and Independents) 4
Athletic Association of Community Colleges
    (Washington/Northwest)

THE FORMER CALIFORNIA COMMUNITY COLLEGE PLAYERS ON MAJOR LEAGUE ROSTERS AT START OF 1981 SEASON

Gary Alexander, L.A. Harbor
Rick Anderson, L.A. Valley
Brian Asselstine, Allen Hancock
Rick Auerbach, L.A. Pierce
Doug Bird, Mt. San Antonio
Dan Boone, Cerritos
Thad Bosley, Mira Costa
Jack Brohamer, Golden West
Mark Brouhard, L.A. Pierce
Warren Brusstar, Napa
Terry Bulling, Golden West
Rick Burleson, Cerritos
Enos Cabell, L.A. Harbor
Bill Campbell, Mt. San Antonio
Bobby Castillo, L.A. Valley
Chris Chambliss, Mira Costa
Bobby Clerk, Riverside CC
Rich Dauer, San Bernardino
    Valley College
Doug DeCinces, L.A. Pierce
Brian Downing, Cypress
Marshall Edwards, L.A.C.C.
Darrell Evans, Pasadena CC
Rollie Fingers, Chaffey
George Foster, El Camino
Dave Frost, Long Beach
Greg Harris, Long Beach

Al Hrabosky, Fullerton
Frank La Corte, Gavilan
Lee Lacey, Laney
Buck Martinez, Sacramento CC
Bob McClure, San Mateo
Tug McGraw, Vallejo
    (now Solano)
Dan Meyer, Santa Ana
Craig Minetto, San Joaquin Delta
Joe Morgan, Merritt
Randy Niemann, College of
    the Redwoods
Mike Norris, San Francisco CC
Rob Picciolo, Santa Monica
Dave Schmidt, L.A. Valley
Tom Seaver, Fresno CC
Jim Slaton, Antelope Valley
Roy Smalley, Los Angeles CC
Fred Stanley, Rio Hondo
Leo Sutherland, Golden West
Dick Tidrow, Chabot
John Urrea, Rio Hondo
Mike Vail, De Anza
Tim Wallach, Saddleback
Reggie Walton, Compton
Bob Watson, L.A. Harbor
Gary Woods, Santa Barbara

Another case in point. Mike Rozier reached the pinnacle as a amateur football player. After completing Woodrow Wilson High School, Camden, New Jersey, he attended Coffeyville Community

College in Kansas "at the suggestion of Nebraska people after his grades made him ineligible for a scholarship."[59]

After one year he transferred to the University of Nebraska. In December 1983 the Downtown Athletic Club of New York awarded the senior running back the distinguished Heisman Trophy for being the most outstanding collegiate football player of the year. He was also the recipient of the Maxwell Award, and was named the UPI player of the year, and running back of the year.

Fred Baer compiled the following:[60]

New Research Shows O. J. Tops in TDs and Points
ROZIER "SUCCEEDS" ALL-TIME COLLEGIATE AND JC SCORING CHAMP O. J. SIMPSON AS HEISMAN WINNER

SAN MATEO, CALIF. (Dec. 7, 1983) — When Mike Rozier formally accepts the Heisman Trophy Thursday evening, he'll become the first ex-JC player since O. J. Simpson (1968) to receive the award. And, ironically, it's the same week during which Simpson is being inducted into the College Football Hall of Fame.

Other than Simpson, no college football player on any level has scored more than 500 points or 70 touchdowns in four years of competition. Simpson tallied 83 touchdowns, including national JC marks of 27 in one season and 50 in a two-year JC career (304 total points) at City College of San Francisco in 1965-66, according to records maintained by the JC Athletic Bureau. Including his two years at USC, O. J. totaled 502 points.

Walter Payton, who competed on the Division II level at Jackson St. from 1971-74, scored 66 touchdowns and 464 total points (including extra points and field goals) to rank second. The next player on the list with major college experience is Rozier — with a total of 60 touchdowns and 360 points.

With 5,969 yards rushing on 825 carries (a 7.24 average per carry and 138.81 yards per game pace), Rozier is the No. 2 career rusher in college football history, just behind Tony Dorsett of Pittsburg, with 6,082 yards on 1,074 rushes in 1973-76. No. 3 is Charles White of USC (1976-79) with 5,598 yards and fourth is Simpson with 5,569 yards on 870 carries (and a 150.51 average per game).

Simpson rushed for 2,445 yards on 249 carries in 18 regular season games at CCSF — a 9.82 average per carry and 135.83 yards per game pace. As a freshman at CCSF in 1965, O. J. established a collegiate record of 11.25 yards per carry (to total 1,080 yards on just 96 carries in nine regular season games). NCAA records still don't show anyone with a better mark.

Rozier scored 10 touchdowns in eight regular season games as a freshman at Coffeyville Community College in Kansas (and rushed for 1,189 yards on 157 carries — a 7.57 average per carry and a 148.6 yards per game pace).

Mike Rozier, Coffeyville Community College (KS), Pittsburg Maulers.
Photo courtesy The Maulers.

Rozier joined the list of sports millionaires when he signed with the Pittsburg Maulers of the United States Football League. It was reported that his three-year contract includes approximately $1.3 million as a signing bonus and the remainder in salaries to total in excess of 3 million dollars.

Also Warren Moon has been the subject of a great deal of attention recently. It resulted from the fact that in six years with the Edmonton Eskimos he led them to five consecutive Grey Cup Championships (equivalent to the NFL Super Bowl). In 1983, he "received the Schenley Trophy as the Canadian Football League outstanding player." As a result, interest swelled among professional football teams in the United States. The Houston Oilers deflated the efforts of all others and public information is he will receive $6 million over the next five years — presently the largest contract in professional football history.

J. Raack, Athletic Director, West Los Angeles Community College (Culver City, CA), stated:[6][1]

> Upon graduating from Hamilton High School (Los Angeles, CA), Moon attended West Los Angeles Community College — then transferred to the University of Washington, and on to the Canadian Football League (CFL) — Edmonton Eskimos.
>
> Moon played for us his freshman year. His achievements while here in 1974 include Honorable Mention All - American, Second Team All - State, ranked the Second Best quarterback in the state in passing, and led West LA to the Western States Conference

Championship. In fact, it was the last time West LA won a football conference championship.

His teammate, Leon Garrett, led the state in receiving and attended the University of Washington along with Moon.

And here is another illustrious example of the "Community College Connection." The spring of 1983 was the historic occasion of the beginning of another sports organization — the United States Football League (USFL). The 12-team league began play on Sunday, March 6, and is scheduled to continue into early summer. Among the reasons for its development was the "belief that our nation's sports fans just can't get enough of the professional gridiron game."[62]

Each team is permitted to have 40 active players, and ten players on the developmental squad.[63] On game days a team may suit up 40 players, plus one extra quarterback. The extra quarterback cannot play unless both of the designated quarterbacks are injured. During each week of the season the 12 teams will publish rosters which will include the names of 480 active players, plus 12 reserve quarterbacks. Probably not listed, but including the 120 developmental players, the USFL will involve a total of 612 players. The lot will be the best of the available talent. Attesting to this, a *USA Today* article quoted John Chaffetz, vice president of the Arizona Wranglers:[64] "The NFL now realizes, if it didn't realize before, that the USFL is real and intends to sign the top college players."

• With the cooperation of the office of the Los Angeles Express (one of the new entries), data revealed that, at the start of the season, 94 of the total USFL players were known to have come via the junior - community colleges. Fifty-nine have roots in the California Association of Community Colleges, and 34 in the National Junior College Athletic Association.

The total number of athletes who have been and presently are in professional sports suggests that as many, or even more, have come via the junior - community colleges en route to professional sports than from any other constituency. There is no public awareness of a comparative measure of any sort and it has never been publicly discussed. Until such time as it is, however, this possibility cannot be denied.

In a superlative degree, this measure is presented in Chapter Four, "National Junior College Athletic Association (NJCAA) Athletes Reported to Have Attained the Ranks of Professional Sports," and Chapter Five, "California Association of Community

Colleges (CACC) Athletes Reported to Have Attained the Ranks of Professional Sports." The names and additional information about some 1,750 athletes listed in these chapters, who came via the .'Cs en route to professional sports, suggested the title for this book — *Professional Sports: The Community College Connection.*

A complete list of the athletes who began in the JCs and later attained the level of professional sports has never been published. This is the first of its kind and its compilation posed many difficulties. It was the remotest thought, in the most futuristic minds, that the JCs would one day be recognized as a major contributor to not only the national pastime, but as a contributor to international pastimes. Therefore, extensive and detailed records were not maintained. Searching for specific information originating several years in the past where there were minimal records, and where the goal is numbers and the objective is accuracy, it was necessary to cross - reference, as much as possible, each bit of information. It was laborious and time - consuming, but necessary in order to establish a beginning.

Numerous resources were utilized to introduce these athletes of the past and present who were reported to have attained the ranks of professional sports. The names and information were obtained with the cooperation of community college athletic directors and coaches, sports departments of the four - year institutions, professional sports teams, professional sports commissioners' offices, newspapers, persons closely associated with athletics, and several professional athletes.

The author has made every reasonable effort to determine that all of the information contained in this book is correct. There is little doubt that it is about 98 percent accurate. The list is far from being conclusive pertaining to the total number of athletes. Hopefully, all names are spelled correctly — though errors do sometimes occur as information passes through the hands (and typewriters) of changing personnel in the various colleges. To those players whose information is incomplete, a sincere apology. The major search was for names, junior - community colleges attended, and professional affiliations. The information was subjected to extensive checks and balances, and a continuous effort is being made to be completely accurate. The author reserves the right to add, amend, or repeal any information in future publications.

Chapter Four
NATIONAL JUNIOR COLLEGE ATHLETIC ASSOCIATION (NJCAA) ATHLETES REPORTED TO HAVE ATTAINED THE RANKS OF PROFESSIONAL SPORTS

PARTICIPANTS	COMMUNITY COLLEGE SPORT	COMMUNITY COLLEGE ATTENDED	FOUR-YEAR INSTITUTION	PROFESSIONAL AFFILIATION
Aadlin, Kirk	Baseball	Johnson County (KS)		Chicago Cubs
Abruzese, Ray	Football	Hinds (MS)	Univ. of Alabama	Buffalo
Abshirer, Loring	Baseball	Manatee (FL)	Georgia Southern	Houston
Acker, Larry	Baseball	Manatee (FL)		Pittsburg
Adam, Brian	Football	Arizona Western (AZ)	Univ. of Alberta	Canada
Adam, Gary	Football	Arizona Western (AZ)	Univ. of Alberta	Canada
Adams, Norman	Baseball	John C. Calhoun (AL)		Cincinnati
Adams, Willis	Football	Navarro (TX)	Univ. of Houston	Cleveland
Adelman, Bill	Baseball	Broward CC (FL)		Atlanta
Adkins, Margene	Football	Henderson (TX		Canada/New Orleans/ Dallas/N.Y. Jets
Ahern, Mike	Baseball	South Georgia (GA)		Atlanta
Aldrich, Russell	Baseball	Chipola (FL)		Cincinnati
Alexander, Doyle	Baseball	Jefferson State (AL)		Texas
Alexander, Glenn	Baseball	Jefferson State (AL)		Texas
Allen, Jeff	Football	Iowa Central (IA)	Iowa State	St. Louis/Chicago
Altman, John	Baseball	Linn-Benton (OR)		Minnesota
Alvarez, Jose	Baseball	Hillsborough CC (FL)	Southwestern Louisiana	Atlanta
Anastasio, Angelo	Soccer	Nassau (NY)	Adelphi Univ.	Pro Soccer
Anderson, Bill	Baseball	South Georgia (GA)	Vanderbilt Univ.	Cincinnati

PARTICIPANTS	COMMUNITY COLLEGE SPORT	COMMUNITY COLLEGE ATTENDED	FOUR-YEAR INSTITUTION	PROFESSIONAL AFFILIATION
Anderson, Billy	Football	Navarro (TX)	Tulsa Univ.	Los Angeles
Anderson, Jerry	Football	NE Oklahoma A&M (OK)	Oklahoma	Canada
Anderson, Larry	Baseball	Bellevue CC (WA)		Cleveland
Anderson, Max	Football	Henderson (TX)		Washington/Buffalo
Andrews, John	Baseball	Lincoln (IL)		San Francisco
Antunes, Gregg	Golf	Temple (TX)	Sam Houston State Univ.	Professional Golf
Archibald, Nate	Basketball	Arizona Western (AZ)	Univ. of Texas, El Paso	New York
Ard, Lloyd	Baseball	Chipola (FL)	Florida International Univ.	Seattle
Arena, Bruce	Lacrosse	Nassau (NY)	Cornell	Pro Lacrosse
Arnold, Gail	Baseball	Linn-Benton (OR)	BYU	California
Arrietia, George	Baseball	Ranger (TX)		Texas
Askew, Sonny	Soccer	Essex (MD)		Montreal
Atkins, Davy	Baseball	John C. Calhoun (AL)	Univ. of Alabama	N. Y. Yankees
Augustine, Dave	Baseball	Miami-Dade South (FL)		Pittsburg
Ault, Doug	Baseball	Panola (TX)	Texas Tech. Univ.	Toronto
Austin, Debbie	Golf	Miami-Dade North (FL)		Women's Pro Golf
Austin, Terry	Baseball	Ranger (TX)		Chicago Cubs
Babb, Carl	Soccer	Bronx (NY)	New Haven Univ.	Cincinnati
Bailey, David	Baseball	Manatee (FL)	Florida Southern Univ.	N. Y. Yankees
Baker, Jay	Baseball	Manatee (FL)		Montreal
Baldwin, Dave	Baseball	Manatee (FL)		Detroit
Ballard, Butch	Baseball	Valencia (FL)		Philadelphia
Banes, David	Baseball	Manatee (FL)	Univ. of Florida	N. Y. Yankees
Bannister, Tim	Baseball	Mercer County (NJ)		Milwaukee
Bare, Ray	Baseball	Miami-Dade North (FL)		St. Louis
Barker, Tom	Basketball	Southern Idaho (ID)	Univ. of Hawaii	Atlanta
Barnes, Jim "Bad News"	Basketball	Cameron (OK)	Univ. of El Paso (TX)	New York/Philadelphia

108

PARTICIPANTS	COMMUNITY COLLEGE SPORT	COMMUNITY COLLEGE ATTENDED	FOUR-YEAR INSTITUTION	PROFESSIONAL AFFILIATION
Barnes, Larry	Football	Northeastern (CO)	Colorado State Univ.	San Francisco
Barrett, Pat	Football	Harford CC (MD)	Towson State	Philadelphia
Bass, Berry	Baseball	Manatee (FL)		Texas
Bassett, Tim	Basketball	Southern Idaho (ID)		New Jersey
Bates, Larry	Football	Arizona Western (AZ)	Univ. of Georgia	San Francisco
Battan, Pat	Football	Ft. Scott (KS)	Miami	Detroit
Baum, Steve	Baseball	Valencia (FL)	Drake	Detroit
Bearden, David	Baseball	Hillsborough (FL)	Univ. of Southern Florida	Atlanta
Beck, Byron	Basketball	Columbia Basin (WA)	Denver Univ.	Denver
Beck, Rich	Baseball	Columbia Basin (WA)	Gonzaga Univ.	New York Yankees
Behagen, Ron	Basketball	Southern Idaho (ID)	Univ. of Minnesota	Kansas City/New Orleans
Bell, Ed	Football	Navarro (TX)	Idaho State Univ.	New York Jets
Bell, Stan	Baseball	Manatee (FL)		Milwaukee/Atlanta
Beltran, Mike	Baseball	Ranger (TX)	Univ. of Texas - El Paso	Philadelphia
Beno, Bill	Baseball	Manatee (FL)		New York Mets
Benson, Wayne	Baseball	Ranger (TX)		New York Yankees
Berger, Ken	Baseball	Valencia (FL)		Philadelphia
Bernadette, Henry	Baseball	Ranger (TX)	Univ. of Texas - El Paso	California
Berry, Reggie	Football	Arizona Western (AZ)	Cal State, Long Beach	Denver/San Diego
Bertulli, Dave	Baseball	Valencia (FL)		Seattle
Bevacqua, Kurt	Football	Miami-Dade North (FL)		Pittsburg
Bishop, Richard	Football	Marshalltown (IA)	Texas Christian Univ.	New England
Blackwood, Lyle	Football	Blinn College (TX)	Iowa State	New York Jets
Blair, Matt	Football	NE Oklahoma A&M (OK)	Univ. of Cincinnati	Minnesota
Bland, Charles	Baseball	Ferrum (VA)	Union Univ.	Houston
Blaylock, Gary	Baseball	Three Rivers (MO)		New York Mets
Blomberg, Ron	Baseball	DeKalb JC (GA)		Chicago
Bock, Lary	Baseball	South Georgia (GA)		Montreal

PARTICIPANTS	COMMUNITY COLLEGE SPORT	COMMUNITY COLLEGE ATTENDED	FOUR-YEAR INSTITUTION	PROFESSIONAL AFFILIATION
Bodkin, Rusty	Baseball	Broward CC (FL)		St. Louis
Boehmer, Bernie	Baseball	Meramac (MO)	Univ. of New Mexico	Oakland
Boland, Tom	Baseball	South Georgia (GA)		Cleveland
Boras, George	Baseball	Valencia (FL)		Montreal
Borgmann, Glenn	Baseball	Miami-Dade North (FL)		Chicago
Bosley, Bob	Baseball	Essex (MD)	Univ. of South. Alabama	Baltimore
Bowen, Sam	Baseball	Brunswick JC (GA)		Boston
Boyd, Jeff	Basketball	Linn-Benton (OR)	Valdosta State	Oakland
Bracey, Steve	Basketball	Kilgore (TX)	Tulsa Univ.	San Francisco/Atlanta
Bradley, Pat	Golf	Miami-Dade North (FL)	Florida International Univ.	Women's Pro Golf Tour
Branch, Cliff	Football/Track	Wharton County (TX)	Colorado	Oakland
Brazell, Ted	Baseball	Meramac (MO)		Detroit
Breiby, Dave	Baseball	Black Hawk (IL)		Minnesota
Brewer, Richard	Football	Henderson (TX)	Cal State, San Diego	Chicago
Brooks, Billy	Football	Navarro (TX)	Oklahoma	Cincinnati/San Diego
Brooks, Chico	Baseball	South Georgia (GA)		Atlanta
Brooks, Hubie	Baseball	Mesa (AZ)	Arizona State	New York Mets
Brooks, Phil	Baseball	South Georgia (GA)		Pittsburg
Broom, Carl	Football	Coffeyville (KS)	Northeast Louisiana Univ.	WFL/Atlanta
Brown, Curtis	Football	Ft. Scott (KS)	Univ. of Missouri	Buffalo
Brown, Fred	Basketball	Burlington (NJ)	Univ. of Iowa	Seattle
Brown, Johnny	Baseball	South Georgia (GA)		Cleveland
Brown, Larry	Football	Dodge City (KS)		Washington
Brown, Tom	Basketball	Indian River (FL)		Harlem Globetrotters
Browning, Dave	Football	Spokane CC (WA)		Oakland
Brunson, Larry	Football	Mesa (CO)	Univ. of Colorado	Kansas City
Brunson, Mike	Football	Mesa (CO)	Arizona State	Atlanta
Bryant, Erwin	Baseball	Columbia State (TN)		Boston
Bryant, Kevin	Baseball	Valencia (FL)	Florida Southern Univ.	Philadelphia

PARTICIPANTS	COMMUNITY COLLEGE SPORT	COMMUNITY COLLEGE ATTENDED	FOUR-YEAR INSTITUTION	PROFESSIONAL AFFILIATION
Bucky, Elroy	Football	Jones County (MS)	South. Mississippi Univ.	Chicago
Bull, Tim	Baseball	Meramac (MO)		San Francisco
Bungarda, Ken	Football	Arizona Western (AZ)	Univ. of Missouri	Canada
Burdette, Ricky	Baseball	Chipola (FL)		Philadelphia
Burgin, Russ	Baseball	Three River (MO)		Kansas City
Burk, Adrian	Football	Kilgore (TX)	Baylor Univ.	Houston/Philadelphia
Burley, Gary	Football	Wharton County (TX)	Pittsburg	Cincinnati
Burrato, Stan	Football	Columbia Basin (WA)		Green Bay
Buston, David	Basketball	Northeastern (CO)	Univ. of Denver	Denver
Butterfield, Brian	Baseball	Valencia (FL)		New York Yankees
Bystrom, Marty	Baseball	Miami-Dade South (FL)		Philadelphia
Calabrese, John	Baseball	Broward (FL)		Chicago/New York
Califano, Ken	Baseball	Essex (MD)		Baltimore
Cameron, Mike	Golf	Temple (TX)	Univ. of Texas	Professional Golf
Camper, Cardell	Baseball/Football			Cleveland
Campbell, Carter	Football	Glendale (AZ) Treasure Valley (OR)	Weber State Univ.	Denver/San Francisco/ New York/WFL
Canoro, Vinnie	Baseball	Kingsborough (NY)		Minnesota
Cannuci, Phil	Baseball	Kingsborough (NY)		San Francisco
Cardieri, Ed	Baseball	Valencia (FL)		Detroit
Carlton, Steve	Baseball	Miami-Dade North (FL)		Philadelphia
Carr, Fred	Football	Phoenix (AZ)	Univ. of Texas - El Paso	Green Bay
Cash, Ron	Baseball	Manatee (FL)	Florida State Univ.	Detroit
Cason, Tommy	Baseball	South Georgia (GA)	Auburn Univ.	Boston
Catchings, Harvey	Basketball	Ranger (TX)	Univ. of Texas	Philadelphia
Cavarretta, Phil	Baseball	Valencia (FL)		Chicago Cubs
Chambers, Jerry	Basketball	Trinidad State (CO)	Univ. of Utah	Los Angeles

Steve Carlton, Miami-Dade Community College (FL), Philadelphia Phillies,
Photo courtesy Philadelphia Phillies.

Don Sutton, Gulf Coast Community College (FL), Milwaukee Brewers,
Photo courtesy Milwaukee Brewers.

PARTICIPANTS	COMMUNITY COLLEGE SPORT	COMMUNITY COLLEGE ATTENDED	FOUR-YEAR INSTITUTION	PROFESSIONAL AFFILIATION
Chappas, Harry	Baseball	Miami-Dade North (FL)		Chicago
Chaves, Lee	Football	Coffeyville (KS)	Kansas State	Detroit
Childers, Terry	Baseball	South Georgia (GA)	Georgia Southern	Chicago Cubs/Montreal
Childs, Mike	Baseball	Ranger (TX)		Texas
Chism, Tom	Baseball	Brandywine (DE)		Baltimore
Church, Lenny	Baseball	Wilbur Wright (IL)		Chicago
Churchill, Norman	Baseball	Hillsborough (FL)		Cleveland
Clark, Frank	Football	Trinidad State (CO)	Univ. of Colorado	Cleveland
Clinton, Kevin	Soccer	Ulster (NY)		Tampa Bay
Clyde, Benny	Basketball	Ellsworth (IA)	Florida State	Boston
Cobb, Ric	Basketball	Ranger (TX)	Marquette	Pro Basketball - France
Coe, Charles	Baseball	Meramac (MO)		Detroit
Colavito, Steve	Football	Wesley College (DE)	Wake Forest	Philadelphia Bell/Eagles
Cole, Linzy	Football	Henderson (TX)	Texas Christian Univ.	Chicago
Collins, Dave	Baseball	Mesa (AZ)		Cincinnati
Collins, Don	Baseball	South Georgia (GA)		Atlanta
Coney, Tyrone	Football	Iowa Central (IA)	Utah State	Dallas
Cook, Tom	Baseball	Manatee (FL)	Florida State	Oakland
Cooper, Cecil	Baseball	Blinn College (TX)	Prairie View	Milwaukee
Cooper, Neal	Basketball	Ranger (TX)	Texas Wesleyan	Philadelphia/Houston
Cornutt, Terry	Baseball	Linn-Benton (OR)		San Francisco
Cosby, John	Baseball	Linn-Benton (OR)	Portland State	Toronto
Costa, Dave	Football	Northeastern (CO)	Univ. of Utah	Oakland/Denver
Cote, Brice	Baseball	Mercer County (NJ)		Boston
Coulson, Steve	Baseball	Three Rivers (MO)	Murray State	New York Yankees
Craig, Jim	Hockey	Massasoit (MA)		Boston
Crews, Tim	Baseball	Valencia (FL)		Milwaukee
Chrisler, Joel	Baseball	South Georgia (GA)		Anaheim

PARTICIPANTS	COMMUNITY COLLEGE SPORT	COMMUNITY COLLEGE ATTENDED	FOUR-YEAR INSTITUTION	PROFESSIONAL AFFILIATION
Criss, Charlie	Basketball	New Mexico (NM)	New Mexico State	Hartford/Atlanta
Cromartie, Warren	Baseball	Miami-Dade North (FL)		Montreal
Culbreath, Jim	Football	Ferrum (VA)	Oklahoma	Green Bay/New York
Culmer, Wilfred	Baseball	Chipola (FL)		Philadelphia
Cupello, Nelson	Soccer	Monroe (NY)	New York State Univ. (SUNY) Brockport	
Daily, Tony	Baseball	Valencia (FL)		Rochester
Daniels, Bobby	Baseball	Kingsborough (NY)	Long Island Univ.	Anaheim
Daniels, Dick	Football	Columbia Basin (WA)	Univ. of Oregon	Minnesota
Daniels, Mel	Basketball	Burlington (NJ)	New Mexico State	Dallas
Dassie, Larry	Basketball	Dodge City (KS)	Kansas State	Indiana
Davidson, Jim	Baseball	Linn-Benton (OR)		Pro Basketball - London, England
Davidson, Parke	Baseball	Ranger (TX)		San Francisco
Davidson, Randy	Baseball	Columbia State (TN)	Texas Christian Univ.	Kansas City
Davis, Glenn	Baseball	Manatee (FL)	Florida State	Cincinnati
Davis, Mike	Basketball	Mercer County (NJ)		Houston
Davis, Ronnie	Baseball	Blinn College (TX)		Italian Pro League, Roma
Dearstone, Mickey	Baseball	Columbia State (TN)	Maryland	New York Yankees
Dees, Greg	Baseball	Manatee (FL)		Atlanta
Dempsey, Pat	Baseball	Columbia State (TN)	Florida Southern	Baltimore
Dent, Bucky	Baseball	Miami-Dade North (FL)		Oakland
Dericco, Dave	Soccer	Mitchell (CT)		New York Yankees
Dickens, Paul	Baseball	Manatee (FL)	Hartwick	No. Amer. Soccer League
Dickerson, Champ	Football	Henderson (TX)		Cleveland
Dickman, Doug	Baseball	Meramac (MD)	Southern Methodist Univ.	Canada/Dallas
Didier, Clint	Football	Columbia Basin (WA)	Portland State	Atlanta
Di Matteo, Frank	Soccer	Mercer County (NJ)		Washington
				New Jersey

115

PARTICIPANTS	COMMUNITY COLLEGE SPORT	COMMUNITY COLLEGE ATTENDED	FOUR-YEAR INSTITUTION	PROFESSIONAL AFFILIATION
Di Venti, Jim	Baseball	Essex (MD)		Cincinnati
Dixon, Zachary	Football	Dean (MA)	Temple Univ.	Baltimore/ Philadelphia/N.Y. Giants
Dolan, Tom	Soccer	Mercer County (NJ)	Bridgeport	New Jersey
Dombroski, Ken	Football	Arizona Western (AZ)	Cameron	Canada
Donckers, Bill	Football	Columbia Basin (WA)	Cal State, San Diego	St. Louis/San Diego
Dorsey, Tony	Baseball	Ranger (TX)		Cincinnati
Douglas, John	Football	Ferrum (VA)	Univ. of Maryland	Buffalo
Driggers, Lee	Baseball	Valencia (FL)		Los Angeles
Dudley, Charles	Basketball	Moberly (MO)		San Francisco
Earnest, Conradt	Soccer	Ulster (NY)	Univ. of Washington	Cleveland
East, Ron	Football	Columbia Basin (WA)	Akron Univ.	Dallas/San Diego
Easom, Tate	Baseball	Valencia (FL)		Chicago White Sox
Ebersole, Keith	Baseball	Manatee (FL)	Montana State	Chicago Cubs
Echols, Eddie	Baseball	Columbia State (TN)	Western Carolina	Chicago
Edward, Ji John	Soccer	Mercer County (NJ)	Jacksonville State	Rochester
Edwards, Eddie	Football	Arizona Western (AZ)	Univ. of Miami (FL)	Cincinnati
Elam, Steve	Baseball	Linn-Benton (OR)		Anaheim
Elliott, Bob	Golf	Temple (TX)		Professional Golf
Ellis, John	Baseball	Mitchell (CT)	Univ. of Arkansas	Texas
Ellis, Gerry	Football	Ft. Scott (KS)		Green Bay
Enea, Aurilio	Soccer	Ulster (NY)	Univ. of Missouri	New York
Enyart, Terry	Baseball	Chipola (FL)	New Haven Univ.	Montreal
Ervey, Albert	Baseball	Massasoit CC (MA)		New York Yankees
Esser, Mark	Baseball	Miami-Dade North (FL)	Florida Atlantic	Chicago White Sox
Ethridge, Bobby	Baseball	Delta (MS)	Mississippi State	San Francisco
Evenson, Jim	Football	Treasure Valley (OR)	Univ. of Oregon	Canada
Fahrow, Bryant	Baseball	Kankakee (IL)	College of St. Francis	California

116

PARTICIPANTS	COMMUNITY COLLEGE SPORT	COMMUNITY COLLEGE ATTENDED	FOUR-YEAR INSTITUTION	PROFESSIONAL AFFILIATION
Falcone, Pete	Baseball	Kingsborough (NY)		San Francisco/St. Louis/ New York Mets
Farmer, Roger	Football	Eastern Ariz. (AZ)	Baker Univ. (KS)	New York Jets
Farrell, David	Soccer	Ulster (NY)	Univ. of Baltimore	Cleveland
Ferguson, Tom	Soccer	Florissant Valley (MO)		St. Louis
Fernandez, Dick	Baseball	Manatee (FL)	Florida State	Oakland
Fiala, Neil	Baseball	Meramac (MO)	Southern Illinois	Cincinnati
Fidelia, Pat	Soccer	Mercer County (NJ)		Montreal
Fields, Bob	Basketball	Brandywine (DE)	La Salle	Portland
Fields, Edgar	Football	Navarro (TX)	Texas A&M	Atlanta
Figueroa, Lou	Baseball	Ranger (TX)		New York Yankees
Fiori, Ed	Golf	Wharton County (TX)	Univ. of Houston	Professional Golf Assoc.
Fiorillo, Nick	Baseball	Brookdale (NJ)	Univ. of Texas - El Paso	Cincinnati (Farm)
Fisher, Glenn	Baseball	Linn-Benton (OR)		San Francisco
Fitzgerald, Tom	Baseball	Kankakee (IL)		Cincinnati
Fitzmorris, Al	Not Known	Johnson County (KS)		Cleveland
Flanders, Mario	Soccer	Mitchell (CT)	South. Conn. State	American Soccer League
Fleisher, Bruce	Golf	Miami-Dade North (FL)		Pro Golf Tour
Fletcher, Scott	Baseball	Valencia (FL)		Chicago Cubs
Flitcraft, Alan	Baseball	Manatee (FL)		California
Flynn, Doug	Baseball	Somerset CC (KY)	Univ. of Kentucky	New York
Folkers, Rich	Baseball	Ellsworth (IA)	Parsons	Milwaukee
Fontes, Frank	Football	Ferrum (VA)	Florida State	Houston
Forte, Ike	Football	Tyler (TX)	Univ. of Arkansas	New England
Foster, Jim	Basketball	Becker (MA)	Univ. of Connecticut	St. Louis/Denver
Foucault, Steve	Baseball	South Georgia (GA)		Detroit
Fowke, Chuck	Baseball	Manatee (FL)		Texas
Franklin, Elliott	Baseball	Ranger (TX)		Milwaukee

PARTICIPANTS	COMMUNITY COLLEGE SPORT	COMMUNITY COLLEGE ATTENDED	FOUR-YEAR INSTITUTION	PROFESSIONAL AFFILIATION
Franklin, Glen	Baseball	Chipola (FL)		Montreal
Franklin, Reggie	Basketball	New Mexico Military Institute (NM)		Harlem Globe Trotters
Frayser, Ashby	Baseball	Manatee (FL)	South. Methodist Univ.	Montreal
Frazier, Cliff	Football	Ft. Scott (KS)	Stetson	Kansas City
Freeman, Clem	Baseball	Manatee (FL)	UCLA	Cincinnati
Frye, John	Baseball	Manatee (FL)	Florida State	Boston
Fuchs, Frank	Soccer	Ulster (NY)	Michigan State	Detroit
Fuller, Tony	Basketball	Vincennes (IN)	Univ. of Tampa	Detroit
Furon, Robin	Baseball	Valencia (FL)	Pepperdine	Cleveland
Gaechter, Mike	Football	Clark (WA)	Oregon	Dallas
Gaglione, Matt	Baseball	Chipola (FL)	Florida Southern	Boston
Gaines, Mumbo	Football	Ferrum (VA)	Cincinnati	Pittsburg/Chicago
Galbreath, Tony	Football	Indian Hills (IA)	Univ. of Missouri	New Orleans
Galen, Mike	Baseball	Ranger (TX)		Boston
Gallagher, Dave	Baseball	Mercer County (NJ)		Cleveland
Garber, Randy	Soccer	Mercer County (NJ)		Tampa Bay
Garland, Wayne	Baseball	Gulf Coast (FL)	Penn State	Cleveland
Garrett, Alvin	Football	Ranger (TX)	Angelo State	New York Giants
Garrett, Lin	Baseball	Manatee (FL)	Florida State	Washington
Gary, Keith	Football	Ferrum (VA)	Oklahoma	Canada
Gastineau, Mark	Football	Eastern Arizona (AZ)	S'eastern Oklahoma State	New York Jets
Gault, Ray	Baseball	Manatee (FL)		Cleveland
George, Ed	Football	Ferrum (VA)	Wake Forest	Canada/Baltimore
Gibbs, Dick	Basketball	Burlington (NJ)	Texas	Washington
Gibson, Ernie	Baseball	South Georgia (GA)		Cleveland
Gilbreath, Rod	Baseball	Jones County (MS)		Atlanta
Gilliam, Melvin	Baseball	Manatee (FL)	Florida A&M	Texas

118

Photos courtesy New York Jets

Mark Gastineau, Eastern Arizona College, New York Jets

Mark Gastineau, New York Jets Defensive End Downs a Raider

Photo courtesy New York Jets.

PARTICIPANTS	COMMUNITY COLLEGE SPORT	COMMUNITY COLLEGE ATTENDED	FOUR-YEAR INSTITUTION	PROFESSIONAL AFFILIATION
Gilmore, Artis	Basketball	Gardner-Webb (NC)	Jacksonville Univ.	Chicago
Glass, Bobby	Baseball	Manatee (FL)		Los Angeles
Goffey, Greg	Baseball	Lincoln (IL)		New York
Gonzalez, Orlando	Baseball	Miami-Dade South (FL)	Univ. of Miami (FL)	Chicago/Oakland/ Philadelphia
Goodman, Norman	Football	Ft. Scott (KS)	Univ. of Missouri	Canada
Goodyear, Chris	Baseball	Hillsborough (FL)		Detroit
Gordon, Ira	Football	Phoenix (AZ)		San Diego
Gorey, Ric	Baseball	Valencia (FL)	Kansas State	Minnesota
Gossett, Bruce	Football	Ferrum (VA)	Univ. of Richmond	Los Angeles/San Francisco
Graham, Dan	Baseball	Mesa (AZ)	La Verne College	Baltimore
Grandy, Eric	Baseball	Essex (MD)		Chicago
Gray, Gary	Baseball	Oklahoma City (OK)		Seattle
Gray, Mel	Football	Ft. Scott (KS)	Univ. of Missouri	St. Louis
Green, Charlie	Football	Coffeyville (KS)	Kansas State	Baltimore
Greent, Eddie	Baseball	South Georgia (GA)		Cleveland
Green, Ken	Basketball	Ranger (TX)	Pan American Univ.	Denver
Green, Ricky	Basketball	Vincennes (IN)	Univ. of Michigan	Golden State/Utah
Grey, Tim	Football	Navarro (TX)	Texas A&M	St. Louis/Kansas
Gronowski, Gary	Baseball	Valencia (FL)		Baltimore
Groover, Larry	Baseball		Pan American Univ.	Chicago
Grier, Dave	Baseball	Valencia (FL)		Milwaukee
Grimsley, Ross	Baseball	Jackson State (TN)		Cleveland/Montreal
Grubb, John	Baseball	Manatee (FL)	Florida State	Texas/San Diego
Guess, Tommy	Baseball	Hillsborough (FL)	Florida Southern	New York Yankees
Guldbjerg, Neils	Soccer	Ulster (NY)		Detroit
Gurzynski, Jim	Baseball	Broward CC (FL)	Florida State	Los Angeles
Hairston, Jerry	Baseball	Lawson State (AL)		Pittsburg

121

PARTICIPANTS	COMMUNITY COLLEGE SPORT	COMMUNITY COLLEGE ATTENDED	FOUR-YEAR INSTITUTION	PROFESSIONAL AFFILIATION
Haddock, Don	Baseball	Valencia (FL)		Atlanta
Hagan, Steve	Baseball	Linn-Benton (OR)		Pittsburg
Hall, Willie	Football	Arizona Western (AZ)	USC	Oakland
Hamilton, Dave	Baseball	Everett (WA)		Pittsburg
Hancock, Gary	Baseball	Hillsborough (FL)	Univ. of South Carolina	Boston
Hansen, George	Football	Delta (MS)	Univ. of Georgia	Canada
Hanslovan, Jeff	Baseball	Linn-Benton (OR)		Kansas
Hanson, Brad	Baseball	Valencia (FL)		Boston
Harden, Leon	Football	Pratt (KS)	Univ. of Texas - El Paso	Green Bay
Hardy, Buster	Baseball	Manatee (FL)	Florida Southern	Detroit
Harley, Woody	Baseball	Columbia State (TN)		Boston
Harlow, Larry	Baseball	Mesa (AZ)		California
Harris, Leroy	Football	Ft. Scott (KS)		Miami/Philadelphia
Harris, Mark	Baseball	Valencia (FL)		New York Yankees
Harris, Monte	Baseball	Ranger (TX)	Arkansas State	Montreal
Harrison, Reggie	Football	Northeastern Oklahoma A&M (OK)		Pittsburg
Hart, Doug	Football	Navarro (TX)	Drake Univ. Univ. of Texas - Arlington	Green Bay
Hart, Mike	Baseball	Kalamazoo Valley (MI)	Western Michigan	Montreal
Hart, Tom	Baseball	Valencia (FL)		Philadelphia
Harvey, John	Football	Tyler (TX)	Univ. of Texas	Memphis
Hatcher, Mickey	Baseball	Mesa (AZ)	Univ. of Oklahoma	Minnesota
Hawkins, Stan	Baseball	Meramac (MO—Ferrum (VA)	Univ. of Nevada - Las Vegas	Toronto
Haywood, Frank	Football		North Carolina State	Cincinnati
Haywood, Spencer	Basketball	Trinidad State (CO)	Univ. of Detroit	Los Angeles/Seattle/Denver
Healy, Bob	Baseball	Meramac (MO)		California

122

PARTICIPANTS	COMMUNITY COLLEGE SPORT	COMMUNITY COLLEGE ATTENDED	FOUR-YEAR INSTITUTION	PROFESSIONAL AFFILIATION
Healy, Francis	None	Holyoke (MA)	American Intern'l Univ.	Kansas City
Helliburton, Jeff	Basketball	San Jacinto Central (TX)	Drake Univ.	Atlanta/Philadelphia
Henderson, Tom	Basketball	San Jacinto Central (TX)	Univ. of Hawaii	Washington/Houston
Hernandez, Charles	Baseball	Hillsborough (FL)		New York Yankees
Herron, Mack	Football	Hutchinson (KS)	Kansas State	New England/Los Angeles
Herman, Ed	Baseball	Mesa (AZ)		Montreal
Hinds, Sam	Baseball	Broward (FL)		Milwaukee
Hinton, Charlie	Football	Arizona Western (AZ)	USC	Denver
Hirson, Gary	Baseball	Hillsborough (FL)	Southwestern Louisiana	Detroit
Hodges, Randy	Baseball	South Georgia (GA)	Georgia Southern	Atlanta
Hodges, Ron	Baseball	Broward (FL)	Southern Illinois Univ.	San Francisco
Hoenstine, Dave	Baseball	South Georgia (GA)	Newberry	Cincinnati
Hogan, Gary	Baseball	Broward (FL)		Chicago
Hollins, Lionel	Basketball	Dixie College (UT)	Arizona State	Portland
Hollowill, Chuck	Baseball	Hillsborough (FL)		Cleveland
Hooper, Richard	Baseball	Ranger (TX)	Texas Christian Univ.	Cleveland
Hopkins, Maury	Baseball	Manatee (FL)	Florida State	New York Mets
Horge, Ira	Basketball	Burlington (NJ)	New Mexico	Miami
Horton, Phil	Golf	Temple (TX)	Univ. of Texas	Professional Golf
Houfek, Keith	Football	Coffeyville (KS)	Arkansas	Oakland
Howard, Fred	Baseball	Miami-Dade South (FL)		Chicago
Howard, Percy	Basketball	Isothermal (NC)	Austin Peay	Dallas
Howell, Eddie	Baseball	Manatee (FL)	Florida State	Oakland
Hubbard, Marv	Football	Mitchell (CT)	Colgate	Oakland
Huddleston, Elgre	Baseball	Meramac (MO)		Atlanta
Hudlow, Floyd	Football	Phoenix (AZ)	Univ. of Arizona	Atlanta
Huff, Jim	Football	Ferrum (VA)	Univ. of Miami (FL)	Green Bay
Hughes, Joe	Baseball	Valencia (FL)		Baltimore

PARTICIPANTS	COMMUNITY COLLEGE SPORT	COMMUNITY COLLEGE ATTENDED	FOUR-YEAR INSTITUTION	PROFESSIONAL AFFILIATION
Huntsinger, Alan	Baseball	Linn-Benton (OR)	Oregon State	St. Louis
Hussey, Bob	Baseball	Kankakee (IL)		Cleveland
Hynko, Gerald	Baseball	South Georgia (GA)	Georgia Southern	Oakland
Iaeger, Richard	Baseball	Ranger (TX)		California
Isleib, Bob	Soccer	Mitchell (CT)	Southern Conn. State	American Soccer League
Ivory, Horace	Football	Navarro (TX)	Oklahoma	New England
Ivy, Gary	Baseball	Oklahoma City (OK)		Philadelphia
Jackson, Eugene	Football	Phoenix (AZ)	Univ. of Texas - El Paso	Cleveland
Jackson, Moody	Football	Phoenix (AZ)	New Mexico State	Canada
Jackson, Robert	Football	Henderson (TX)	Texas A & M	Cleveland
Jackson, Rudy	Basketball	Hutchinson (KS)	Wichita State	New York/Europe
Jacobs, Ray	Football	Navarro (TX)	Howard Payne	Houston/Denver/Miami
Jacoby, Don	Baseball	Brookdale (NJ)	Florida Int'l Univ.	St. Louis
James, Art	Baseball	Macomb (MI)		Detroit
Jean-Baptiste, Ernst	Soccer	Miami-Dade South (FL)		Phoenix/New England
Jeffcoat, Larry	Baseball	Ferrum (VA)		Philadelphia
Jefferson, Jeff	Baseball	John Tyler CC (VA)		Toronto
Jendra, Rick	Baseball	Kankakee (IL)	Florida Int'l Univ.	Cincinnati
Jenkins, Bill	Basketball	Essex (MO)	Adams State	Pro Basketball - Italy
John, Bob	Football	Trinidad State (CO)	Univ. of Wisconsin	Los Angeles/Phoenix
Johnson, Carl	Football	Phoenix (AZ)	Univ. of Nebraska	New Orleans/Washington
Johnson, Chip	Basketball	Isothermal (NC)	Augusta	Hartfield/France
Johnson, Cleo	Football	Ferrum (VA)	Georgia Tech	Dallas
Johnson, Cliff	Baseball	Massasoit (MA)	Boston State	Pittsburg
Johnson, Jerry	Baseball	Temple (TX)		St. Louis
Johnson, John	Basketball	Northwest (WY)	Univ. of Iowa	Seattle
Johnson, Lamar	Baseball	Lawson State (AL)		Chicago
Johnson, Ollie	Basketball	CC of Philadelphia (PA)		Chicago/Portland

PARTICIPANTS	COMMUNITY COLLEGE SPORT	COMMUNITY COLLEGE ATTENDED	FOUR-YEAR INSTITUTION	PROFESSIONAL AFFILIATION
Johnson, Randy	Baseball	Miami-Dade South (FL)		Chicago
Johnson, Raymond	Football	Ferrum (VA)		New York Giants
Johnston, Bill	Football	Tyler (TX)	Texas A & M	Tampa Bay
Jonas, Tony	Baseball	Kingsborough (NY)	Long Island Univ.	Detroit
James, Cody	Football/Basketball			
Jones, Dicky	Football	Trinidad State (CO)	Cal State, San Jose	Los Angeles
Jones, Jimmy	Football	Ferrum (VA)	Univ. of Richmond	New Orleans
Jones, Joe	Baseball	Trinidad State (CO)	Univ. of Wisconsin	Atlanta
Jones, Ronny	Football	Ranger (TX)		Philadelphia
Jordan, Kip	Soccer	Henderson (TX)	Univ. of Texas - El Paso	Green Bay/Atlanta
Justice, Marshall	Baseball	Monroe (NY)	Cornell	Rochester
Kaage, George	Baseball/Basketball	South Georgia (GA)	Gorgia Southern	Atlanta
Kadupski, Charles	Soccer	Kankakee (IL)		Los Angeles
Kalinas, Mick	Football	Mitchell (CT)		American Soccer League
Kastelic, Bruce	Baseball	Coffeyville (KS)	Hartwick	Pittsburg
Keeton, Burwood	Football	Ranger (TX)	Oklahoma State	New York Mets
Kelleher, Mick	Baseball/Basketball	Navarro (TX)	Oklahoma State	New England
Kelly, Dickie	Basketball	Wenatchee (WA)	Puget Sound	Chicago
Kelly, William	Basketball	Bay (MD)		Philadelphia
Kemp, Rick	Baseball	Mercer County (NJ)		Cincinnati
Kennedy, Mike	Baseball	Kankakee (IL)		Texas
Kenon, Larry	Basketball	Linn-Benton (OR)		Oakland
Kern, Jim	None	Amarillo (TX)	Memphis State	New York/San Antonio
Kerrigan, Joe	Baseball	Delta (MI)	Michigan State	Cleveland
Kinder, Bruce	Baseball	Temple (TX)		Baltimore
	Baseball	Broward CC (FL)	Florida Southern	Montreal/St. Louis

125

PARTICIPANTS	COMMUNITY COLLEGE SPORT	COMMUNITY COLLEGE ATTENDED	FOUR-YEAR INSTITUTION	PROFESSIONAL AFFILIATION
Kindsfather, Vern	Baseball	Clark (WA)	Portland State	Seattle
King, Travis	Baseball	South Georgia (GA)		Los Angeles
Kinney, Ron	Baseball	Meramac (MO)		St. Louis
Kirkland, Ronnie	Baseball	South Georgia (GA)		Cincinnati
Kinson, Bruce	Football	Manatee (FL)	Central Washington State	Pittsburg
Klank, Bill	Baseball	Mercer County (NJ)		Cleveland
Klein, Mark	Baseball	Broward CC (FL)		Philadelphia
Knapp, Chris	Baseball/ Basketball	Kalamazoo Valley (MI)	Univ. of Central Michigan	California
Knight, Barry	Baseball	Hillsborough (FL)		Seattle
Knight, Bobby	Baseball	South Georgia (GA)	Emory Univ.	Baltimore
Knight, Ray	Baseball	Chipola (FL)		Cincinnati
Knight, Tim	Baseball	Valencia (FL)		New York Yankees
Knoles, Gene	Basketball	Ranger (TX)	Texas Tech.	Pro Basketball - Europe
Kotchman, Tom	Baseball	Chipola (FL)	Georgia Southern	Cincinnati
Kosmos, Mike	Football	Eastern Oklahoma		
Kosa, David	Baseball	Eastern Oklahoma State (OK)		
Krebs, Kris	Baseball	Manatee (FL)		Boston
Krueger, Rick	Baseball	Grand Rapids (MI)		Boston
Kubit, Joe	Baseball	Valencia (FL)		Boston
Kuiper, Duane	Baseball	Indian Hills (IA)	Michigan State	Minnesota
Kupich, Ron	Football	Wilbur Wright (IL)	Southern Illinois	Cleveland
Lackey, Bob	Basketball	Casper (WY)	Marquette	Chicago
Lackey, John	Baseball	Chipola (FL)	Florida Southern	New York
Lamont, King	Basketball	Southeastern (IA)	Cal State, Long Beach	Detroit
Landrum, Terry	Baseball	Eastern Oklahoma State (OK)		Denver
				St. Louis

PARTICIPANTS	COMMUNITY COLLEGE SPORT	COMMUNITY COLLEGE ATTENDED	FOUR-YEAR INSTITUTION	PROFESSIONAL AFFILIATION
Langford, Rick	Baseball	Manatee (FL)	Florida State	Oakland
Lane, Dick "Night Train"				
Larson, Bill	Football	Nebraska Western (NB)		Los Angeles
Larson, Lynn	Football	Pratt (KS)	Colorado State	Green Bay
Lasck, James	Football	Phoenix (AZ)	Kansas State	Baltimore
Latimer, Al	Baseball	Black Hawk (IL)		Philadelphia/
	Football	Ferrum (VA)	Clemson	Philadelphia/ San Francisco/Canada
Lattimore, Mo	Football	Hutchinson (KS)	Kansas State	Canada
Lavell, Gary	Baseball	Northhampton (PA)		San Francisco
Layton, Dennis	Basketball	Phoenix (AZ)	USC	Phoenix/New York/ San Antonio
Lear, Ric	Baseball	Valencia (FL)		Cincinnati
Leckie, Dave	Soccer	Mercer County (NJ)	Alderson-Broaddus	Cleveland
Ledbetter, Jack	Baseball	Valencia (FL)		Chicago Cubs
Lee, Ice	Baseball	Johnson County (KS)	Univ. of Kansas	Kansas City
Lee, Robert	Football	Iowa Central (IA)	Northern Iowa	Denver
Leeper, Curtis	Soccer	Miami-Dade South (FL)	Florida Intern'l Univ.	Ft. Lauderdale/ Philadelphia
Leggett, Earl	Football	Hinds (MS)	Louisiana State	Chicago
Lein, Chris	Baseball	Valencia (FL)		New York Yankees
Lesslie, Bob	Baseball	Meramac (MO)		Los Angeles
LeWallyn, Dennis	Baseball	Chipola (FL)	Kansas State	Los Angeles
Lewis, Freddie	Basketball	Eastern Arizona (AZ)	Arizona State	Indiana
Lighos, John	Soccer	Ulster (NY)		New England
Lindblad, Paul	Baseball/ Track			
Lipsey, Dan	Baseball	Neosho County (KS)	Univ. of Kansas	Texas
		Linn-Benton (OR)	Puget Sound	Cincinnati

PARTICIPANTS	COMMUNITY COLLEGE SPORT	COMMUNITY COLLEGE ATTENDED	FOUR-YEAR INSTITUTION	PROFESSIONAL AFFILIATION
Littell, Mark	Baseball	Longview (MO)		Kansas City
Livingston, Andy	Football	Phoenix (AZ)		Chicago/New Orleans
Lloyd, Lewis	Basketball	New Mexico Military Institute (NM)		
Lollar, Tim	Baseball	Mineral Area (MO)	Drake Univ.	California
Looney, Joe Don	Football	Cameron (OK)	Univ. of Arkansas	San Diego
Lorch, Karl	Football	Arizona Western (AZ)	Univ. of Oklahoma	Detroit
Lurtsema, Bob	Baseball/Football		USC	Washington
Mack, Ollie	Basketball	Grand Rapids (MI)	Western Michigan	Minnesota
Mackey, Cliff	Baseball	San Jacinto Central (TX)		Dallas
Madlock, Bill	Baseball	Linn-Benton (OR)		Chicago
		Southeastern (IA)		San Francisco/Texas/Chicago Cubs
Magness, Mike	Baseball	Manatee (FL)		Atlanta
Manley, Steve	Baseball	Kingsborough (NY)		Kansas City
Manor, Brison	Football	Pratt (KS)	Arkansas	Denver
Mantooth, Billy Joe	Football	Ferrum (VA)	West Virginia	Philadelphia
Marshall, Ed	Football	Ranger (TX)	Cameron State	Memphis/New York Giants
Martell, Tom	Baseball	Linn-Benton (OR)		San Francisco
Martin, Jerry	Baseball	Spartanburg Methodist (SC)	Furman	Philadelphia/Chicago Cubs/San Francisco
Martin, Melvin	Football	Ferrum (VA)	William and Mary	Detroit
Martin, Mike	Baseball	Linn-Benton (OR)		San Diego
Martinez, R.	Baseball	Hillsborough (FL)		Philadelphia
Martinez, Randy	Baseball	Hillsborough (FL)		Seattle
Martino, Marty	Baseball	Black Hawk (IL)		Kansas City
Marquez, Raul	Baseball	Ranger (TX)		Saltillo

128

PARTICIPANTS	COMMUNITY COLLEGE SPORT	COMMUNITY COLLEGE ATTENDED	FOUR-YEAR INSTITUTION	PROFESSIONAL AFFILIATION
Mathewson, Christy	Baseball	Keystone (PA)	Bucknell	New York
Mathis, Reggie	Football	Navarro (TX)	Univ. of Oklahoma	New Orleans
Matuszak, John	Football	Iowa Central (IA)	Univ. of Tampa	Oakland/Houston/ Kansas City
May, Milt	Baseball	Manatee (FL)		Detroit
May, Ted	Baseball	Valencia (FL)		Chicago Cubs
Mays, Henry	Baseball	South Georgia (GA)	Georgia Southern	St. Louis
Mawhinney, Mike	Baseball	Broward CC (FL)		Baltimore
Maxwell, Jim	Baseball	Mercer County (NJ)		Texas
Meely, Clifford	Basketball	Northeastern (CO)	Univ. of Colorado	Houston
Melillo, Phil	Basketball	Goldey Beacom (DE)		Pro Basketball - Italy
Melvin, Ray	Baseball	Chipola (FL)		Detroit
Mercado, John	Baseball	Ranger (TX)		New York
Mesoroll, Mark	Baseball	Wesley (DE)	Florida State	Oakland
Messino, Shep	Soccer	Nassau (NY)	Harvard	Pro Soccer
Metcalf, Terry	Football	Everett (WA)	Cal State, Long Beach	St. Louis/Canada/ Washington
Meyer, Marty	Baseball	Broward (FL)	Florida State	New York
Meyers, Ken	Baseball	Ranger (TX)		Minnesota
Milam, Wayne	Baseball	Broward CC (FL)		Boston
Milbourne, Larry	Baseball	Cumberland (NJ)	Glassboro State	N.Y. Yankees/Seattle
Milledge, Tony	Baseball	Manatee (FL)		St. Louis
Miller, Mark	Basketball	Ranger (TX)	Univ. of Texas - El Paso	Texas
Miller, Mike	Baseball	Valencia (FL)		Atlanta
Mitchell, Charlie	Baseball	Chipola (FL)		Pittsburg
Mitchell, H.	Football	Ferrum (VA)		Canada
Moates, David	Baseball	Manatee (FL)	Florida State	Washington/ Texas/N.Y. Yankees

PARTICIPANTS	COMMUNITY COLLEGE SPORT	COMMUNITY COLLEGE ATTENDED	FOUR-YEAR INSTITUTION	PROFESSIONAL AFFILIATION
Monroe, Danny	Golf	Temple (TX)		Professional Golf
Montgomery, Randy	Football	Everett (WA)	Weber State	Chicago/Denver
Moore, Alvin	Baseball	South Georgia (GA)		Atlanta
Moore, Donnie	Baseball	Ranger (TX)		Chicago Cubs
Moriarity, Dermont	Baseball	Massasoit (MA)		Kansas City
Moroff, Dan	Baseball	Valencia (FL)		New York Yankees
Morrison, Jim	Baseball	South Georgia (GA)	Georgia Southern	Chicago White Sox
Mosser, Phil	Football	Ferrum (VA)	William and Mary	Canada
Montefusco, John "The Count"	Baseball	Brookdale (NJ)		San Francisco
Moxley, Bob	Baseball	Manatee (FL)		Chicago White Sox
Moya, Ernie	Baseball	Hillsborough (FL)		Detroit
Mulroy, Tom	Soccer	Ulster (NY)		Miami
Muncie, Chuck	Football	Arizona Western (AZ)	U. C. Berkeley	New Orleans/San Diego
Murray, Dale	Baseball	Blinn College (TX)		New York Mets
Murphy, Dan	Baseball	Meramac (MO)		Texas
Murphy, Mike	Baseball	Meramac (MO)		St. Louis
Murrell, Willie	Basketball	Eastern Oklahoma State (OK)	Univ. of Nevada - Las Vegas	
Myatt, Gene	Baseball	Manatee (FL)	Kansas State	Denver
Myernick, Glenn	Soccer	Mercer County (NJ)	Parsons	Philadelphia
McAdoo, Bob	Basketball	Vincennes (IN)	Hartwick	Dallas/Portland
			North Carolina	Buffalo/New York/Detroit
McCann, Jim	Football	Phoenix (AZ)	Arizona State	San Francisco
McCarthy, Jim	Football	Wilbur Wright (IL)		Green Bay
McCatty, Steve	Baseball	Macomb (MI)		Oakland
McClanahan, Randy	Football	Glendale (AZ)	Southwestern Louisiana	Oakland
McDougal, Rick	Baseball	Temple (TX)		Philadelphia

PARTICIPANTS	COMMUNITY COLLEGE SPORT	COMMUNITY COLLEGE ATTENDED	FOUR-YEAR INSTITUTION	PROFESSIONAL AFFILIATION
McElroy, Bucky	Football	Hinds (MS)	Southern Mississippi	Chicago
McGill, Ralph	Football	N'eastern A&M (OK)	Tulsa	New Orleans
McGinnis, Jim	Football	Ferrum (VA)	Univ. of Richmond	Washington
McIntyre, Jim	Baseball	Aquinas JC (TN)		St. Louis
McIver, Gerald	Baseball	Brunswick (GA)		New York Mets
McKay, Dave	Baseball	Columbia Basin (WA)	Creighton Univ.	Toronto
McKay, Tom	Baseball	Manatee (FL)	Louisiana State	Montreal
McMath, Herb	Football	Ellsworth (IA)	Morningside Univ.	Green Bay
McRae, Bill	Baseball	South Georgia (GA)		Oakland
McWilliams, Larry	Baseball	Paris (TX)		Atlanta
Nash, Bob	Basketball	San Jacinto Central (TX)	Univ. of Hawaii	Detroit
Nelson, Doug	Baseball	Manatee (FL)		Pittsburgh
Nelson, Shane	Football	Blinn College (TX)	Baylor	Buffalo
Newhouser, Don	Baseball	Broward CC (FL)		Boston
Nordhagen, Wayne	Baseball	Treasure Valley (OR)	Portland State	Chicago
Norrid, Tim	Baseball	Hillsborough (FL)		Cleveland
Nuss, Ed	Baseball	Valencia (FL)		Boston
Oberkfell, Steve	Baseball	Belleville (IL)		St. Louis
Ochal, Mark	Baseball	Brookdale (NJ)		N.Y. Yankees
O'Connor, Billy	Baseball	Kingsborough (NY)		Minnesota
O'Day, Tom	Baseball	Broward CC (FL)		San Diego
Odum, Joe	Football	Ferrum (VA)	North Carolina	Canada
Oestriech, Mark	Baseball	Valencia (FL)		Seattle
Oglivie, Ben	Baseball	Bronx (NY)	Wichita State	Milwaukee
Okoniewski, Steve	Football	Everett (WA)	Wayne State Univ.	Atlanta/Green Bay/
			Univ. of Montana	St. Louis
O'Leary, Bob	Soccer	Florissant Valley (MO)	St. Louis Univ.	St. Louis
Oliva, Mario	Soccer	Ulster (NY)	New Haven Univ.	Connecticut

PARTICIPANTS	COMMUNITY COLLEGE SPORT	COMMUNITY COLLEGE ATTENDED	FOUR-YEAR INSTITUTION	PROFESSIONAL AFFILIATION
Ortiz, George	Baseball	Valencia (FL)		Cleveland
Osborne, Pat	Baseball	Manatee (FL)	Florida State Univ.	Cincinnati/Detroit
Otten, Jim	Baseball	Mesa (AZ)	Arizona State	St. Louis
Outland, Clifford	Track	John C. Calhoun (AL)	Auburn	Pro Track
Pagan, Dave	Baseball	Bellevue (WA)		N.Y. Yankees/Baltimore
Pagel, Karl	Baseball/Football			
Paglione, Al	Baseball	Glendale (AZ)		Cleveland
Parker, Jackie	Football	Valencia (FL)		Chicago Cubs
Parker, Sonny	Basketball	Jones County (MS)	Mississippi State	Canada
Parker, Willie	Football	Mineral Area (MO)	Texas A & M	San Francisco
Parrish, Larry	Baseball	Wharton County TX	North Texas State	Detroit
Patterson, Gilbert	Baseball	Seminole CC (FL)		Montreal
Patterson, Scott	Baseball	Miami-Dade South (FL)		New York Yankees
	Baseball	Valencia (FL		Atlanta
Pate, Bob	Baseball	Mesa (AZ)	Arizona State	Montreal
Paulas, Tim	Football	Phoenix (AZ)	Kansas State	Washington
Paultz, Billy	Basketball	Cameron (OK)	St. John Univ.	San Antonio
Pecka, Keith	Baseball	Kankakee (IL)		Boston
Pena, Robert	Football	Dean (MA)	Univ. of Massachusetts	Cleveland
Peiffer, Dan	Football	Ellsworth (IA)	Southeast Missouri State	Chicago
Perdoni, Rock	Football	Ferrum (VA)	Georgia Tech	Canada
Perez, Dale	Baseball	Manatee (FL)		St. Louis
Perkins, Johnny	Football	Ranger (TX)	Abilene Christian	New York Giants
Pesa, Njego	Soccer	Ulster (NY)		Dallas
Peters, Tony	Football	N'eastern Oklahoma A & M (OK)	Oklahoma	Washington
Peterson, Dale	Soccer	Massasoit CC (MA)	Southern Methodist	New England
Peterson, Les	Soccer	Miami-Dade South (FL)	Florida Intern'l Univ.	Fort Lauderdale

132

PARTICIPANTS	COMMUNITY COLLEGE SPORT	COMMUNITY COLLEGE ATTENDED	FOUR-YEAR INSTITUTION	PROFESSIONAL AFFILIATION
Peterson, Rod	Baseball	Black Hawk (IL)		San Diego
Pette, Jimmy	Baseball	Manatee (FL)		St. Louis
Pettes, Andrew	Basketball	New Mexico (NM)	Univ. of Oklahoma	Kentucky
Phelps, Ken	Baseball	Mesa (AZ)	Arizona State	Kansas City
Pinckney, Chuck	Baseball	Kingsborough (NY)		Boston
Phillips, Bill	Soccer	Nassau (NY)	Adelphi	Pro Soccer
Powell, Hoskin	Baseball	Chipola (FL)		Minnesota
Powell, Ted	Football	Ferrum (VA)	Ohio State	Birmingham
Poythress, Richard	Baseball	South Georgia (GA)		Chicago Cubs
Pride, Dexter	Football	Ferrum (VA)	Univ. of Minnesota	Miami
Prilo, James	Baseball	Wilbur Wright (IL)		Cincinnati
Powell, Joe	Baseball	Valencia (FL)		Baltimore
Quiltor, Charles	Football	Tyler (TX)	Stephen F. Austin	Canada/San Francisco
Rasmussen, Eric	Baseball	Indian Hills (IA)	Louisiana State	St. Louis
Rawley, Shane	Baseball	Indian Hills (IA)		Seattle
Reamon, Tommy	Football	Ft. Scott (KS)	Univ. of Missouri	Chicago Fire/Pittsburg/Washington/Kansas City
Reasonover, Larry	Baseball	Hillsborough (FL)	Univ. of Tampa	Texas
Redus, Gary	Baseball	John C. Calhoun (AL)	Athens State	Cincinnati
Reed, Henry	Football	Iowa Central (IA)	Weber State	New York
Regan, Frank	Baseball	Valencia (FL)		Cleveland
Regensburger, Bill	None	Holyoke (MA)		Pittsburg
Reid, Steve	Soccer	Mercer County (NJ)	Penn State	New England
Reiter, Jack	Baseball	Meramac (MO)		Chicago Cubs
Reyes, Louis	Baseball	Hillsborough (FL)	Univ. of Tampa	Philadelphia
Richardson, Ron	Baseball	Linn-Benton (OR)		Philadelphia
Rielly, Jim	Baseball	Longview (MO)		Philadelphia

PARTICIPANTS	COMMUNITY COLLEGE SPORT	COMMUNITY COLLEGE ATTENDED	FOUR-YEAR INSTITUTION	PROFESSIONAL AFFILIATION
Rivera, Carmen	Women's Basketball	Bronx DD (NY)	Long Island Univ.	New York Gems (Women's Pro)
Rivers, Larry	Basketball	Moberly (MO)	Missouri Western	Harlem Globetrotters
Rivers, Mickey	Baseball	Miami-Dade North (FL)		Texas/ N.Y. Yankees
Rizzo, Phil	Baseball	Manatee (FL)		Chicago White Sox
Robbins, Steve	Baseball	South Georgia (GA)		Cleveland
Robert, Terry	Baseball	South Georgia (GA)	Augusta	Chicago Cubs
Roberts, Bill	Basketball/ Baseball	Kalamazoo Valley (MI)	Univ. of Western Michigan	Houston
Rodriquez, Rodolfo	Baseball	Ranger (TX)		Nueva Laredo
Robinson, Craig	Baseball	Chipola (FL)	Southern Illinois	Chicago Cubs
Robinson, Flynn	Basketball	Casper (WY)	Univ. of Wyoming	Milwaukee/Chicago/ Cincinnati/Los Angeles
Robinson, Larry	Football	Ferrum (VA)	Tennessee	Dallas
Robinson, Paul	Football	Eastern Arizona (AZ)	Univ. of Arizona	Cincinnati
Romes, Charles	Track	Lake City (FL)	North Carolina Central Univ.	Buffalo
Rudacille, Cleve	Basketball	Essex (MD)		Pro Basketball - Luxembourg
Rum, Steve	Baseball	Valencia (FL)		Pro Baseball - Japan
Runyon, Curtis	Baseball	Temple (TX)		Cincinnati
Rudolph, Victor	Baseball	Florissant Valley (MO)	Univ. of Missouri	St. Louis
Russo, John	Baseball	Meramac (MO)		Atlanta
Ryan, Nolan	Baseball	Alvin (TX)		California/Houston
Rozema, Dave	Baseball	Grand Rapids (MI)		Detroit
Rozmus, Jerry	Baseball	Wilbur Wright (IL)		Chicago
Saber, Mark	Baseball	Manatee (FL)	Univ. of Georgia	Pittsburg
Sacks, Nathan	Soccer	Miami-Dade South (FL)		Dallas

PARTICIPANTS	COMMUNITY COLLEGE SPORT	COMMUNITY COLLEGE ATTENDED	FOUR-YEAR INSTITUTION	PROFESSIONAL AFFILIATION
Safewright, Harry	Baseball	Manatee (FL)	Florida State	Philadelphia/ Atlanta/Pittsburg
Sakata, Lea	Baseball	Treasure Valley (OR)	Gonzaga	Baltimore
Sansosti, Fran	Baseball	Essex (MD)	Towson State	Cincinnati
Sarrett, Dan	Baseball	Valencia (FL)		Cincinnati
Scarber, Sam	Football	Northeastern (CO)	Univ. of New Mexico	San Diego
Scarce, Mac	Baseball	Manatee (FL)	Florida State	Philadelphia/ Cincinnati/Texas
Scanlon, James "Pat"	Baseball	St. Petersburg (FL)	Univ. of Minnesota	San Diego
Schaeffer, Jim	Baseball	Meramac (MO)	Southwest Missouri	Kansas
Scheller, Dave	Baseball	Ranger (TX)		Boston
Schields, Steve	Baseball	Ranger (TX)	Tulsa	Oakland
Schneck, Steve	Baseball	Kalamazoo Valley (MI)		Boston
Schneider, Orville	Football	Grand Rapids (MI)	Western Michigan	Washington
Schoendienst, Kevin	Baseball	Meramac (MO)		Chicago
Scott, James	Football	Henderson (TX)		Chicago
Scott, Jeff	Basketball	Kankakee (IL)	Univ. of Illinois	Texas
Scott, Louis	Football	Henderson (TX)	Univ. of Houston	Canada
Scott, Marty	Baseball	Paris (TX)		Dallas
Scrivener, Chuck	Baseball	Baltimore (MD)	Univ. of Baltimore	Detroit
Sheats, Eddie	Football	Hutchinson (KS)	Univ. of Kansas	Washington
Shelby, John	Baseball	Columbia State (TN)		Baltimore
Sherbina, Lorne	Football	Columbia Basin (WA)	Idaho	Canada
Showalter, Nat	Baseball	Chipola (FL)	Mississippi State	New York Yankees
Shopay, Tom	Baseball	Dean (MA)	Univ. of Bridgeport	Baltimore
Sievers, Bill	Baseball	Wilbur Wright (IL)		Detroit
Sims, Mike	Baseball	Johnson County (KS)		Philadelphia
Sitten, Ken	Football	Navarro (TX)	Univ. of Oklahoma	Baltimore

135

PARTICIPANTS	COMMUNITY COLLEGE SPORT	COMMUNITY COLLEGE ATTENDED	FOUR-YEAR INSTITUTION	PROFESSIONAL AFFILIATION
Skok, Craig	Baseball	Broward CC (FL)	Florida State	Boston
Slinker, Bill	Baseball	Hillsborough (FL)		Philadelphia
Smith, Bobby	Baseball	Manatee (FL)		New York Mets
Smith, Darryl	Soccer	Florissant Valley (MO)		St. Louis
Smith, Gary	Baseball	Valencia (FL)		New York Yankees
Smith, Glenn	Baseball	Columbia State (TN)	David Lipscomb	Atlanta
Smith, Jackie	Baseball	Manatee (FL)	Florida State	Chicago White Sox
Smith, James T.	Baseball	Chipola (FL)		St. Louis
Smith, Jerry	Football	Eastern Arizona (AZ)	Arizona State	Washington
Smith, Keith	Baseball	Manatee (FL)		Texas/St. Louis
Smith, Ken	Football	Navarro (TX)	New Mexico	Cleveland
Smith, Perry	Football	Mesa (CO)	Colorado State	Green Bay
Smith, Randy	Baseball	Lincoln (IL)		San Francisco
Smith, Randy	Baseball	Three Rivers (MO)		California
Sobers, Ricky	Basketball	Southern Idaho (ID)	Univ. of Nevada - Las Vegas	Phoenix
Soderholm, Eric	Baseball	South Georgia (GA)	Univ. of Nevada - Las Vegas	Minneapolis/Texas/N.Y. Yankees
Sondergaard, Bob	Football	Worthing (MN)		Pittsburg
Spagnola, Mike	Baseball	Valencia (FL)		Texas
Sparks, Randy	Baseball	Pratt (KS)	Missouri Southern	Kansas City
Spence, John	Baseball	Hillsborough (FL)		Cleveland
Spriggs, Larry	Basketball	San Jacinto Central (TX)		Houston
Spring, Ronnie	None	Coffeyville (KS)		Dallas
Squires, Mike	Baseball	Kalamazoo Valley (MI)	Western Michigan	Chicago
Stanley, Mickey	Baseball	Grand Rapids (MI)		Detroit
Stanton, Mike	Baseball	Miami-Dade South (FL)		Cleveland
Staubach, Roger	Football	New Mexico Military Institute (NM)	U.S. Naval Academy	Dallas

PARTICIPANTS	COMMUNITY COLLEGE SPORT	COMMUNITY COLLEGE ATTENDED	FOUR-YEAR INSTITUTION	PROFESSIONAL AFFILIATION
Stegman, Dennis	Baseball	Florissant Valley (MO)		Oakland
Steidl, Bill	Baseball	South Georgia (GA)		Oakland
Stein, Bill	Baseball	Brevard (FL)	Southern Illinois	Seattle
Stein, Jim	Baseball	Everett (WA)	Univ. of Washington	San Diego
Stepther, Harrison	Basketball	Moberly (MO)	Michigan State	Harlem Globetrotters
Stinson, Bob	Baseball	Miami-Dade North (FL)		Seattle/Los Angeles
St. Clair, Mike	Football	Iowa Central (IA)	Grambling	Cleveland/ New England/Cincinnati
Stovall, Paul	Basketball	Pratt (KS)	Arizona State	Phoenix
Strickland, Lawrence	Football	Tyler (TX)	North Texas State	Chicago
Strolk, Bill	Baseball	Manatee (FL)		Minnesota
Sturm, Randy	Baseball	Mercer County (NJ)		Kansas City
Styles, Tony	Basketball	Iowa Central (IA)	Univ. of San Francisco	Los Angeles
Sucarichi, George	Baseball	Hillsborough (FL)		Cincinnati
Suchy, Larry	Football	Jones County (MS)	Mississippi College	Atlanta
Sutton, Don	Baseball	Gulf Coast (FL)	Whittier	Los Angeles
Sutton, Mitch	Football	Ft. Scott (KS)	Univ. of Kansas	Philadelphia
Swayne, Bill	Football	Clark (WA)	Oregon	St. Louis/New York
Sweder, Dave	Baseball	Hillsborough (FL)		New York Yankees
Sweetan, Karl	Football	Navarro (TX)	Wake Forest	Detroit
Sykes, Bob	Baseball	Miami-Dade North (FL)		St. Louis
Tamargo, John	Baseball	Miami-Dade North (FL)		Montreal
Tanzi, Robert	Baseball	Massasoit (MA)		Texas
Tate, Randy	Baseball	John C. Calhoun (AL)		New York
Taylor, Jim	Football	Hinds (MS)	Louisiana State Univ.	Green Bay
Taylor, Ollie	Basketball	San Jacinto Central (TX)	Univ. of Houston	San Diego
Taylor, Roland	Basketball	Dodge City (KS)	La Salle	Virginia/Denver
Taylor, Scott	Baseball	Manatee (FL)	South Florida	Atlanta

137

PARTICIPANTS	COMMUNITY COLLEGE SPORT	COMMUNITY COLLEGE ATTENDED	FOUR-YEAR INSTITUTION	PROFESSIONAL AFFILIATION
Teegarden, Rob	Baseball	Valencia (FL)	USC	New York Yankees
Thomas, Alonzo "Skip"	Football	Arizona Western (AZ)		Oakland
Thomas, Earl	Football	Mesa (CO)	Univ. of Houston	St. Louis
Thomas, Paul	Baseball	Ranger (TX)	Pan American	Reynosa
Thomas, Ron	Basketball	Henderson (TX)	Univ. of Louisville	Kentucky
Thompson, Bobby	Football	Arizona Western (AZ)	Univ. of Oklahoma	Detroit
Thompson, Don	Football	Ferrum (VA)	Univ. of Richmond	Baltimore/ Philadelphia/St. Louis
Thompson, Leonard	Football	Arizona Western (AZ)	Oklahoma State	Detroit
Thornton, Bubba	Football	Navarro (TX)	Texas Christian Univ.	Buffalo
Tillman, Faddie	Football	Arizona Western (AZ)	Boise State	Dallas
Tompkins, Jimmy	Baseball	Ranger (TX)	Univ. of Texas	Atlanta
Torres, George	Basketball	Oklahoma City (OK)	Bethany Nazarene	Utah
Townsend, Curtis	Football	Hutchinson (KS)	Univ. of Arkanssa	San Diego
Treadway, Dick	Baseball	Manatee (FL)		Minnesota
Trevino, Margo	Baseball	Ranger (TX)		Mexico City
Triplett, Tony	Basketball/ Baseball			
Tullish, Bill	Baseball	Johnson County (KS)	Kansas State	Texas
Turner, Ed	Baseball	Manatee (FL)	Florida Southern	San Francisco
Tuttle, John	Basketball	Indian River (FL)	Texas A & I	Houston
Twitchell, Wayne	Football	Coffeyville (KS)	Kansas	Canada
Tyler, Maurice	Baseball	Portland (OR)		Montreal
Tyrone, Jim	Football	Baltimore (MD)		New York/Denver
Tyrone, Wayne	Baseball	Ranger (TX)	Pan American	Chicago Cubs/Oakland
Tyson, Michael	Baseball	Ranger (TX)	Pan American	Chicago
Upchurch, Rick	Baseball	Indian River (FL)		St. Louis
Valdez, Nelson	Football	Indian Hills (IA)	Univ. of Minnesota	Denver
	Baseball	Hillsborough (FL)		Chicago

PARTICIPANTS	COMMUNITY COLLEGE SPORT	COMMUNITY COLLEGE ATTENDED	FOUR-YEAR INSTITUTION	PROFESSIONAL AFFILIATION
Vande Casteele, Mark	Baseball	Black Hawk (IL)		New York Mets
Vann, Jesse	Baseball	Johnson County (KS)	Univ. of Kansas	New York Mets
Vanniger, Denny	Soccer	Florissant Valley (MO)	Harris Stowe	St. Louis
Vassilaris, George	Soccer	Ulster (NY)	Florida Tech	Pro Soccer - Greece
Vencent, Ernie	Baseball	Manatee (FL)	Univ. of Georgia	Kansas City
Venner, Gary	Baseball	Ranger (TX)	Texas Wesleyan	Texas
Verrano, Michael	Baseball	Massasoit (MA)		Boston
Vickers, Butch	Baseball	Ranger (TX)	Univ. of Kansas	Kansas City
Viefhaus, Steve	Baseball	Meramac (MO)		Detroit
Von Ahnen, Billy	Baseball	Kingsborough (NY)		Chicago Cubs
Wagner, Brad	Football	Coffeyville (KS)	Kansas State	Canada
Waiters, Jim	Baseball	Manatee (FL)	Georgia Southern	Minnesota
Wakefield, Andre	Basketball	Southern Idaho (ID)	Loyola Univ. - Chicago	Chicago/Utah
Walker, Clarence "Foots"	Basketball	Vincennes (IN)	West Georgia	Cleveland/New Jersey
Walker, Dwayne	Basketball	San Jacinto Central (TX)		Cincinnati
Wall, Art, Jr.	Golf	Keystone (PA)	Duke	Pro Golf Tour
Wallace, Bob	Football	Phoenix (AZ)	Univ. of Texas - El Paso	Chicago
Wallace, Michael	Basketball	Keystone (PA)	Univ. of Scranton	Boston
Walling, Dennis	Basketball	Brookdale (NJ)	Clemson	Houston
Walls, Tyrone	Football	Ft. Scott (KS)	Univ. of Missouri	Canada
Walthour, Jim	Baseball	Meramac (MO)		St. Louis
Walton, Larry	Football	Trinidad State (CO)	Arizona State	Detroit
Walton, Lloyd	Basketball	Moberly (MO)	Marquette	Milwaukee
Ward, Joey	Baseball	Manatee (FL)	Univ. of Florida	San Francisco
Wark, Doug	Soccer	Mitchell (CT)	Hartwick	No. Amer. Soccer League
Washburn, Ray	Baseball	Columbia Basin (WA)	Whitworth	St. Louis
Watkins, Jim	Baseball	Valencia (FL)		Boston
Watson, Steve	Baseball	Manatee (FL)	Florida Southern	Texas

139

PARTICIPANTS	COMMUNITY COLLEGE SPORT	COMMUNITY COLLEGE ATTENDED	FOUR-YEAR INSTITUTION	PROFESSIONAL AFFILIATION
Watts, Don	Basketball	Burlington (NJ)	Univ. of Iowa	Seattle
Watts, Sam	Basketball	Northwest (WY)	Great Falls	Pittsburg
Watts, Ted	None	Coffeyville (KS)	Texas Tech.	Oakland
Weaver, Charlie	Football	Arizona Western (AZ)	USC	Detroit
Weaver, Gary	Football	Trinidad State (CO)	Cal State, Fresno	Green Bay
Weaver, Jimmy	Baseball	Manatee (FL)	Florida State	Minnesota
Weldon, Mel	Basketball	Mercer County (NJ)	Boston College	Pro League - Venezuela
Westmoreland, Henry	Soccer	Miami-Dade South (FL)	Florida Intern'l Univ.	Phoenix
Whaley, Gary	Baseball	Valencia (FL)		Chicago White Sox
White, Charlie	Football	Iowa Central (IA)		New York Jets/Tampa Bay
White, Connie	Basketball	Mercer County (NJ)	Bethune Cookman	Pro Basketball — Europe
White, Frank	Baseball	Manatee (FL)		Kansas City
White, Lee	Football	Arizona Western (AZ)	U.C. Berkeley	San Diego/ New York Jets
White, Walter	Football	Mesa (CO)	Weber State	Kansas City
Whitt, Ernie	Baseball	Macomb (MI)		Boston/Toronto
Wickenfuss, Ernie	Baseball	Goldey Beacom (DE)	Univ. of Maryland	Detroit
Wickerson, Al	Baseball	Johnson County (KS)	Colorado	New York Mets
Wickstrom, Ernie	Football	Wilbur Wright (IL)		Chicago/Green Bay
Wiegand, Rick	Soccer	Macomb (MI)	Northern Illinois	Ft. Lauderdale
Wiggins, Dick	Baseball	Valencia (FL)	Cleveland State	Detroit
Wilkins, Jeff	Basketball	Black Hawk (IL)	Illinois State	San Antonio
Williams, Bob	Baseball	Meramac (MO)		Montreal
Williams, Joe	Baseball	Hillsborough (FL)	Florida Southern	Oakland
Williams, Joe	Baseball	Manatee (FL)	Southern Florida	Oakland
Williams, Mark	Baseball	Hillsborough (FL)	Western Kentucky	Detroit
Williams, Mike	Baseball	Temple (TX)		Kansas City
Williams, Ray	Basketball	San Jacinto Central (TX)	Univ. of Minnesota	New York

PARTICIPANTS	COMMUNITY COLLEGE SPORT	COMMUNITY COLLEGE ATTENDED	FOUR-YEAR INSTITUTION	PROFESSIONAL AFFILIATION
Williams, Willie	Basketball	Miami-Dade North (FL)	Florida State	Nat'l Basketball League
Wilson, Jerrel	Football	Pearl River (MS)	Southern Mississippi	Kansas City
Wilson, Mark	Baseball	Linn-Bendon (OR)		Minnesota
Wilson, Mookie	Baseball	Spartanburg Methodist (SC)		New York Mets
Wilson, Robert "Bob"	Basketball	Northeastern (CO)	Univ. of South Carolina	Chicago/Boston
Wilson, Steve	Baseball	South Georgia (GA)	Wichita State	Los Angeles
Wilson, Ward	Baseball	Valencia (FL)	Georgia State	New York Mets
Winston, Scott	Baseball	Chipola (FL)		New York Mets
Wood, Chris	Baseball	South Georgia (GA)	Montreal	
Worth, Dennis	Baseball	Lincoln (IL)	Southern Illinois - Edwardsville	
Wright, Joe	Soccer	Florissant Valley (MO)		New York
Wyszynski, Dennis	Baseball	Mercer County (NJ)		St. Louis
Yankowski, Ron	Football	N'eastern Oklahoma A & M (OK)		Oakland
Yarbrough, Buddy	Baseball	Manatee (FL)		St. Louis
Young, Gary	Baseball	Ranger (TX)		Kansas City
Young, Jerome	Basketball	Mercer County (NJ)		Philadelphia
Young, Kevin	Baseball	Valencia (FL)	U.C. Berkeley	Pro Basketball - Europe
Zabel, Steve	Football	New Mexico Military Institute (NM)		Detroit
Zamora, Oscar	Baseball	Miami-Dade North (FL)	Oklahoma	Philadelphia
Zimmer, Tom	Baseball	Manatee (FL)		Chicago
Zoeller, Fuzzy	Golf	Edison CC (FL)		St. Louis
Zurburg, Wayne	Baseball	Broward CC (FL)		Pro Golf
				Chicago

NATIONAL JUNIOR COLLEGE ATHLETIC ASSOCIATION (NJCAA) ATHLETES REPORTED TO BE AFFILIATED WITH THE UNITED STATES FOOTBALL LEAGUE (USFL)

PARTICIPANTS	COMMUNITY COLLEGE SPORT	COMMUNITY COLLEGE ATTENDED	FOUR-YEAR INSTITUTION	AFFILIATION
Albright, Ira	Football	Tyler (TX)	Northeastern State	Michigan Panthers
Baxley, Ed	Football	Arizona Western (AZ)	South Carolina	Kansas City/ Washington Federals
Bell, Duane	Football	Hudson (NY)	Temple	Philadelphia Stars
Breathett, Sherdell	Football	Northeastern Oklahoma A & M (OK)		
Cobb, Robert L.	Football	Northeast (MS)	Oklahoma	Canada/New Jersey
Crump, Richard	Football	Miami Dade (FL)	Cincinnati/Arizona Jacksonville	Tampa Bay/Chicago Blitz Canada/ Boston Breakers
Dark, Frank	Football	Ferrum (VA)	Virginia	Baltimore/Canada/ Philadelphia Stars
Dunek, Ken	Football	Paducah (KY)	Memphis State	Philadelphia Eagles/ Baltimore/ Philadelphia Stars
Durrettem, Mike	Football	Ferrum (VA)	West Virginia	Los Angeles Express
Friede, Mike	Football	Garden City (KS)	Indiana	New Jersey Generals
Gerdon, Steve	Football	Ferrum (VA)	Richmond	Cleveland/ Washington Federals
Gibson, Antonio	Football	Hinds (MS)	Cincinnati	Philadelphia Stars
Goddard, Derrick	Football	Iowa Central (IA)	Drake	Tampa Bay/Canada/ Philadelphia
Goosby, Darryl	Football	Ellsworth (IA)	Cincinnati	Denver Gold

142

PARTICIPANTS	COMMUNITY COLLEGE SPORT	COMMUNITY COLLEGE ATTENDED	FOUR-YEAR INSTITUTION	AFFILIATION
Greene, Doug	Football	Lakewood (MN)	Texas A & I	St. Louis/Buffalo/ New Orleans/Houston/ Green Bay/Washington Federals
Hagen, Mike	Football	Walla Walla (WA)	Montana Univ.	Michigan Panthers
Happe, Joe	Football	Ferrum (VA)	Georgia	Philadelphia Eagles/ Philadelphia Stars
Jackson, Roger	Football	Middlesex (NJ)	Penn State	Philadelphia Stars
Jones, Tim	Football	Fort Scott (KS)	Kansas	Canada/Denver Gold
Jordinelli, Kris	Football	Mesa (AZ)		Houston/Denver Gold
Keel, Mark	Football	Olympia (WA)	Arizona	Arizona Wranglers
Logan, Fred	Football	Jones (MS)	Cincinnati	Michigan Panthers
Manucci, Dan	Football	Mesa (AZ)	Kansas State	Buffalo Bills/ Toronto Argonauts/ Arizona Wranglers
McConnaughy, Tom	Football	Spokane Falls (WA)	Central Arkansas	New Orleans/N.Y. Jets/ New Jersey Generals
Melontree, Andres Richard, Jr.	Football	Tyler (TX)	Baylor	Cincinnati/Tampa Bay/ Chicago Blitz
Melontree, Lester	Football	Tyler (TX)	Stephen F. Austin	Pittsburg/ Philadelphia Stars
Mitchell, Mike	Football	Ferrum (VA)		New York Coronets/Canada/ New Jersey Generals
Norris, Bob	Football	Iowa Central (IA)	Eastern Illinois	Tampa Bay Bandits
Overly, Bobby	Football	Snow (UT)	San Jose	Oakland Invaders
Peters, Joel	Football	Mesa (AZ)	Arizona	New York Jets/Buffalo/ Baltimore/Arizona Wranglers

PARTICIPANTS	COMMUNITY COLLEGE SPORT	COMMUNITY COLLEGE ATTENDED	FOUR-YEAR INSTITUTION	AFFILIATION
Purifoy, Bill	Football	New Mexico Military Academy (NM)	Tulsa	Dallas Cowboys/ Arizona Wranglers
Testermans, Don	Football	Ferrum (VA)	Clemson	Seattle/Miami/ Philadelphia/ Washington Federals
Worsham, Dave	Football	Ranger (TX)	Arkansas Tech.	Birmingham Stallions

Chapter Five
CALIFORNIA ASSOCIATION OF COMMUNITY COLLEGES (CACC) ATHLETES REPORTED TO HAVE ATTAINED THE RANKS OF PROFESSIONAL SPORTS

PARTICIPANT	COMMUNITY COLLEGE SPORT	COMMUNITY COLLEGE ATTENDED	FOUR-YEAR INSTITUTION	PROFESSIONAL AFFILIATION
Adams, Bob	Football	San Mateo		New Orleans
Adams, John	Football	Santa Monica	UCLA	Los Angeles/Chicago
Adams, Mike	Baseball	Fullerton		Chicago
Adams, Pete	Football	San Diego City	USC	Cleveland
Adams, Steve	Baseball	San Bernardino		Chicago
Adams, Tony	Football	Riverside	Utah State	Kansas City
Agajanian, Ben	Football	Compton	New Mexico	Los Angeles
Aker, Jack	Baseball	College of Sequoias	U.C. Berkeley	New York
Aker, John	Baseball	College of Sequoias		Atlanta
Alcorn, Gary	Basketball	Fresno	Cal State, Fresno	Los Angeles
Alexakos, Steve	Football	Diablo Valley	Cal State, San Jose	New York Giants
Allen, Duane	Football	Santa Ana		Los Angeles
Allen, Jimmy	Football	L.A. Pierce	UCLA	Pittsburg
Alexander, Gary	Baseball	L.A. Harbor		Cleveland
Allison, Henry	Football	College of Sequoias	Cal State, San Diego	Philadelphia
Allison, Otis	Basketball	Laney	Nevada	San Francisco
Allred, Ray	Football	Consumnes River		Canada
Ames, Billy	Basketball	De Anza		Germany
Anderson, Billy	Football/Track			
Anderson, Ralph	Football	Compton		Chicago
Andrew, Kim	Baseball	L.A. Valley	Cal State, L. A.	Chicago
Andrews, Al	Football	L.A. Valley		Boston
	Football	Laney	New Mexico State	Buffalo

145

PARTICIPANTS	COMMUNITY COLLEGE SPORT	COMMUNITY COLLEGE ATTENDED	FOUR-YEAR INSTITUTION	PROFESSIONAL AFFILIATION
Andrews, Rob	Baseball	El Camino		San Francisco
Anglin, Gary	Baseball	Ventura		New York Mets
Apodaca, Jim	Baseball	Cerritos	UCLA/USC	New York Mets
Argee, Dan	Baseball	Consumnes River	Chapman	Oakland
Ashby, Allen	Baseball	L.A. Harbor		Toronto/Houston
Askea, Mike	Football	College of Sequoias	Stanford	Denver
Asselstine, Brian	Baseball	Allan Hancock		Atlanta
Auerbach, Rick	Baseball	L.A. Pierce		Cincinnati
Austin, Rick	Baseball	Cerritos		Minnesota
Babb, Lance	Track	L.A. City		Intern'l Track Assn.
Baez, Jessie	Baseball	Cerritos	USC	Los Angeles
Baccaglio, Martin	Football	College of Marin	Cal State, San Jose	Cincinnati
Baker, Dusty	Baseball	American River		Los Angeles/San Francisco
Baker, Jeff	Football	Fullerton	U.S. Intern'l Univ.	Green Bay
Baker, Stan	Baseball	Antelope Valley	Dallas Baptist	Texas Rangers
Balderrama, Sal	Baseball	Yuba	U.C. Davis	Kansas City
Ballanger, Don	Basketball	Merced		Philadelphia
Baltzer, Tom	Football	San Diego		Continental League
Bandy, Bert	Baseball	Fresno		Philadelphia
Barber, Steve	Baseball	Riverside	Azusa Pacific	Minnesota
Barnes, Bennie	Football	Contra Costa	Stanford	Dallas
Barnes, Jeff	Football	Chabot	U.C. Berkley	Oakland
Barr, Mark	Baseball	Golden West	USC	Boston
Barton, Greg	Football	Long Beach City	Tulsa	Detroit
Basinger, Mike	Football	Gavilan	U.C. Riverside	Green Bay
Batcha, Frank	Baseball	Riverside City		Los Angeles
Battle, Mike	Football	Long Beach City	USC	Detroit/New York
Bauckman, Tony	Football	L.A. City	Cal State, San Diego	Canada

146

PARTICIPANTS	COMMUNITY COLLEGE SPORT	COMMUNITY COLLEGE ATTENDED	FOUR-YEAR INSTITUTION	PROFESSIONAL AFFILIATION
Bauers, Wayne	Baseball	San Jose		New York Mets
Baugh, Dean	Baseball	Butte/Hartnell		Philadelphia
Beadell, George	Football	Cerritos	Cal State, San Jose	San Francisco
Beare, Gary	Baseball	San Diego Mesa	Boston	
Beene, Charlie	Baseball	College of Sequoias		Chicago Cubs
Belelski, Bronco	Football	L.A. City	Texas - El Paso	Dallas
Bell, Eddie	Football	Compton	Idaho State	Buffalo
Bell, Kevin	Baseball	Mt. San Antonio		Chicago
Berry, Dan	Football	San Diego	U.C. Berkeley	Philadelphia
Berry, Gerald	Football	Compton	UCLA	Detroit
Berry, Ken	Football	Foothill	Cal State, San Jose	Los Angeles/Canada
Besana, Fred	Football	Sierra	U.C. Berkeley	Buffalo/New York
Bessey, Stan	Baseball	College of Sequoias		Philadelphia
Bettiga, Mike	Football/Basketball/Track	College of Redwoods	Cal State, Humbolt	San Francisco
Bienhoff, Wayne	Football	Cerritos	Cal State, San Diego	San Diego
Bird, Doug	Baseball	Mt. San Antonio		Kansas
Bishop, Don	Football	L.A. City		Dallas
Blackledge, Walter	Football	San Diego City		Baltimore
Blackwell, Tim	Baseball	San Diego Mesa		Montreal
Blanche, Amos	Baseball	Antelope Valley		
Block, John	Basketball	Glendale	Oakland	
Bloomendale, Allen	Football	Barstow	USC	Kansas City
Boitano, Dan	Baseball	Fresno		Canada
Bokamper, Kim	Football	San Jose	Cal State, San Jose	Philadelphia
Booker, Bill	Football	San Diego City	Univ. of Nevada - Las Vegas	Miami
Boone, Dan	Baseball	Cerritos	Cal State, Fullerton	Canada
Bonham, Bill	Baseball	L.A. Valley		California/San Diego
				Chicago

PARTICIPANTS	COMMUNITY COLLEGE SPORT	COMMUNITY COLLEGE ATTENDED	FOUR-YEAR INSTITUTION	PROFESSIONAL AFFILIATION
Bordner, Mike	Basketball/Tennis	Merritt	USC	San Diego
Borjas, Phil	Football	Fresno	Cal State, Fresno	Portland
Bosetti, Rick	Baseball	Shasta		New York/Philadelphia
Bosley, Thad	Baseball	Mira Costa		Chicago
Bothwell, Monte	Baseball	Cypress		Oakland
Bourdet, Len	Baseball	Gavilan	Cal State, Fresno	Chicago Cubs
Bowa, Larry	Baseball	Sacramento City		Philadelphia
Bowers, Gary	Baseball	Fullerton	Azusa Pacific	Philadelphia
Box, Bob	Baseball	College of Redwoods		Atlanta
Boyd, Greg	Football	Fresno City	Cal State, San Diego	New England
Boyett, Arvel	Baseball	Taft		Boston
Bradley, Otha	Football	L.A. City	USC	San Diego
Branch, Ken	Baseball	Siskiyous		St. Louis
Branyan, Tyrone	Basketball	Cypress	Univ. of Texas	Germany
Bratz, Mike	Basketball	Allan Hancock	Stanford	Phoenix
Braziel, Larry	Football	Compton		Baltimore
Brett, George	Baseball	El Camino		Kansas City
Brewster, Rich	Baseball	San Bernardino		Oakland
Brice, Lawrence	Football	Delta	Cal State, San Jose	San Francisco
Brohamer, Jack	Baseball	Golden West		Boston
Brooks, Bob	Baseball	L.A. Harbor		New York
Brouhard, Mark	Baseball	L.A. Pierce		Milwaukee
Brown, Bill	Baseball	Fresno	Cal State, Fresno	Boston
Brown, Booker	Football	Santa Barbara	USC	California/Houston/San Diego
Brown, Ed	Baseball	Butte/Hartness	U.C. San Francisco	Houston
Brown, Elton	Football	San Diego	Utah State	Denver

PARTICIPANTS	COMMUNITY COLLEGE SPORT	COMMUNITY COLLEGE ATTENDED	FOUR-YEAR INSTITUTION	PROFESSIONAL AFFILIATION
Brown, Fred	Football	American River		Philadelphia
Brown, Ollie	Baseball	Long Beach		Philadelphia
Brown, Sam	Football	Contra Costa		Cleveland
Brown, Warren	Baseball	American River	UCLA	Portland (NW League)
Brownlee, Dave	Golf	Citrus		PGA Tour
Bruce, Dwaine	Baseball	Cypress		San Francisco
Brustar, Warren	Baseball	Napa	Fresno State	Philadelphia
Byrant, Jim	Baseball	Merced		Baltimore
Byrant, Larkin	Basketball	Allan Hancock	Univ. of Pacific	Belgium
Buchanan, Dave	Football	Pasadena City	Arizona State	Canada
Buchannon, Willie	Football	Mira Costa	Cal State, San Diego	Green Bay/San Diego
Buford, Don	Football/Baseball	L.A. City	USC	Chicago/Baltimore/Japan
Bulling, Terry	Baseball	Golden West	Cal State, L.A.	Minnesota
Bunce, Larry	Basketball	Riverside City	Utah State	Los Angeles
Buncom, Framk	Football	East L.A.	USC	San Diego
Burgess, Buddy	Baseball	College of Sequoias		New York Yankees
Burke, Glenn	Baseball	Merritt		Oakland
Burke, Mike	Football	Chabot	Univ. of Miami (FL)	Los Angeles
Burleson, Rick	Baseball	Cerritos	So'western Okla. State	Boston
Burns, Leon	Football	Laney	Cal State, Long Beach	St. Louis
Burroul, Jeff	Baseball	Barstow		San Francisco
Burroughs, Don	Football	Ventura	Colorado State	Los Angeles/Philadelphia
Burtt, Dennis	Baseball	Santa Ana		Boston
Cabell, Enos	Baseball	L.A. Harbor		Houston
Cadile, Jim	Football	San Jose	Cal State, San Jose	Chicago/Hawaii
Calderan, Kent	Baseball	Chabot		Los Angeles/St. Louis

PARTICIPANTS	COMMUNITY COLLEGE SPORT	COMMUNITY COLLEGE ATTENDED	FOUR-YEAR INSTITUTION	PROFESSIONAL AFFILIATION
Caldwell, Rex	Golf	Allan Hancock		PGA Tour
Calzia, Gary	Baseball	College of Sequoias	Cal State, Northridge	Chicago White Sox
Cain, Lynn	Football	East L.A.	Cal State, Fullerton	Atlanta
Calvin, Mack	Basketball	Long Beach	USC	Denver
Campanaro, Mark	Basketball	Cypress	USC	Harlem Globetrotters
Campbell, Bill	Baseball	Mt. San Antonio	U.C. Santa Barbara	Boston
Capilla, Douglas	Baseball	West Balley		St. Louis/Chicago Cubs
Carderilli, Glen	Football	Cypress	Cal State, Fullerton	New York Jets
Cardoza, Anthony	Baseball	College of Sequoias		San Francisco
Cardoza, Don	Baseball	College of Sequoias		Los Angeles
Carlos, Cisco	Baseball	Citrus		Chicago White Sox
Carlson, Tim	Baseball	American River		Los Angeles
Carmichael, Al	Football	Santa Ana	USC	Green Bay
Carter, Kent	Football	L.A. City	USC	New England/St. Louis
Carter, Milton	Football	Monterey	Cal State, Fullerton	Kansas City
Case, Bill	Baseball	Antelope Valley		Anaheim
Cash, Sam	Basketball	San Bernardino	U.C. Riverside	Cleveland/Memphis
Cashore, Randy	Basketball	Butte		Oakland
Casillas, Rich	Baseball	San Bernardino		Oakland
Cassell, Charles	Baseball	Barstow		Anaheim
Cassidy, Ron	Football	Fullerton	Cal State, San Diego	Denver
Castillo, Robert (Bobby)	Baseball	L.A. Valley		Los Angeles
Cataldo, Ron	Baseball	San Jose		Detroit
Causey, Jerry	Baseball	Solano		Houston
Cavatalo, Pat	Baseball	San Jose		Philadelphia
Chamberlin, Craig	Baseball	Cypress/Long Beach	Arizona	Kansas
Chambliss, Chris	Baseball	Mira Costa	UCLA	New York
Charboneau, Joe	Baseball	West Valley		Cleveland

PARTICIPANTS	COMMUNITY COLLEGE SPORT	COMMUNITY COLLEGE ATTENDED	FOUR-YEAR INSTITUTION	PROFESSIONAL AFFILIATION
Cheatham, Ron	Football	L.A. Harbor	Washington State	Canada
Chelander, Hal	Football	Taft	Mississippi State	Minnesota
Childs, Rich	Baseball	Sacramento City		Minnesota
Chiott, Gary	Football	Foothill	Cal State, San Francisco	San Francisco
Chris, Mike	Baseball	L.A. Pierce	Oakland/Detroit	
Clark, Robert	Baseball	Riverside City		California
Codiroli, Chris	Baseball	San Jose		Detroit
Colchico, Dan	Football	Diablo Valley	Cal State, San Jose	San Francisco
Collett, Elmer	Football	College of Marin	Cal State, San Francisco	Baltimore
Collins, Al	Football	San Francisco City	USC	Los Angeles
Cook, Hank	Football	Allan Hancock	New Mexico State	Chicago
Combs, Jim	Baseball	American River		Boston
Copess, Mike	Baseball	Chaffey		New York
Copper, Michael	Basketball	Pasadena	Univ. of New Mexico	Los Angeles
Corcorall, Tim	Baseball	Mt. San Antonio	Cal State, Los Angeles	Detroit
Coulon, Dan	Baseball	College of sequoias		Los Angeles
Courtney, Matt	Baseball	DeAnza		Texas
Couton, Jim	Football	Gavilan		Hawaii
Cowan, Billy	Baseball	Bakersfield	U.C. Riverside	Chicago Cubs/ Los Angeles
Cowling, Al	Football	San Francisco City	USC	Houston
Crabbe, Claude	Football	Monterey	Colorado	Los Angeles
Cram, Jerry	Baseball	Riverside City		New York
Crane, Denni	Football	San Bernardino	USC	Washington
Crittendon, Willie	Football	Taft	Univ. of Tulsa	New Orleans
Crosby, Eddie	Baseball	Long Beach		Cleveland

PARTICIPANTS	COMMUNITY COLLEGE SPORT	COMMUNITY COLLEGE ATTENDED	FOUR-YEAR INSTITUTION	PROFESSIONAL AFFILIATION
Crossan, Marshall	Baseball	San Jose		Oakland
Crtalic, Don	Football	L.A. Harbor	Cal State, Fullerton	Portland (WFL)
Crump, Dwayne	Football	Fresno	Cal State, Fresno	St. Louis
Cruz, Julio	Baseball	San Bernardino		Seattle
Cureton, Hardiman	Football	L.A. Valley	UCLA	Canada
Curran, Pat	Baseball	Golden West	Chapman College	Kansas City
Daniels, Benny	Baseball	Compton		Washington
Darnell, Rick	Basketball	Cypress		Virginia/Italy
Dauer, Rich	Baseball	San Bernardino	Cal State, San Jose	Baltimore
Davidson, Ben	Football	East L.A.	USC	Oakland
Davis, Clarence	Football	East L.A.	Univ. of Washington	Oakland
Davis, Don	Football	Santa Ana	USC	New York
Davis, Gary	Football	Cerritos		Cincinnati
Davis, Keni	Basketball	Consumnes River	Cal State, Fullerton	Switzerland
Davis, Mark	Baseball	Chabot		Philadelphia
Davis, Mike	Football	East L.A.	Colorado	Oakland
Davis, Milton	Football	L.A. City	UCLA	Baltimore
Davis, Stan	Baseball	Riverside		St. Louis
Davis, Tom	Baseball	San Jose		Los Angeles
Dawkin, Joe	Football	L.A. City	Wisconsin	Houston
DeBerg, Steve	Football	Fullerton	Cal State, San Jose	San Francisco
DeCinces, Doug	Baseball	L.A. Pierce		Baltimore/California
Deek, Dennis	Baseball	Barstow		Portland
Dejurnett, Charles Ray	Football	West L.A.	Cal State, San Jose	San Diego
DeLaney, Tim	Football	Mt. San Antonio	Cal State, San Diego	St. Louis
Degan, Dick	Football	Cerritos	Cal State, Long Beach	San Diego
Dempsey, Tom	Football	Palomar	Cal Western	Los Angeles
Dennis, Pete	Football	Laney	Cal State, San Francisco	Florida

152

Dusty Baker, American River College, Los Angeles Dodgers/ San Francisco Giants. *Photo courtesy San Francisco Giants.*

Brian Downing, Cypress College, California Angels.
Photo courtesy *California Angels.*

PARTICIPANTS	COMMUNITY COLLEGE SPORT	COMMUNITY COLLEGE ATTENDED	FOUR-YEAR INSTITUTION	PROFESSIONAL AFFILIATION
Denton, Dave	Baseball	Chabot	Univ. of Nevada - Las Vegas	Boston
DeSanti, Leonard	Football	San Diego City	U.S. Intern'l Univ.	New Orleans
DeVanon, Frank	Baseball	San Diego Mesa	Westmont	St. Louis
DeVine, Rusty	Baseball	College of Sequoias		Chicago White Sox
Diaz, Carlos	Baseball	Allan Hancock	Stanford	San Francisco
Kierks, Larry	Baseball	College of Sequoias	Univ. of Arizona	California/Detroit
DiPietro, Fred	Baseball	San Jose		Detroit
Dixon, John	Baseball	Siskiyous	Cal State, Sacramento	Kansas City
Doek, Dennis	Baseball	Barstow		Portland
Doepker, Dick	Baseball	College of Sequoias	Cal State, Fresno	Pittsburg
Dolf, Mike	Baseball	College of Redwoods		Reno (Cleveland Organization)
Downing, Brian	Baseball	Cypress		California
Draper, Jim	Baseball	Allan Hancock	U.C. Riverside	Detroit
Dressler, Doug	Football/ Wrestling	College of Marin	Cal State, Chico	Cincinnati
Dryer, Fred	Football	El Camino	Cal State, San Diego	Los Angeles
DuBois, Phil	Football	Cerritos	Cal State, San Diego	Washington
Dummitt, Dennis	Football	Long Beach	UCLA	Los Angeles
Dungy, Dennis	Baseball	San Jose		Los Angeles
Dunn, Paul	Football	San Diego City	U.S. Intern'l Univ.	Cincinnati
Dupree, Mike	Baseball	Fresno City		San Diego
Duren, Clarence	Football	L.A. City	U.C. Berkeley	St. Louis/San Diego
Eason, Charles Carroll "Tony"	Football/ Baseball	American River	Univ. of Illinois	New England
Eastwood, Bob	Golf	Delta	Cal State, San Jose	Pro Golf
Edelsen, Tom	Tennis	Merritt	USC	L.A. Tennis Club
Edmonson, Warren	Track	Merritt	Cal State, Los Angeles	Pro Track

PARTICIPANTS	COMMUNITY COLLEGE SPORT	COMMUNITY COLLEGE ATTENDED	FOUR-YEAR INSTITUTION	PROFESSIONAL AFFILIATION
Edward, Herman	Football	Monterey	U.C. Berkeley/ Cal State, San Diego	Philadelphia
Edward, Lloyd	Football	L.A. Harbor	Cal State, San Diego	Oakland
Edwards, Vinc	Football	L.A. City	USC	Chicago
Eichholts, John	Baseball	Fresno		Minnesota
Elderklin, Joel	Baseball	Chabot		New York/Montreal
Ellis, Doc	Baseball	L.A. Harbor		Texas
Engelhart, Jim	Baseball	Chabot	Brigham Young Univ.	Los Angeles
Erichson, Keith	Basketball	El Camino	UCLA	Phoenix
Ernst, Michael Paul	Football	Cerritos	Cal State, Fullerton	Denver
Estrada, Manny	Baseball	Mt. San Antonio		Chicago White Sox
Etchandy, Curtis	Baseball	Golden West		Chicago White Sox
Evans, Darrell	Baseball	Pasadena		San Francisco
Evans, Lee	Track	San Jose	Cal State, San Jose	Intern'l Track Assn.
Fairchild, John	Basketball	Palomar	Brigham Young Univ.	Los Angeles
Fairley, Rusty	Football	Long Beach	Denver	Canada
Farmer, George	Football	Santa Monica	Southern Univ.	Los Angeles
Farmer, Karl	Track	L.A. Southwest	Univ. of Pittsburg	Pro Football - Canada
Farmer, Teddy	Football	Mt. San Antonio	Oregon	Seattle/Los Angeles
Farr, Mel	Football	Santa Monica	UCLA	Detroit
Farris, John	Football	Cerritos	Cal State, San Diego	San Diego
Fassel, Jim	Football	Fullerton	USC/ Cal State, Long Beach	
Feramisco, Jeff	Baseball	Fresno City		Hawaii
Fergeson, Clarence	Football	Merced		Baltimore
Ferguson, Bill	Football	Grossmont	Cal State, San Diego	Portland
Ferguson, Duke	Football	Merced	Cal State, San Diego	New York
Ferguson, Nate	Football	Merced	Cal State, San Diego	Seattle
				Portland

PARTICIPANTS	COMMUNITY COLLEGE SPORT	COMMUNITY COLLEGE ATTENDED	FOUR-YEAR INSTITUTION	PROFESSIONAL AFFILIATION
Fernandez, Manny	Football	Chabot	Univ. of Utah	Miami
Ferro, Tom	Baseball	Riverside	Cal State, Pomona	Minnesota
Fezler, Forrest	Golf	San Jose City	Cal State, San Jose	Pro Golf
Figueroa, Fred	Football	Fresno	Cal State, Fresno	Green Bay
Fischlin, Mike	Baseball	Consumnes River		Houston
Fingers, Rollie	Baseball	Chaffey		San Diego
Fisher, Doug	Football	Reedley	Cal State, San Diego	Pittsburg
Fletcher, Rick	Track	Fresno	UCLA	Intern'l Track Assn.
Flisher, Ron	Football	San Diego City	Cal State, San Diego	Canada
Flores, Tom	Football	Fresno	Univ. of Pacific	Oakland
Fopma, Ev	Basketball	Cerritos	Idaho	Madrid
Ford, Don	Basketball	Santa Barbara	Pepperdine	Seattle
Forsch, Bob	Baseball	Sacramento City		Houston/St. Louis
Forsch, Ken	Baseball	Sacramento City		St. Louis
Forster, Terry	Baseball	Grossmont		Los Angeles
Foster, Bob	Baseball	El Camino		Cincinnati
Foster, George	Basketball	Allan Hancock	Drake Univ.	Belgium
Foster, Jerry	Football	Santa Ana	USC	Los Angeles
Fouch, Ed	Football	Siskiyous		Canada
Fraietta, Emilio	Baseball	San Bernardino		California
Fraley, Dave	Football	Mt. San Antonio	Univ. of Hawaii	Los Angeles
Fralick, Lance	Baseball	Fresno		Pittsburg
Frankfort, Ken	Baseball	Mt. San Antonio		St. Louis
Freed, Roger	Football	Fresno	Cal State, Fresno	Atlanta
Freeman, Mike	Baseball	San Mateo		San Diego
Frizella, Dan	Football	Cerritos	Baylor	Houston
Frongilio, John	Basketball	Long Beach City	Stanford	California
Frost, Dave	Baseball	Chabot	Brigham Young Univ.	California
Fuderaro, Bob				

157

PARTICIPANTS	COMMUNITY COLLEGE SPORT	COMMUNITY COLLEGE ATTENDED	FOUR-YEAR INSTITUTION	PROFESSIONAL AFFILIATION
Fuller, Ken	Baseball	Chabot		Philadelphia
Gage, Ralph	Baseball	Canada		Baltimore
Galagher, Ed	Football	Chabot	UCLA	New York Giants/ San Francisco
Gallagher, Dennis	Baseball	Yuba	Chapman	Kansas City
Galbreath, Tony	Football	Indian Hills	Univ. of Nebraska	New Orleans
Gama, Tim	Baseball	San Jose		Atlanta
Gambero, Darrell	Baseball	Fresno	Cal State, Fresno	Kansas City
Gamble, John	Football	Modesto	Univ. of Pacific	Detroit
Garcia, Bob	Baseball	College of Sequoias		Minnesota
Garcia, Frank	Baseball	DeAnza		Texas
Garcia, Henry	Baseball	Gavilan		Boston
Garcia, Jess	Football	Merced		Philadelphia
Garcia, Mike	Baseball	College of Sequoias		Cleveland
Garner, Bob	Golf	Long Beach City		Tour Tournament
Garrison, Gary	Football	Long Beach City	Cal State, Fresno	San Diego
Garvin, Jerry	Baseball	Merced	Cal State, San Diego	Toronto
Gators, Robert	Football	Santa Ana	New Mexico State	New York
Gay, Bill	Football	San Diego City	USC	Denver/Detroit
Geddes, Bob	Football	Riverside City	UCLA	Boston
Geech, Jeff	Baseball	American River		Atlanta
George, Nattie	Baseball	Lee	San Jose	Toronto
Gifford, Frank	Football	Bakersfield	USC	New York
Gillette, Fred	Football	L.A. Valley	Cal State, Los Angeles	San Diego
Gilmore, Art	Football	Riverside City	Oregon State	Dallas
Gilson, Harold	Baseball	San Jose		St. Louis
Givler, Bob	Baseball	Canada		Tri-City NW Indiana
Gladden, Dan	Baseball	DeAnza		San Francisco

158

PARTICIPANTS	COMMUNITY COLLEGE SPORT	COMMUNITY COLLEGE ATTENDED	FOUR-YEAR INSTITUTION	PROFESSIONAL AFFILIATION
Goich, Dau	Football	West Hills	U.C. Berkeley	Detroit/St. Louis/ New York
Gooch, Ken	Baseball	Yuba		California
Goodman, Brian	Football	L.A. Valley	UCLA	Houston
Goodman, Harvey	Football	L.A. City	Colorado	St. Louis
Gotshalt, Len	Football	Santa Rosa		Atlanta
Goularte, Greg	Baseball	Gavilan		Atlanta
Grady, Kevin	Football	Orange Coast	Tulsa	Los Angeles
Graham, Jack	Football	Foothill	Oklahoma	Miami
Graham, Ken	Football	Sacramento City	Colorado State	San Diego
Gray, Alexander	Baseball	L.A. Harbor	Univ. of Washington	San Francisco
Gray, Harold	Football	Cerritos	USC	Green Bay
Gray, Johnny	Football	Allan Hancock	Cal State, Los Angeles	Green Bay
Gray, Mel	Football	Santa Rosa	Cal State, Fullerton	St. Louis
Green, Cornell	Basketball	Contra Costa		Dallas
Gregory, Ken	Football	Cerritos	Utah State	Baltimore
Gregory, Leroy	Baseball	West Hills	Whittier	Chicago
Griffin, Greg	Basketball	Pasadena City	Cal State, Fresno	Phoenix
Griffin, Hank	Baseball	Merced	Idaho State	Boston
Griffin, Tom	Baseball	L.A. Pierce		San Francisco
Griggs, Larry	Golf	Long Beach City		Tour Tournament
Gross, Bobby	Basketball	L.A. Harbor		Portland
Grosscup, Lee	Football	Santa Monica	Utah	New York
Guillory, John	Football	Merritt	Stanford	Cincinnati
Gunn, Jimmy	Football	San Diego City	USC	Chicago
Hackley, Ricardo	Football	San Diego City	Univ. of Mexico	Kansas City
Hale, Tom	Baseball	Riverside		Cincinnati
Hall, Tom	Baseball	Riverside		Cincinnati

PARTICIPANTS	COMMUNITY COLLEGE SPORT	COMMUNITY COLLEGE ATTENDED	FOUR-YEAR INSTITUTION	PROFESSIONAL AFFILIATION
Hallberg, Lance	Baseball	San Bernardino		Minnesota
Hallimon, Shaller	Basketball	Imperial Valley		Chicago
Hammett, Bill	Football	Chabot	Utah State	Portland (WFL)
Hansen, Doug	Baseball	Fresno	Cal State, San Diego	New York
Hansen, Jim	Baseball	College of Sequoias		Chicago Cubs
Hargan, Steve	Baseball	College of the Desert	Ball State	Atlanta
Harper, Tommie	Football	Santa Rosa		Cincinnati
Harper, Wayne	Baseball	San Jose		Chicago Cubs
Harris, Leroy	Baseball	Fresno		St. Louis/Chicago
Harris, Louis	Football	Sacramento City	USC	Canada
Harris, Ricky	Football	East L.A.	Arizona State	Washington/ New England
Harris, Vic	Baseball	L.A. Valley		San Francisco
Harrison, Roric	Baseball	L.A. Valley/ Santa Monica		
Harroway, Charles	Football	Monterey	Houston	St. Louis
Hartwig, Dan	Baseball	Antelope Valley	Cal State, San Jose	Washington
Hauhoe, Bill	Football	L.A. Valley	USC	San Francisco
Hayes, Thomas	Football	Riverside City	Cal State, San Diego	Green Bay
Hayes, Wendell	Football/ Baseball/Track			Atlanta/San Diego
Hazzard, Walt	Basketball	Merritt	Cal State, Humbolt	Kansas City
Heaton, Mike	Baseball	Santa Monica	UCLA	Los Angeles
Hecklenberg, Marvin	Baseball	Butte		California
Heenan, John	Baseball	San Jose		St. Louis
Heise, Bob	Baseball	San Jose		St. Louis
Henard, Gailen	Baseball	Solano		Kansas City
Henderson, Bobby	Football	College of Sequoias L.A. City	Cal State, San Diego	California California

PARTICIPANTS	COMMUNITY COLLEGE SPORT	COMMUNITY COLLEGE ATTENDED	FOUR-YEAR INSTITUTION	PROFESSIONAL AFFILIATION
Henderson, Ken	Baseball	West Valley		Chicago Cubs
Hendrick, George	Baseball	East L.A.		St. Louis
Hendricks, Eric	Baseball	Chabot		Kansas City
Henke, Karl	Football	Ventura	Chapman	New York
Henry, Wally	Football	San Diego City	Tulsa	Philadelphia
Hergenraden, Steve	Baseball	Fresno	UCLA	New York Yankees
Hermmeling, Terry	Football	Allan Hancock		Washington
Hernandez, Keith	None	San Mateo		St. Louis
Herron, Bill	Football	Fresno City	Univ. of Nevada - Reno	Canada
Hewett, Bill	Basketball	Mt. San Antonio	Univ. of Georgia	Chicago
Heydeman, Greg	Baseball	Monterey	USC	Los Angeles
Hicks, Richard	Football	West L.A.	Cal State, Humbolt	Detroit
Heinz, Bob	Football	Delta	Univ. of Pacific	Miami
Hientz, Chris	Baseball	Fresno		Chicago
Hill, Donny	Baseball	Orange Coast		Oakland
Hines, Henry	Track	Sacramento City	USC	Pro Track
Hinzenraeder, Terry	Baseball	Fresno	Cal State, Fresno	Los Angeles
Hodge, Ed	Baseball	Cerritos		Minnesota
Hoffman, Ross	Baseball	College of Sequoias	UCLA	Montreal
Holland, Cliff	Baseball	Canada	USC	Chicago
Hollyfield, Larry	Basketball	Compton	UCLA	Germany
Holt, Darren	Baseball	College of Sequoias	Cal State, Fresno	New York Yankees
Holt, Dave	Baseball	College of Sequoias	Cal State, Fresno	Boston
Hooker, Fair	Football	Pasadena City	Stanford	Cleveland
Hoover, Bucky	Baseball	Fresno	Cal State, Fresno	Los Angeles
Horn, Alvin	Baseball	College of Sequoias		San Francisco
Horn, Don	Football	L.A. Harbor	Cal State, San Diego	San Diego/Green Bay
Horrow, Larry	Baseball	San Jose		Chicago Cubs

PARTICIPANTS	COMMUNITY COLLEGE SPORT	COMMUNITY COLLEGE ATTENDED	FOUR-YEAR INSTITUTION	PROFESSIONAL AFFILIATION
Hosteler, Dave	Baseball	Citrus	USC	Cleveland
Houghton, Mark	Football	Siskiyous	U.C. Berkeley	Canada
Houston, Gary	Baseball	San Jose		Kansas City
Houston, Jerry	Baseball	San Jose		Philadelphia
Howard, Bob	Football	San Bernardino	Cal State, San Diego	San Diego
Howard, Gary	Baseball	Yuba		Houston
Howard, Luther	Football	Imperial Valley	Deleware	Canada
Hoxie, Randall	Baseball	Riverside City		Chicago
Hrabosky, Alan	Baseball	Fullerton		Kansas City
Hubbard, Dave	Baseball	Consumnes River		Los Angeles
Hudson, Tyrone	Football	L.A. City	USC	New England
Huff, Doug	Football	L.A. City	UCLA	Atlanta
Humphries, Ray	Baseball	San Bernardino		Kansas City
Humphries, Terry	Baseball	L.A. City		Montreal
Hunt, Ervin	Football	Fresno	Cal State, Fresno	Green Bay
Hunter, Logan	Football	Chabot	Brigham Young Univ.	Canada
Hunziker, Kent	Baseball	Golden West		Chicago
Huppert, Dave	Baseball	Cypress		Baltimore
Hutton, Tommy	Baseball	Pasadena		Montreal
Iorg, Garth	Baseball	College of Redwoods		New York
Ireland, Tim	Baseball	Chabot		Canada
Jackson, Bernard	Football	L.A. Pierce	Washington State	Denver
Jackson, Bob	Football	Riverside City	New Mexico State	San Diego
Jackson, Honor	Football/Track	College of Marin	Univ. of Pacific	New York
Jackson, Kenneth	Football	L.A. City	Cal State, San Diego	California
Jackson, Mike	Basketball	Allan Hancock	Cal State, Northridge	Chicago
Jackson, Monte	Football	San Diego Mesa	Cal State, San Diego	Oakland
Jackson, Terry	Football	San Diego City	Cal State, San Diego	New York Giants

PARTICIPANTS	COMMUNITY COLLEGE SPORT	COMMUNITY COLLEGE ATTENDED	FOUR-YEAR INSTITUTION	PROFESSIONAL AFFILIATION
Jacobs, Proverb	Football	Modesto	U.C. Berkeley	Oakland
Jacobsen, Joe	Baseball	Fresno		Minnesota
Jacobsen, Mike	Baseball	Fresno		Minnesota
Jankovich, Keever	Football	Santa Ana		Chicago
Jarmon, Lawrence	Football	L.A. Harbor	Cal State, Los Angeles	Chicago
Jefferies, Clay	Football	Cerritos		California
Jessie, Ron	Football	Imperial Valley	Kansas	Detroit
Jessup, Bill	Football	Long Beach		San Francisco
Jett, Rod	Baseball	Cypress		San Diego
Johnson, Dennis	Basketball	L.A. Harbor	Pepperdine	Seattle
Johnson, Greg	Baseball	Santa Ana		California
Johnson, Jim	Football	Santa Monica City		San Francisco
Johnson, Mike	Baseball	Cypress	UCLA	Boston
Jones, Bob	Football	Mt. San Antonio		Chicago
Jones, Clarence	Baseball	Santa Ana		Chicago
Jones, Cody	Football	San Francisco City		Los Angeles
Jones, Dick	Football	Chabot	Univ. of Pacific	Minnesota
Jones, Doak	Baseball	Chabot		St. Louis
Jones, Donnie	Baseball	Barstow		California
Jones, Doug	Football	San Diego City	Cal State, Northridge	Kansas City/ Buffalo
Jones, Guy	Baseball	College of Sequoias		California
Jones, Homer	Football	L.A. City	Syracuse	New York
Jones, Leanell	Football	Laney	Cal State, Long Beach	Chicago
Joseph, John	Baseball	Chabot		Kansas
Joyce, Kevan	Baseball	Chabot		Canada
Joshua, Von	Baseball	Laney		San Francisco

163

Doug De Cinces, L. A. Pierce, California Angels.
Photo courtesy California Angels.

Mike Davis, East L. A., Los Angeles Raiders *Photo courtesy Los Angeles Raiders.*

PARTICIPANTS	COMMUNITY COLLEGE SPORT	COMMUNITY COLLEGE ATTENDED	FOUR-YEAR INSTITUTION	PROFESSIONAL AFFILIATION
Kahler, John	Football	Long Beach		Kansas City
Kane, Kevin	Baseball	Cuesta		Boston
Keener, Joe	Baseball	Antelope Valley		Montreal
Keilig, Roger	Baseball	Canada	Cal State, Chico	Los Angeles
Kelley, Mike	Baseball	Allan Hancock	Hawaii	Toronto
Kemp, Rod	Baseball	College of Sequoias	Cal State, San Jose	Los Angeles
Kendricks, Marvin	Football	Riverside City	U.C. Riverside	Portland
Kennedy, Junior	Baseball	Bakersfield		Cincinnati
Keough, Joe	Baseball	Mt. San Antonio		Kansas City
Kerry, Gary	Football	Chabot	Cal State, San Luis Obispo	Canada
Keys, Bobby	Football	Antelope Valley	Univ. of San Diego	San Francisco
Keyes, Brady	Football	East L.A.	Colorado	Pittsburg
Kilmer, Billy	Football	Citrus/East L.A.	UCLA	Washington
Kilson, Dave	Football	Sacramento City	Univ. of Nevada - Reno	Buffalo
Kimble, Ray	Football	Chabot	Washington State	San Francisco
Kinney, Steve	Football	San Jose City	Utah State	Chicago
Kirner, Gary	Football	Santa Monica		San Diego
Knight, Ron	Basketball	L.A. Harbor	Cal State, Long Beach	Portland
Kozlowski, Mike	Football	Mira Costa	Univ. of Colorado	Miami
Kramer, Bill	Football	L.A. City	Cal State, San Diego	California
Kreig, Jim	Football	Taft	Univ. of Washington	Denver
Kukulica, Rick	Football	Chabot	UCLA	Miami
Kuiper, Duane	Baseball	Indian Hills	Southern Illinois	Cleveland
Kuntz, Rusty	Baseball	Cuesta		Chicago White Sox
LaCock, Pete	Baseball	L.A. City		Chicago
LaCorte, Frank	Baseball	Gavilan		Atlanta/Houston
Lacy, Lee	Baseball	Laney		Los Angeles
Landsberger, Mark	Basketball	Allan Hancock	Minnesota/ Arizona State	Los Angeles

PARTICIPANTS	COMMUNITY COLLEGE SPORT	COMMUNITY COLLEGE ATTENDED	FOUR-YEAR INSTITUTION	PROFESSIONAL AFFILIATION
Lane, Bob	Football	Cerritos	Baylor	San Diego
Lane, MacArthur	Football	Laney	Utah State	Green Bay/Kansas
Laney, Duff	Baseball	Antelope Valley		Baltimore
Lanon, Bill	Baseball	West Hills		Boston
Latzke, Paul	Football	Menlo	Univ. of Pacific	San Diego/Denver
Lauer, Jim	Baseball	Butte	Washington State	New York Mets
Lavender, Joe	Football	Imperial Valley	Cal State, San Diego	Philadelphia
Lavender, Tim	Football	San Diego City		Dallas
Lawson, Bob	Football	West Hills	Cal State, San Luis Obispo	Detroit
LeBaron, Eddie	Football	San Joaquin Delta	College of Pacific	Washington/Dallas
Lee, Bob	Football	San Francisco	Univ. of Pacific	Atlanta/Minnesota
Lee, Michael	Football	San Diego Mesa	Univ. of Nevada - Las Vegas	San Diego
Leicht, Jim	Baseball	Fullerton	Cal State, San Diego	Montreal
LeMendola, Greg	Baseball	Cypress		St. Louis
Lemley, Don	Baseball	Fresno		New York
Lemoine, Jim	Football	Chabot		Dallas/Oakland
Lettrich, Stephen	Baseball	San Jose City		California
Lewis, David	Football	San Diego City	USC	Miami
Lewis, Joe	Football	Compton		Pittsburg
Lewis, Woodley	Football	L.A. City	Oregon	Los Angeles
Lillywhite, Verle	Football	Modesto	USC	San Francisco
Liggins, Danny	Baseball	Laney		St. Louis
Lindsey, Terry	Football	San Diego Mesa	Cal State, Fullerton	Kansas City/California
Lintz, Larry	Baseball	Laney	Cal State, San Jose	Oakland
Lloyd, Craig	Baseball	Consumnes River	Brigham Young Univ.	Philadelphia

PARTICIPANTS	COMMUNITY COLLEGE SPORT	COMMUNITY COLLEGE ATTENDED	FOUR-YEAR INSTITUTION	PROFESSIONAL AFFILIATION
Lohse, John	Baseball	Butte		Philadelphia
Lomas, Mark	Football	Golden West	Northern Arizona	New York
Lomax, Tony	Football	Laney	Washington State	Florida
Lorick, Tony	Football	East L.A.	Arizona	Baltimore
Loscotoff, Jim	Basketball	American River	Oregon	Boston
Loudd, Rommie	Football	L.A. Valley	UCLA	San Diego/Boston
Love, Dave	Baseball	San Bernardino		Oakland
Lowe, Reggie	Football	L.A. City		Baltimore
Lowery, Marvin	Football	San Diego City	Utah State	Canada
Lozano, Dave	Baseball	Delta		New York
Lucas, Gary	Baseball	Riverside	Chapman	San Diego
Lung, John	Baseball	Fresno	UCLA	Chicago
Lusk, Herb	Football	Monterey	Cal State, Long Beach	Philadelphia
Lycaak, Ray	Football	Foothill	Cal State, San Jose	Canada
Lyle, Dan	Baseball	Consumnes River		Cincinnati
MacElhenney, Hugh	Football	Compton	Univ. of Washington	San Francisco
Maddox, Jerry	Baseball	Cerritos	Arizona State	Atlanta/Cleveland
Maloney, Jim	Baseball	Fresno		Cincinnati
Maltbie, Roger	Golf	San Jose	Cal State, San Jose	Pro Golf
Marchetti, Gino	Football	Modesto	Univ. of San Francisco	Baltimore
Marion, Gary	Baseball	San Jose		St. Louis
Marone, Lou	Baseball	San Diego Mesa		Pittsburg
Marshall, Dave	Baseball	Long Beach		Chicago
Marslowski, Matt	Football	San Diego Mesa	Univ. of San Diego	Los Angeles
Martin, Darrell	Baseball	College of Sequoias		Boston
Martin, Denny	Football	L.A. Valley		Montreal
Martin, Howard	Baseball	Fresno	Santa Clara	New York
Martin, Rod	Football	L.A. City	USC	Oakland

PARTICIPANTS	COMMUNITY COLLEGE SPORT	COMMUNITY COLLEGE ATTENDED	FOUR-YEAR INSTITUTION	PROFESSIONAL AFFILIATION
Martin, Saladin	Football	San Diego		New York Giants
Martinez, Buck	Baseball	Sacramento City	Cal State, Sacramento	Milwaukee
Martinez, Mike	Baseball	Gavilan	Cal State, San Diego	San Francisco
Matson, Ollie	Football/Track	San Francisco	Univ. of San Francisco	Chicago
May, Ray	Football	L.A. City	USC	Baltimore
Mayfield, Wayne	Baseball	College of Sequoias		Chicago White Sox
Mayo, Rick	Baseball	Merced		Baltimore
McCall, Don	Baseball	L.A. City	USC	Denver
McClure, Bob	Baseball	San Mateo		Milwaukee
McCord, Gary	Golf	Riverside	U.C. Riverside	PGA
McComish, John	Golf	Allan Hancock	Cal State, Northridge	PGA
McCoy, Mike	Football	West L.A.	Univ. of Colorado	Green Bay
McCullough, Earl	Football	Long Beach	USC	Detroit
McCraken, Paul	Basketball	L.A. City		Houston
McCraw, Tom	Baseball	Santa Monica		Cleveland
McDonald, Dwight	Football	San Diego	USIU/Cal State, San Diego	San Diego
McDonald, Rusty	Baseball	DeAnza		Los Angeles
McGraw, Tug	Baseball	Solano		Philadelphia
McHenry, Vance	Baseball	Butte	Univ. of Nevada - Las Vegas	Seattle
McIntyre, Jeff	Football	L.A. Southwest	Arizona State	San Francisco
McKiney, Odis	Football	L.A. Vallwy	Colorado	New York Giants
McLain, Kevin	Football	Fullerton		Los Angeles
McMillan, Jim	Football	Diablo Valley	Colorado State	Denver/Oakland
McNulty, Bill	Baseball	American River		Oakland
McShane, Charles	Football	Long Beach	Cal Lutheran	Seattle
Meier, Cal	Baseball	Grossmont	USC	Kansas City
Melton, Bill	Baseball	Citrus		Chicago
Mendez, Mario	Football	Cerritos	Cal State, San Diego	San Diego

169

PARTICIPANTS	COMMUNITY COLLEGE SPORT	COMMUNITY COLLEGE ATTENDED	FOUR-YEAR INSTITUTION	PROFESSIONAL AFFILIATION
Menyard, Dewitt	Basketball	Allan Hancock	Utah	Houston
Merlo, Jim	Football	Fresno	Stanford	San Francisco
Messer, Dale	Football	College of Sequoias	Cal State, Fresno	San Francisco
Meyer, Dan	Baseball	Santa Ana	Univ. of Arizona	Seattle
Meyer, Steven	Football	Mt. San Antonio	Univ. of New Mexico	Seattle
Miller, Chris	Football	San Diego City	Cal State, San Diego	St. Louis
Miller, Greg	Baseball	Butte	Cal State, Chico	California
Miller, Kevin	Baseball	Cerritos		Minnesota
Miller, Rich	Football	San Mateo		San Francisco
Mills, Brad	Baseball	College of Sequoias	Univ. of Arizona	Montreal
Milks, Jack	Football	Cerritos	Cal State, San Diego	San Diego
Mims, Jess	Football	Laney	New Mexico State	Detroit
Minor, Claude	Football	Mt. San Antonio	Cal State, San Diego	Denver
Minton, Greg	Baseball	San Diego		San Francisco
Mitchell, Curt	Baseball	Barstow		St. Louis
Mitchell, Emory	Baseball	American River		Chicago White Sox
Mitchell, West	Baseball	San Jose		Cleveland
Mitterwald, George	Baseball	Chabot		Chicago
Moline, Stan	Baseball	San Jose		San Francisco
Montgomery, Marv	None	L.A. Valley	USC	Denver
Montoya, Max	Football	Mt. San Antonio	UCLA	Cincinnati
Moon, Warren	Football	West L.A.	Univ. of Washington	Edmonton (Canada)
Moore, Renard	Football	L.A. City	UCLA	Los Angeles
Moore, Tony	Football	L.A. Valley	Cal State, Long Beach	San Diego
Morales, Rich	Baseball	San Mateo		San Diego
Morgan, Joe	Baseball	Merritt		Cincinnati
Morton, Craig	Football	San Francisco	U.C. Berkeley	Denver
Moses, Greg	Football	L.A. City	Cal State, San Diego	California

PARTICIPANTS	COMMUNITY COLLEGE SPORT	COMMUNITY COLLEGE ATTENDED	FOUR-YEAR INSTITUTION	PROFESSIONAL AFFILIATION
Moses, Haven	Football	L.A. Harbor	Cal State, San Diego	Denver
Moyer, Greg	Baseball	Cerritos		San Francisco
Mulligan, John "Muggs"	Basketball	DeAnza		Italy
Mulliniks, Harvey	Baseball	College of Sequoias		Pittsburg
Muniz, Armando	Boxing	Cerritos		Pro Boxing
Murphy, Rod	Baseball	Antelope Valley	UCLA	Seattle
Murphy, Tim	Baseball	Delta	Univ. of Nevada - Reno	Montreal
Murray, Mike	Baseball	Cypress		Detroit
Muser, Tony	Baseball	San Diego Mesa		Milwaukee
Myers, Dennis	Baseball	American River		Oakland
Nater, Swen	Basketball	Cypress	UCLA	San Diego
Nelson, Bill	Football	Cerritos	USC	Cleveland
Nelson, Dave	Baseball	Compton	Cal State	Kansas City
Nelson, Jamie	Baseball	Orange Coast		Seattle
Nelson, Terry	Baseball	Antelope Valley		Cincinnati
Nen, Richard	Baseball	L.A. Harbor	Cal State, Long Beach	Washington
Nettles, Craig	Baseball	San Diego City		New York
Nettles, Tom	Baseball	San Diego City	Cal State, San Diego	Kansas City/Canada
Newton, Tom	Football	San Jose	U.C. Berkeley	New York Jets
Nicklas, Pete	Football	Cerritos	Baylor	Oakland
Nieman, Randy	Baseball	College of Redwoods		New York Yankees
Norm, Angelini	Baseball	San Mateo		Kansas City
Norman, Dan	Baseball	Barstow		New York Mets
Norris, Mike	Baseball	San Francisco		Oakland
O'Bardovich, Jim	Football	El Camino	USC	Oakland
O'Brien, Bob	Baseball	Fresno		Los Angeles
O'Conner, Tom	Baseball	San Bernardino	U.C. Irvine	Kansas City
Office, Rowland	Baseball	Sacramento City	U.C. Irvine	Atlanta

PARTICIPANTS	COMMUNITY COLLEGE SPORT	COMMUNITY COLLEGE ATTENDED	FOUR-YEAR INSTITUTION	PROFESSIONAL AFFILIATION
Ojeda, Bob	Baseball	College of Sequoias		Boston
Oliver, Al	Football	Cerritos	UCLA	Los Angeles
Oliver, Bob	Baseball	American River		California
Oliver, Nate	Baseball	Canada		Los Angeles/ San Francisco
Oliver, Ralph	Football	San Diego		Oakland
Oliver, Rick	Baseball	Santa Ana	USC	California
Olmeda, Alex	Tennis	Modesto		Pro Tour
Olson, Rich	Baseball	Fresno	USC	Pittsburg
Otterson, Jerry	Football	Cerritos	Cal State, Long Beach	Green Bay
Ottima, Dave	Football	Gavilan	Stanford	Los Angeles
Owens, Brig	Football	Fullerton	Univ. of Cincinnati	Washington
Owens, Jim	Baseball/ Basketball	San Jose	Cal State, San Jose	Texas
Palamino, Carlos	Boxing	Orange Coast	Cal State, Long Beach	World Boxing Council/ Welterweight Champ.
Palma, Jim	Baseball	San Jose		New York Yankees
Pane, Chris	Football	Chabot	Cal State, Humbolt	Denver
Pao Pao, Joe	Football	Mira Costa	Cal State, Long Beach	Canada
Parks, Billy	Football	Santa Monica	Cal State Long Beach	Chicago
Parsons, Bill	Baseball	Riverside City	Utah State	Milwaukee
Pasillas, Andy	Baseball	Cerritos		Chicago White Sox
Patterson, Darryl	Baseball	College of Sequoias		Detroit
Patterson, Dave	Baseball	Cerritos		Los Angeles
Patterson, Roderick	Baseball	Santa Monica		Oakland
Paul, Dewey	Basketball	DeAnza		Australia
Payne, Ceasar	Football	L.A. Valley	Cal State, San Diego	New York
Peak, Gerald	Football	L.A. Pierce	UCLA	Pittsburg

George Brett, El Camino College, Kansas City Royals
Photo courtesy Kansas City Royals.

173

Rick Burleson, Cerritos, California Angels.
Photo courtesy California Angels.

PARTICIPANTS	COMMUNITY COLLEGE SPORT	COMMUNITY COLLEGE ATTENDED	FOUR-YEAR INSTITUTION	PROFESSIONAL AFFILIATION
Pearson, Barney	Football	San Diego	UCLA	Philadelphia
Pearson, Paul	Football	Siskiyous	U.C. Berkeley	Canada
Pecota, Andy	Basketball	DeAnza		Switzerland
Pender, Jerry	Basketball	Merced	Cal State, Fresno	San Diego
Perez, Jose	Baseball	Laney		St. Louis
Perkins, Tom	Baseball	San Bernardino	Cal State, Los Angeles	Detroit
Perkov, Jackson	Football	L.A. Pierce	Cal State, San Diego	Cleveland
Perry, Joe	Football/Track	Compton		San Francisco
Perry, Rod	Football	Fresno	Colorado	Los Angeles
Peteas, Jay	Baseball	San Bernardino		California
Peterson, Tyrone	Football	L.A. City	Cal State, Northridge	Dallas
Pettigrew, Leon	Football	L.A. City	Cal State, Northridge	New England
Pettis, Gary	Baseball	Laney		California
Picciolo, Rob	Baseball	Santa Monica	Pepperdine	Oakland
Pidgeon, Harold	Baseball	College of Redwoods		Philadelphia
Pierce, Jack	Baseball	San Jose		Atlanta
Platt, Chris	Basketball	DeAnza	Cal State, Bakersfield	Holland
Platt, Mitch	Basketball	DeAnza	Cal State, Bakersfield	Holland
Plummer, Bill	Baseball	Shasta		Seattle
Plummer, Tony	Football	San Mateo		New Orleans
Plump, Dave	Football	Solano	Cal State, Fresno	San Diego
Porkorski, Tom	Baseball	Mt. San Antonio		Chicago
Post, Homer	Football	L.A. City	Cal State, Long Beach	New England
Powell, Jerry	Football	San Diego	Cal State, Northridge	San Diego
Presley, Bob	Basketball	Mt. San Jacinto	U.C. Berkeley	Denver
Pritchett, Jerry	Baseball	Reedley	Cal State, Fresno	AAA Baseball
Prude, Woody	Football	Compton	Pepperdine	San Francisco
Quinjian, Brendon	Baseball	Fresno		Boston/Los Angeles

PARTICIPANTS	COMMUNITY COLLEGE SPORT	COMMUNITY COLLEGE ATTENDED	FOUR-YEAR INSTITUTION	PROFESSIONAL AFFILIATION
Quisenberry, Dan	Baseball	Orange Coast		Kansas City
Rader, David	Baseball	Bakersfield		Chicago
Rainey, Charles	Baseball	San Diego Mesa		Boston
Randel, Larry	Baseball	Fullerton		Detroit
Randolph, Bob	Baseball	Butte	Arizona State	Seattle
Reddick, Hal	Baseball	American River		Minor League (Independent)
Redmond, Rudy	Football	Riverside	Univ. of Pacific	Detroit
Reed, Ken	Football	Cerritos	Tulsa	Canadian Pro League
Reed, Tony	Football	Antelope Valley	Colorado	Kansas City
Reid, Bill	Football	Long Beach	Stanford	San Francisco
Reniker, Ben	Baseball	College of Sequoias		New York Yankees
Reynolds, Tom	Football	El Camino	Cal State, San Diego	New England
Ricardo, Bennie	Football	Orange Coast		New Orleans
Richardt, Mike	Baseball	Fresno		Texas
Ridge, Houston	Football	Reedley	Cal State, San Diego	San Diego
Righetti, Dave	Baseball	San Jose		Texas
Righetti, Steve	Baseball	San Jose		Texas
Rivas, Ray	Baseball	Chabot	Santa Clara	St. Louis
Roberson, Hiawatha	Baseball	Canada		Los Angeles
Roberts, Gerry	Football	College of Desert	UCLA	Miami
Robertson, Steve	Soccer	San Diego	Cal State, San Diego	San Diego (NASL)
Robino, Tony	Baseball	San Jose	Detroit	
Robinson, Jackie	Baseball/Football	Pasadena	UCLA	Brooklyn Dodgers
Robinson, Jerry	Baseball	Fresno		Philadelphia
Robinson, Joe	Baseball	College of Sequoias		San Francisco
Robinson, Sam	Basketball	Pasadena	Cal State, Long Beach	Florida

PARTICIPANTS	COMMUNITY COLLEGE SPORT	COMMUNITY COLLEGE ATTENDED	FOUR-YEAR INSTITUTION	PROFESSIONAL AFFILIATION
Robison, Jerry	Baseball	Fresno	Cal State, Fresno	Los Angeles
Rodich, Jerry	Football	L.A. Harbor		Portland
Rogers, Darrell	Football	Long Beach		Los Angeles
Romar, Lorenzo	Basketball	Cerritos		Golden State
Rosette, John	Football	Chabot	Univ. of Washington	Dallas
Ross, Dave	Football	Cerritos	Univ. of Oregon	Canadian Pro League
Rowland, Ron	Football	San Jose		Canada League
Roy, Frank	Basketball	Long Beach	Univ. of Washington	St. Louis
Rudometkin, Terry	Basketball	Allan Hancock	USC	New York
Ruffner, Paul	Basketball	Cerritos	Utah State	Denver
Rule, Bob	Basketball	Riverside	Colorado State	Seattle
Rusco, Dave	Baseball	Cuesta		Philadelphia
Rutledge, Weldon	Football	Riverside		St. Louis
Sandeman, Bill	Football	Delta	New Mexico State	Atlanta
Sander, Rick	Baseball	San Bernardino	Univ. of Pacific	New York Mets
Sandifer, Bill	Football	Mira Costa		San Francisco
Sandoval, Dennis	Baseball	Fullerton	UCLA	New York
Savage, Tim	Baseball	San Bernardino		Minnesota
Scapellino, Barry	Baseball	College of Redwoods	Cal State, Humbolt	Texas
Schmidt, Jim	Football	College of Marin	Cal State, San Francisco	Canada
Schmidt, Henry	Football	East L.A.	Trinity Univ. (TX)	San Diego
Sconiers, Daryl	Baseball	Orange Coast		California
Scott, Willard	Football	L.A. City	USC	Oakland
Scoville, Mack	Baseball	Consumnes River		Minnesota
Scribner, Rick	Football	Riverside	Idaho State	Green Bay
Seagren, Bob	Track	Mt. San Antonio	USC	Intern'l Track Assn.
Seaver, Tom	Baseball	Fresno	USC	Cincinnati
See, Larry	Baseball	Cerritos		Los Angeles

177

PARTICIPANTS	COMMUNITY COLLEGE SPORT	COMMUNITY COLLEGE ATTENDED	FOUR-YEAR INSTITUTION	PROFESSIONAL AFFILIATION
Sellesiger, John	Baseball	College of Redwoods		New York Yankees
Sells, Dave	Baseball	Solano		California
Selma, Dick	Baseball	Fresno		New York Mets/ San Diego/Chicago
Semerly, Jim	Baseball	Consumnes River	Chapman	Oakland
Severson, Jeff	Football	Long Beach	Cal State, Long Beach	Houston
Sevy, Jeff	Football	DeAnza	U.C. Berkeley	Chicago/Seattle
Shafer, Steve	Football	College of Sequoias	Utah State	Canada
Shanze, Bob	Baseball	Fresno		St. Louis
Shaw, Bryan	Football	Mt. San Antonio	Cal State, Long Beach	San Francisco
Shaw, Dennis	Football	Mt. San Antonio	Cal State, San Diego	St. Louis
Shaw, Mike	Football	San Diego	Univ. of New Mexico	Philadelphia
Shaw, Nate	Football	San Diego	USC	Los Angeles
Shellabarger, Tom	Football	Ventura	Cal State, San Diego	Philadelphia
Sherman, Ray	Football	Laney	Cal State, Fresno	Portland
Sherman, Rod	Football/Track	Pasadena	USC	Oakland
Shinnick, Don	Football	L.A. Valley	UCLA	Baltimore
Shipley, Mike	Baseball	Barstow		California
Shy, Don	Football	Mt. San Antonio	Cal State, San Diego	Atlanta
Shy, Les	Football	Mt. San Antonio	Cal State, Long Beach	Dallas
Siebler, Bill	Baseball	Antelope Valley		Baltimore
Silva, Mel	Baseball	College of Sequoias		Boston
Simon, Walt	Basketball	Fullerton		Philadelphia
Simone, Mike	Football	Golden West	Utah	Denver
Simpson, O. J.	Football	San Francisco	Stanford	Buffalo
Simpson, Travis	Baseball	College of Sequoias	USC	San Francisco
Sims, James	Football	L.A. Harbor	Cal State, Fresno	Charlotte
Singer, Bill	Baseball	Mt. San Antonio	USC	Toronto

PARTICIPANTS	COMMUNITY COLLEGE SPORT	COMMUNITY COLLEGE ATTENDED	FOUR-YEAR INSTITUTION	PROFESSIONAL AFFILIATION
Sipe, Brian	Football	Grossmont	Cal State, San Diego	Cleveland
Slaton, Frank	Baseball	Antelope Valley	Cal State, Northridge	Milwaukee
Slaton, Jim	Baseball	Antelope Valley		Detroit
Slaughter, Greg	Football	San Diego Mesa	USC	Oakland
Slough, Greg	Football	San Diego City	USC	Oakland
Smalley, Roy	Baseball	L.A. City	USC	Minnesota
Smith, Bobby	Football	Compton	UCLA	Detroit/Los Angeles
Smith, Bryn	Baseball	Allan Hancock		Montreal
Smith, Charlie	Baseball	Bakersfield		Oakland
Smith, Earl	Football	San Francisco City/ Riverside City		
Smith, James	Football	Compton	UCLA	Canada
Smith, Jeff	Football	Long Beach	USC	Chicago
Smith, Kevin	Baseball	Antelope Valley		New York
Smith, King David	Boxing	West L.A.	Dallas Baptist	Toronto
Smith, Mike	Baseball	DeAnza	Cleveland	Pro Boxing (IBC)
Smith, Waddell	Track	L.A. Southwest	Univ. of Kansas	Kansas City/Canada
Souza, Ron	Baseball	Butte		New York Mets
Sox, Dave	Baseball	Consumnes River		Los Angeles
Speier, Chris	Baseball	Santa Barbara		Montreal
Spiller, Phil	Football	Orange Coast		St. Louis
Spratt, George	Volleyball	L.A. Valley	USC	Santa Barbara Spikers
Spriggs, Dave	Football	Cypress	New Mexico State	Toronto
Springer, Paul	Baseball	College of Sequoias		St. Louis
Springman, Bill	Baseball	Cerritos		Cleveland
Staggers, Jon	Football	Merritt	Univ. of Missouri	Pittsburg
Staggs, Jeff	Football	San Diego	Cal State, San Diego	San Diego/ Los Angeles

PARTICIPANTS	COMMUNITY COLLEGE SPORT	COMMUNITY COLLEGE ATTENDED	FOUR-YEAR INSTITUTION	PROFESSIONAL AFFILIATION
Staggs, Steve	Baseball	Cerritos		Oakland
Stanfield, Kevin	Baseball	San Bernardino		Minnesota
Stanley, Fred	Baseball	Rio Hondo		New York
Stanley, John	Basketball	Palomar	Brigham Young Univ.	Denver
Stelle, Harold	Football	San Diego	USC	San Diego
Steptoe, Jack	Football	L.A. Valley	Utah	San Francisco
Stevens, Dave	Baseball	American River		Atlanta
Stillman, Royle	Baseball	El Camino		Chicago
Stone, Ron	Baseball	Delta		Philadelphia
Strable, Ray	Baseball	College of Sequoias	Cal State, Fresno	Minnesota
Strict, James	Football	L.A. City	Univ. of Utah	Green Bay
Stringer, Scott	Football	Delta	U.C. Berkeley	St. Louis
Strom, Brent	Baseball	San Diego		San Diego
Stroughter, Steve	Baseball	College of Sequoias		San Francisco
Stuckey, Henry	Football	Merritt		New York
Sutherland, Matt	Baseball	Cypress		San Francisco
Taggart, Dwayne	Football/Track	L.A. Southwest	Texas Southern	Kansas City
Tapier, Al	Golf	Cerritos	USC	Pro Golf
Tarver, John	Football	Bakersfield	Colorado State	New England
Tautolo, Terry	Football	Long Beach	UCLA	Philadelphia
Taylor, Altie	Football	Diablo Valley	Utah State	Detroit
Taylor, Mike	Football	San Francisco	USC	Washington
Terry, Chuck	Basketball	Long Beach	Cal State, Long Beach	San Antonio/ Milwaukee
Thiessen, Don	Football	Reedley		Cleveland
Thomas, Lee	Baseball	College of Redwoods	Cal State Humbolt	California
Thomas, Louie	Football	Laney	Utah Univ.	New Orleans
Thomas, Norm	Football	Laney	Utah Univ.	St. Louis

PARTICIPANTS	COMMUNITY COLLEGE SPORT	COMMUNITY COLLEGE ATTENDED	FOUR-YEAR INSTITUTION	PROFESSIONAL AFFILIATION
Thomas, Speedy	Football	Laney		Houston
Thompson, Bobby	Football	Compton		Detroit
Thormodsgard, Paul	Baseball	Mt. San Jacinto		Minnesota
Throop George	Baseball	Pasadena	Cal State, Long Beach	Kansas City
Tidrow, Dick	Baseball	Chabot		New York
Tipton, Dave	Football	Gavilan	Stanford	New York/San Diego
Timberlake, George	Football	Long Beach		Green Bay
Tippitt, Don	Baseball	Antelope Valley		Baltimore
Toler, Burl	Football	San Francisco	Univ. of San Francisco	Chicago
Tom, Mel	Football	San Francisco		Philadelphia
Tordsian, Scott	Baseball	Fresno		St. Louis
Townley, Robin	Baseball	San Bernardino	Cal State, Long Beach	Kansas City
Trapp, George	Basketball	Pasadena	Cal State, Long Beach	Detroit
Trapp, John	Basketball	Pasadena	Cal State, Long Beach	Los Angeles
Travis, John	Football	Foothill	Cal State, San Jose	San Diego
Tucker, Len	Baseball	College of Sequoias	Cal State, Fresno	St. Louis
Turner, Cecil	Football	Allan Hancock	Cal State, San Luis Obispo	Cincinnati
Turner, David	Football	Bakersfield	Cal State, San Diego	Chicago
Turner, John	Football	Taft	Cal State, Long Beach	New England
Tyack, Jim	Baseball	Bakersfield	Cal State, Fresno	Philadelphia
Ulrich, Jeff	Baseball	Fresno		Philadelphia
Urrea, John	Baseball	Rio Hondo		St. Louis
VacBuena, Gary	Football	Golden West	Stanford	New England
Vail, Mike	Baseball	DeAnza		Chicago
Valdez, Vern	Football	Antelope Valley	Univ. of San Diego	Los Angeles
Vallely, John	Basketball	Orange Coast	UCLA	Houston/Atlanta
Vallone, Jim	Football	Cerritos	USC	Minnesota
Van Deren, Steve	Baseball	College of Redwoods	Cal State, Humbolt	Anaheim

PARTICIPANTS	COMMUNITY COLLEGE SPORT	COMMUNITY COLLEGE ATTENDED	FOUR-YEAR INSTITUTION	PROFESSIONAL AFFILIATION
Vanderstock, Jeff	Track	Mt. San Antonio		Pro Track
Vasquez, Dennis	Baseball	San Bernardino	LaVerne	California
Vataha, Randy	Football	Golden West	Stanford	New England/Green Bay
Vaughn, Steve	Baseball	L.A. Valley		Detroit
Vicker, Mike	Football	L.A. City	Cal State, Northridge	New York
Villanueva, Danny	Football	Reedley	New Mexico State	Los Angeles/Dallas
Von Lossow, Jim	Golf	Citrus		PGA Tour
Voss, Bill	Baseball	Orange Coast	Cal State, Long Beach	California
Vukovich, John	Baseball	American River		Philadelphia
Walk, Bob	Baseball	College of Canyons		Philadelphia
Walker, Louie	Football	L.A. West	Colorado State	Dallas
Walker, Rick	Football	Santa Ana		Cincinnati
Walters, Mike	Baseball	Chaffey		Los Angeles
Wantz, Doug	Baseball	San Jose		Portland
Ward, Bruce	Football	San Diego	Cal State, San Diego	San Diego
Ward, Chris	Baseball	Chabot		Chicago
Ward, Stan	Boxing	American River		California
Warren, Don	Football	Mt. San Antonio	Cal State, San Diego	Washington
Washington, Otis	Football	L.A. City	Washington State	Minnesota
Washington, Spencer	Football	L.A. City	North Texas State	New York Giants
Watson, Bobby	Baseball	L.A. Harbor		Houston
Watson, Russ	Baseball	Chabot		Kansas City
Weathers, Carl	Football	Long Beach	Cal State, San Diego	Oakland
Weatherwax, Jim	Football	San Bernardino	Cal State, Los Angeles	Green Bay
Wellman, Brad	Baseball	Chabot		Kansas City
Wells, George	Football	Laney	New Mexico State	Canada
Wersching, Raimund	Football	Cerritos	U.C. Berkeley	San Diego

PARTICIPANTS	COMMUNITY COLLEGE SPORT	COMMUNITY COLLEGE ATTENDED	FOUR-YEAR INSTITUTION	PROFESSIONAL AFFILIATION
Werzel, Ralph	Football	Foothill	Cal State, San Jose	Philadelphia
West, Robert	Football	San Diego Mesa	Cal State, San Diego	San Francisco
Wheelock, Gary	Baseball	Fullerton	U.C. Irvine	Seattle
White, Alvin	Football	Orange Coast	Oregon State	California
White, Roy	Baseball	Compton		New York
White, Sherman	Football	Laney	U.C. Berkeley	Cincinnati
Whitehead, Jerome	Basketball	Riverside	Marquette	NBA
Whitmer, Dan	Baseball	San Bernardino	Cal State, Fullerton	Anaheim
Whitol, Sandy	Baseball	DeAnza		Cleveland
Wicks, Sidney	Basketball	Santa Monica	UCLA	Boston
Wiggins, Paul	Football	Modesto		Cleveland
Wilborn, Chuck	Baseball	Consumnes River	Stanford	San Diego
Williams, Arthur "Hambone"	Basketball	San Diego	Cal State, Pomona	Boston
Williams, Homer	Football	Long Beach	USC	Los Angeles
Williams, John	Football	Reedley	Cal State, San Diego	Philadelphia
Williams, Rich	Baseball	Merced		Houston
Williams, Travis	Football/Track	Contra Costa	Arizona State	Green Bay
Williams, Walter	Baseball	San Francisco		Cleveland
Wilson, Bob	Baseball	College of Redwoods		Philadelphia
Wilson, Dave	Football	Fullerton	Univ. of Illinois	New Orlean
Wilson, Jack	Baseball	Riverside		Minnesota
Wilson, Jim	Baseball	Cerritos		Boston
Winans, Jeff	Football	Modesto	Cal State, Chico	Cincinnati
Wing, Harry	Baseball	Cypress	Chapman	San Francisco
Winters, Van	Baseball	Fresno		St. Louis
Wise, Willie	Basketball	San Francisco	Drake	Utah
Wiseman, Jim	Baseball	Yuba		Kansas City

183

PARTICIPANTS	COMMUNITY COLLEGE SPORT	COMMUNITY COLLEGE ATTENDED	FOUR-YEAR INSTITUTION	PROFESSIONAL AFFILIATION
Witcher, Dick	Football	Bakersfield	U.C. Berkeley	San Francisco
Wohlford, Jim	Baseball	College of Sequoias	Cal State, Fresno	Milwaukee
Wojcik, Greg	Football/Wrestling			
Wolfe, Larry	Baseball	Orange Coast		San Diego
Womack, Joe	Football	Sacramento	USC	Boston
Woods, Al	Baseball	L.A. City	Cal State, Los Angeles	Pittsburg
Woods, Gary	Baseball	Laney		Toronto
Woods, Willie	Football	Santa Barbara	USC	Toronto
Wright, Louie	Football	West Hills		Green Bay
Wright, Nate	Football/Basketball	Bakersfield		Denver
Wright, Steve	Baseball	Monterey	Cal State, San Diego	Minnesota
Yary, Ron	Football	San Jose	USC	New York Mets
York, Jim	Baseball	Cerritos	UCLA	Minnesota
Zeller, Gary	Basketball	Cerritos	Drake	Houston
Zimmerer, George	Baseball	Long Beach		Baltimore
Zorn, Jim	Football	San Jose	Cal State, Pomona	New York Yankees
Zouras, Mike	Baseball	Cerritos		Seattle
		El Camino		Pittsburg

Bill Kilmer, Citrus College, Washington Redskins. When asked for a picture to use in this publication, Kilmer responded with this photo — including the shot of him at Citrus (then Citrus Junior College).

CALIFORNIA ASSOCIATION OF COMMUNITY COLLEGES (CACC) ATHLETES REPORTED TO BE AFFILIATED WITH THE UNITED STATES FOOTBALL LEAGUE (USFL)

PARTICIPANTS	COMMUNITY COLLEGE SPORT	COMMUNITY COLLEGE ATTENDED	FOUR-YEAR INSTITUTION	AFFILIATION
Allen, Carl	Football	Los Medanos	Cal State, Long Beach	L. A. Express
Barnett, John	Football	Southwestern	Oregon Tech.	L. A. Express
Bayle, David	Football	Pasadena	Washington	Seattle/Buffalo/ Boston Breakers
Berry, Raymond	Football	San Diego Mesa	Texas Christian	Oakland Invaders
Biedermann, Leo	Football	Diablo Valley	California	Canada/Cleveland/ San Francisco/ Oakland Invaders
Bledsoe, Curtis	Football	Chabot	San Diego State	Kansas City Chiefs/ Arizona Wranglers
Corral, Frank	Football	Riverside	UCLA	L. A. Rams/Chicago Blitz
Croudip, David	Football	Ventura	Cal State, San Diego	L. A. Express
Daniel, Kenny	Football	Contra Costa	San Jose State	Oakland Invaders
Darby, Eric	Football	Imperial Valley	Tennessee State	Oakland Invaders
Darrow, Scott	Football	College of Sequoias	Fresno State	Oakland Invaders
Ellis, Rickey	Football	L. A. City	Cal State, Fullerton	L. A. Express
Fiedler, Don	Football	Golden West	Kentucky	Pittsburg/ Philadelphia Stars
Fields, Greg	Football	Hartnell	Grambling	L. A. Express
Flanagan, Orlando	Football	Long Beach	Oklahoma	Boston Breakers
Ford, Mariet	Football	Diablo Valley	California	Oakland Invaders

PARTICIPANTS	COMMUNITY COLLEGE SPORT	COMMUNITY COLLEGE ATTENDED	FOUR-YEAR INSTITUTION	AFFILIATION
Franey, Jerome	Football	Bakersfield	Cal State, San Diego	L. A. Express
Gibson, Gary	Football	Long Beach	Arizona	San Francisco/ Boston Breakers
Gortz, Steve	Football	Saddleback	Las Vegas	Denver Broncs/ Minnesota/Denver Gold
Grant, Steve	Football	Chabot	Washington State	Canada/ Oakland Invaders
Harris, Mike	Football	Fullerton	Purdue	L. A. Express
Henderson, Wyatt	Football	L. A. Valley	Fresno State	Los Angeles/San Diego/ Oakland Invaders
Henderson, Wymon	Football	Allan Hancock	Las Vegas	L. A. Express
Hickman, Dallas	Football	Reedley	U.C. Berkeley	Washington/Baltimore/ Washington Federals
Horton, Myke	Football	Gavilan	UCLA	Washington Redskins/ Canada/Philadelphia/ Washington Federals
Hosea, Bobby	Football	San Bernardino	UCLA	L. A. Express
Houston, Steve	Football	Golden West	Fresno State	Oakland Invaders
Howell, Wes	Football	Chabot	California	Oakland Invaders
James, Elmer	Football	Long Beach	San Francisco State	Oakland Invaders
James, Victor	Football	L. A. Valley	Colorado	Denver Gold
Jones, Kevin	Football	Chaffey/Citrus	Fresno State	Oakland Invaders
Justin, Tyrone	Football	L.A. Southwest	Cal State, Fullerton	L. A. Express
Kampa, Bob	Football	Gavilan	California	Denver/ Oakland Invaders
Larry, Admiral D.	Football	Contra Costa	Las Vegas	N. Y. Jets/ Arizona Wranglers
Lathrop, Kit	Football	West Valley	Arizona State	Chicago Blitz

PARTICIPANTS	COMMUNITY COLLEGE SPORT	COMMUNITY COLLEGE ATTENDED	FOUR-YEAR INSTITUTION	PROFESSIONAL AFFILIATION
Lockett, Frank	Football/Wrestling	Contra Costa	Nebraska	Green Bay/Miami/Boston Breakers
Looney, James	Football	L.A. Southwest	Purdue	San Francisco/Arizona Wranglers
Love, Terry	Football	College of Canyons	Murray State	Kansas/Buffalo/Boston Breakers
Maher, Tom	Football	Pasadena	Cal State, Los Angeles	Oakland Invaders
Manumaleuga, Frank	Football	DeAnza	San Jose State	Kansas City/Oakland Invaders
Miller, Nathaniel	Football	San Bernardino	Cameron	Atlanta/Denver Gold
Mitchell, Aaron	Football	College of Canyons	Las Vegas	Tampa Bay/Dallas Cowboys/Arizona Wranglers
Newton, Robert	Football	Cerritos	Nebraska	Chicago Bears/Seattle/Boston Breakers
Norris, Sam	Football	San Francisco	East Carolina	Arizona Wranglers
O'Brien, Mike	Football	Olympic (WA)	California	Oakland Invaders
Orange, Rick	Football	L.A. Harbor	Cal State, San Diego	L. A. Express
Paige, Stephone	Football	Saddleback	Fresno State	Oakland Invaders
Plummer, Gary	Football	Ohlone	California	Oakland Invaders
Porras, Tom	Football	Ventura	Washington	Oakland Raiders/Chicago Blitz
Shaw, David	Football	Long Beach	California	Oakland Invaders
Taylor, Drew	Football	Long Beach/Golden West	San Jose State	Portland (WFL)/Green Bay/Canada/Washington Federals
Tolbert, Mark	Football	El Camino		L. A. Express
Townsend, Greg	Football	Long Beach	Texas Christian	Oakland Invaders

PARTICIPANTS	COMMUNITY COLLEGE SPORT	COMMUNITY COLLEGE ATTENDED	FOUR-YEAR INSTITUTION	PROFESSIONAL AFFILIATION
Turner, Lonnie	Football	L.A. City	Cal State, Pomona	L. A. Express
Walker, Glen	Football	L.A. Harbor	USC	L. A. Express
Williams, Greg	Football	Long Beach	Washington	L. A. Express
Wilson, Lee	Football	Compton	San Diego State	Los Angeles Rams/ Arizona Wranglers
Wright, Eddie	Football	Pasadena	Wake Forest	New England/Canada/ New Jersey Generals
Yancy, Bill	Football	Saddleback	Fresno State	Detroit/ Oakland Invaders

Chapter Six
POSTSCRIPT: A CASE FOR JUNIOR-COMMUNITY COLLEGE INTER-SCHOLASTIC ATHLETICS

Junior - community colleges are experiencing one of the toughest times in their history in terms of finances. According to many authorities, these times are the worst. They are being forced to cut back in all areas.

Major decisions must be made as to the specific areas that will have to be sacrificed due to the lack of finances. Those at the governance — decision making — level will be pondering many questions, a major one being what it is the junior-community colleges ought to be doing.

Some of the challenges with which they may be faced will be the ability to provide access, maintain open admissions policies, provide services, and continue to offer a wide variety of programs.

The missions of the junior - community colleges will be undergoing scrutiny. Of their varied missions, the early three were the transfer function, which prepares students to continue their education in four - year institutions; the vocational / occupational function, to prepare students for immediate employment and job advancement; and the continuing education function, which provides cultural, educational, and recreational programs to meet the personal needs and interests of students. In the early days the continuing education function was not as prevalent. California, with the community - college concept, expanded that function. During this economical crisis, functions related to the community college concept are causing a great deal of criticism in California — they are not the state's most vital interest.

In recent years the historical transfer function has been of major concern to the junior - community colleges. An *Inglewood News* article published in October 1981, stated:[1] "Why the community colleges stopped becoming the ever - increasing feeding ground for universities is unclear to education officials." Amidst the uncertainty, and the threat to this function, some districts have taken steps to deal with this concern by scrutinizing each of their functions.

Among others, some questions will be: Has the role of the junior - community college changed? If not, in light of compelled cutbacks, in what manner should the junior - community colleges function to best assure the possibility of achieving all of the mandates? If so, they will have the same concern, but in addition, where should the greater emphasis be placed?

Regardless of what decisions are made, hopefully they will not be "rattled" by the negative charges sometimes directed at interscholastic athletics. JC-CC intercollegiate athletics have been, still are, and will continue to be one of the most viable programs among their offerings as long as there is a world-wide demand for those skills. In spite of claims that overall there is a decline in JC-CC transfers to four - year institutions, their interscholastic athletic programs are maintaining.

This significant point deserves further elaboration. Two-year colleges cannot afford the luxury of associating their interscholastic athletic problems, issues, and concerns with those of their four - year counterparts. Many authorities feel they do. Four - year institutions with big-time college athletic programs have enormous budgets which include: athletic scholarships; recruiting expenses; large coaching staffs; resources for coaching staffs; massive facilities; maintenance for those facilities; scheduling; travel, lodging, and boarding; an abundance of playing equipment; training equipment; office budget; publicity budget; filming; scouts; and numerous other items.

During the best of times the two-year colleges operated on far less. And this book, *Professional Sports: The Community College Connection*, contains sufficient documentation to support the fact that they were successful in their endeavors.

The fact that a large number of athletes transfer to four - year institutions is not an end in itself for the junior - community colleges. They have a greater concern. That concern is to provide the best training, information, and education possible while the student is in their domain. This is their educational philosophy. Echoing Chancellor Leslie Koltai, Los Angeles Community College District, and Chancellor Gerald Hayward, Chancellor's Office, California Community Colleges, in an article in the *Inglewood*

News, October 22, 1981,[2] there should be "increased concern about the quality of the transfer program and we should be working to improve that."

But when the student-athlete feels comfortable about attending a four-year institution, negotiates toward that end, then elects to transfer, a mission of the two-year college has been accomplished. It is not the decision of the two-year colleges; for them mere acceptance of their students by the four-year institutions means a job well done. And this should be noted: no program other than intercollegiate athletics has the honor of having their immediate products hand-picked by the four-year institutions.

To use a familiar phrase, "the ball is now in the court" of the four-year institutions. Because they now have responsibility for the social, emotional, and educational outcomes of the student-athlete. Some things which they are to be accountable for are: To what extent did this activity / experience affect the student socially, emotionally, educationally? What effect did it or will it have on the student? Is the student better off as a result of the experience? Have we dealt with the student ethically, morally, and legally as we are expected to do?

Wherein, then, lies the guilt of the two-year institutions? Is it because some of the student-athletes did not achieve the educational requirements at that level? Is it because some did not achieve professional sports careers as they expected? Neither one is the mission, goal, or objective of the junior-community colleges. The basic promise was — a chance.

Wherein lies the reason for abandoning the interscholastic athletic program? Money? A lack of resources? Are the junior-community colleges less sensitive, ingenious, creative, and tenacious now than in previous years? Their growth and development resulted from the application of those virtues. They exhibited those virtues so well that, through the years, millions of students opted to attend the junior-community colleges rather than other segments of higher education or other institutions which offer the same specialized training. The students expressed their faith by embracing the junior-community-college concept.

There are many who feel that it would be an indictment against the junior-community colleges if they were any less than they have been. It would be a betrayal. They have been more than just colleges — they have been pillars of society. It would be a further indictment to dismantle a program which has always fulfilled their mission and given them a high level of visibility and pride in the community.

It is readily understandable that the present financial crisis will necessitate the junior - community colleges adapting to change, but not necessarily that they destroy one of their most productive programs. The brink of destruction for these great institutions may be the willingness — hopefully, not the lack of wisdom — to destroy the program and put nothing comparable in its place.

NOTES

Chapter One

1. Wallace Albertson, President, Los Angeles Community College District Board of Trustees. Statement made in an address to the Los Angeles Community College District Administrators' Association, Ambassador Hotel, Los Angeles, California, November 16, 1978.
2. Norka Manning, Public Information Officer, Pasadena City College, Pasadena, California, "PCC Olympians: Past and Present." In: *Pasadena City College Spring Schedule of Classes, February 6, 1984 - June 16, 1984*, pp. 3-5.
3. William Thomas, Sports Information Director, Compton College, Compton, CA. Personal communication, April 17, 1984.
4. Fred Baer, Director, J. C. Athletic Bureau, San Mateo, CA. "National (TAC/AAU) Champions While Students at San Jose CC," May 19, 1983.
5. *Ibid.*, "Petranoff Symbolic of Community College Impact on World of Track & Field," May 19, 1983.
6. James R. "Jimmie" Smith, retired Water Polo and Swimming Coach, Fullerton College (CA), and author, Foster City, CA. Personal communication, May 2, 1984.
7. Ken Pivernetz, "U.S. Water Polo Squad Will Increase Training," *Press-Telegram*, Long Beach (CA), August 1, 1983, Section C, p. 3.
8. *Op. cit.*, Norka Manning.
9. Jack Flanagan, Swimming and Water Polo Coach, Diablo Valley College, Pleasant Hills, CA. Personal communication, May 16, 1984.
10. *Op. cit.*, James Smith.
11. Bob Tisdale, Sports Information Officer, Long Beach City College, Long Beach (CA). Personal communication, May 3, 1984.
12. Bob Kelley, Associate Dean, Physical Education, and Athletic Director, Hartnell College, Salinas, CA. Personal communication, April 17, 1984.
13. Jim Corfield, General Manager, National Intercollegiate Rodeo Association (NIRA), Walla Walla, WA. Personal communications, April 17 and 19, 1984.
14. George Vizvary, Engineering Professor, Soccer Coach, and Staff Coach of the U.S. Soccer Federation, Ulster County Community College, Stone Ridge, NY. Personal communication, April 25, 1984.
15. Terry Martin, Ice Hockey Coach, Canton Agricultural and Technical College (State University of New York). Personal communication, April 26, 1984.
16. A publication of the California Community College Football Coaches Association — Hall of Fame Bulletin, Fall 1984.
17. Bob Gomperz, Director, Public Information Office, Pasadena City College, Pasadena, CA. Personal communication, May 2, 1984.
18. Copyright 1977, *Los Angeles Times*. Reprinted by permission. John Hall, "Ratless Race," December 7, 1977, Part III, p. 3.

19. Copyright 1974, *Los Angeles Times*. Reprinted by permission. Al Carr, "JC Brand of Football Getting Better, But Crowds are Slimming," November 8, 1974, Part III, p. 14.
20. *Ibid.*
21. *Op. cit.*, Fred Baer.
22. *Ibid.*
23. George E. Killian, Executive Director, National Junior College Athletic Association (NJCAA), Hutchinson, KS. Personal interview, November 12, 1982.
24. Wayne Unruh, Assistant Director, National Junior College Athletic Association (NJCAA), Hutchinson, KS. Personal interview, November 12, 1982.
25. Walter Rilliet, Commissioner of Athletics, California Association of Community Colleges (CACC), Sacramento, CA. Information was in a statement entitled "A Note Concerning California Community College Basketball Coaches," received by the author November 12, 1982.
26. Copyright, 1983, *The Sacramento Union* (CA). Reprinted by permission. Glen Crevier, "SAC City's Sullivan Paying the High Price of Success," November 30, 1983, Section F, p. 1.
27. *Op. cit.*, John Hall.
28. *Ibid.*
29. Bill Sandstrom, Athletic Director, Pasadena City College, Pasadena, CA. Personal interview, May 18, 1982.
30. George E. Killian, "In the Sports Spotlight," *Community and Junior College Journal*, 43:54, February 1973.
31. *Ibid.*
32. Lloyd Messersmith, Past Director, California Community and Junior College Association, Sacramento, CA. Personal interview, October 23, 1980. Since that time the name has been changed to California Association of Community Colleges (CACC).
33. *Op. cit.*, Walter Rilliet.
34. *Op. cit.*, George E. Killian.

Chapter Two

1. Copyright, 1983, *USA Today*. Reprinted by permission. Susan Fornoff, "State of union in JCs still divided," March 8, 1983, Section C, p. 5.
2. "History of the National Junior College Association." *National Junior College Association 1982-1983 Handbook and Casebook*. Revised August 1, 1982, pp. 19-23.
3. *Ibid.*, p. 23.
4. *Ibid.*
5. Lee Samuel Vokes. Taken from "A Historical Study of the California Junior College State Athletic Committee: Years 1946-1972." Doctoral dissertation, United States International University, 1973, Chapters III, IV, and V, pp. 60-162.

6. *Ibid.*
7. *Ibid.*, p. 92.
8. *Ibid.* p. 67.
9. *Ibid.*, p. 73.
10. *Ibid.*, p. 74.
11. *Ibid.*
12. *Ibid.*
13. *Ibid.*, p. 75.
14. *Ibid.*
15. *Ibid.*, p. 73.
16. *Ibid.*, p. 76.
17. *Ibid.*, p. 77.
18. *Ibid.*, p. 79.
19. *Ibid.*, p. 80.
20. *Ibid.*, p. 101.
21. *Ibid.*, p. 80.
22. *Ibid.*
23. *Ibid.*
24. *Ibid.*, p. 88.
25. *Ibid.*, pp. 89-90.
26. *Ibid.*, p. 90.
27. *Ibid.*, pp. 121-122.
28. *Ibid.*, pp. 122-123.
29. *Ibid.*, 146-147.
30. *Ibid.*, 149-150.
31. "Junior Rose Bowl Football Classic December 10." *California Community and Junior College Association News.* Sacramento, CA, Vol. 22, No. 3, May 1977, p. 1.
32. *Ibid.*
33. Copyright 1976, *Los Angeles Times.* Reprinted by permission. "Junior Rose Bowl Revived," July 2, 1976, Part III, p. 1.
34. *Op. cit.*, Note. No. 31 above.
35. *Ibid.*

Chapter Three

1. Joseph B. Iantorno, Dean of Students, College of the Desert, Palm Desert, CA. Personal interviews, April 10, 1979 and May 4, 1983.
2. Gene Mazzei, Head Football Coach, San Bernardino Valley College, San Bernardino, CA. Personal interviews. November 12, 1978 and February 11, 1983.

3. Lloyd McCullough, Research Consultant, Sacramento, CA. Personal interviews, March 3, 1979 and August 20, 1982.
4. Gary S. Belkins and Jerry L. Gray. *Educational Psychology.* Dubuque, IA: Wm. C. Brown Co., 1977, pp. 245 - 246.
5. Richard L. Moore, President, Santa Monica College, Santa Monica, CA. Personal interview, September 12, 1979, and correspondence, November 2, 1982.
6. Freddie Goss, Head Basketball Coach, United States International University, San Diego, CA. Personal interview, September 24, 1980, and correspondence, February 9, 1983.
7. "Wellman Analyzed Chabot Success," *The Spectator*, February 11, 1975. (*The Spectator* is a weekly publication compiled and edited by the journalism students of Chabot College, Hayward, California. *Spectator* sports writers Obrey Brown and Jim Gonsalves, and sports editor Jeff Lane, conducted the interview. Gene Wellman's coaching experience spans some 20 years. The author corresponded with Coach Wellman November 3, 1982.)
8. Copyright 1983, *The Tribune* (Oakland, CA). Reprinted by permission. Paul McCarthy, "Community colleges worthwhile for many athletes," May 29, 1983, Section F, p. 7.
9. Alvin Toffler, *Future Shock.* New York: Bantam Books, 1970, p. 2.
10. William Proctor, *Survival on Campus.* Old Tappan, New Jersey: Spire Books, 1973, p. 32.
11. *Ibid.*, p. 13.
12. *Ibid.*, p. 9.
13. George B. Dintiman and Jerrold S. Greenberg. *Health Through Discovery.* Massachusetts: Addison - Wesley Publishing Company, 1980, pp. 168, 170-171.
14. Paul M. Insel and Walton T. Roth, *Health in a Changing Society.* Palo Alto, California: Mayfield Publishing Company, 1976, p. 77.
15. *Op. cit.*, Dintiman and Greenberg, p. 155.
16. *Ibid.*, p. 171.
17. Copyright 1978. *San Francisco Chronicle.* Reprinted by permission. Al Moss, "A Bitter Loss for Stanford — It's Becoming a Habit," October 16, 1978, p. 48.
18. Copyright 1978. *Sun Telegram* (San Bernardino, CA). Reprinted by permission. Dan Sewell, "Williams Heart in S.F. but Miami Has His Body," November 16, 1978, Section D, p. 8.
19. Leon Henry, Head Basketball Coach, Los Angeles Southwest College, Los Angeles, CA. Personal interview, December 2, 1978 and telephone communication, November 17, 1982.
20. Lloyd Messersmith, Past Director, California Community and Junior College Association, Sacramento, CA. Personal interview, October 20, 1978 and telephone communication, November 12, 1982.
21. Roy Sommers, Athletic Director, Niagara County Community College, Sanborn, NY. Personal interview, October 20, 1978 and telephone communication, October 28, 1982.

22. Wayne Unruh, Assistant Director, National Junior College Athletic Association, Hutchinson, KS. Personal interviews, October 5, 1978 and September 1, 1982, and correspondence, November 24, 1982.
23. "The Open Door Colleges — Policies for Community Colleges (June 1970)." Taken from: *A Digest of Reports of the Carnegie Commission on Higher Education.* New York: McGraw - Hill, 1974, p. 23.
24. Copyright 1983, *Los Angeles Times.* Reprinted by permission. Richard Hoffer, "College Basketball Creates Vagabonds Class," March 6, 1983, Part III, p. 3.
25. *Ibid.*
26. *Ibid.*, p. 12.
27. *Ibid.*
28. Copyright 1983, *Los Angeles Times.* Reprinted by permission. Mike Hiserman, "JC Track Coaches Voicing Concern on Foreign Affair," July 10, 1983, Part III, p. 3.
29. *Ibid.*
30. *Op. cit.*, Gene Mazzei.
31. J. Raack, Athletic Director, West Los Angeles Community College, Culver City, CA., and Chairman of the Los Angeles Community College District Athletic Director's Research Committee. Personal interview, February 18, 1983.

    Other members of the research committee were Diedra Stark, Los Angeles Valley Community College, Van Nuys, CA, and Lawrence Jarmon, Los Angeles Southwest Community College.
32. John McKay, *McKay: A Coach's Story.* New York: Atheneum, 1974, pp. 292 - 294.
33. Joseph Durso and the New York Times Sports Department, *The Sports Factory: An Investigation into College Sports.* New York: Quadrangle, The New York Times Book Company, 1975, pp. 69-71.
34. Lawrence Jarmon, Athletic Director, and Ron Mims, Head Football Coach, Los Angeles Southwest College, Los Angeles, CA. Personal interview, October 21, 1978.
35. Mike Fleming, Staff Writer, *The Commercial Appeal,* Memphis, TN, personal communication, February 1984; and Joanne Bliss, Librarian, City of Inglewood Library, Inglewood, CA. Personal communication, February 12, 1984.
36. Copyright 1983, *Los Angeles Times.* Reprinted by permission. Mark Heisler, "But Look Who's In The Rose Bowl," December 25, 1983, Part III, P. 1.
37. Copyright 1983, *Los Angeles Times.* Reprinted by permission. Mark Heisler, "It Took the Illini 20 Years To Fight Back," December 21, 1983, Part III, p. 1.
38. *Ibid.*
39. Copyright 1983, *The Sacramento Bee.* Reprinted by permission. Gary Voet, "Illini's Return: Fluke or White's Genius?" December 30, 1983, Section E, p. 1.

40. Copyright 1983, *Los Angeles Times.* Reprinted by permission. Mark Heisler, "Illinois Feels Right at Home in Pasadena," December 29, 1983, Part III, p. 1.
41. *Ibid.*
42. Jim Newman, Assistant Athletic Director, Arizona State University, Tempe, AZ. Personal interviews March 15, 1978; September 17, 1978; November 9, 1982; and April 14, 1983.

    During the five years Newman served as Head Basketball Coach at Compton Community College, Compton, CA, he established a 140-24 record, including five league and two state championships. Also, among his records are: his 1969 - 1970 team was the first time a JC in California was undefeated for an entire season; his team scored 166 points against West Los Angeles Community College to set a California Community College Basketball scoring record. Newman was assistant basketball coach at Compton High School, Compton, CA, when that school set a record by winning 42 consecutive games.
43. "Cal State L.A. Brings Newman Back Home," *Los Angeles Sentinel,* June 9, 1983, Section B, p. 2.
44. *Op. cit.,* Jim Newman.
45. *Ibid.*
46. Haskell Cohen, "Parade's All-American High School Basketball Team," *Parade,* a supplement from *The Sacramento Bee* (Sacramento, CA), March 28, 1976, p. 23.
47. *Ibid.*
48. *Ibid.*
49. Copyright 1983, *Los Angeles Times.* Reprinted by permission. Randy Harvey, "One More Time: It's the Lakers and the 76ers," May 22, 1983, Part III, p. 1.
50. Copyright 1983, *Los Angeles Times.* Reprinted by permission. Randy Harvey "76ers Big Finish Finishes Lakers," June 1, 1983, Part III, p. 1.
51. Haskell Cohen, "Parade's All-American High School Tennis Team," *Parade,* a supplement from *The Sacramento Bee* (Sacramento, CA), June 8, 1975, p. 16.
52. Haskell Cohen, "Parade's All-American High School Football Team," *Parade,* a supplement from *The Sacramento Bee* (Sacramento, CA), December 29, 1974, p. 8.
53. Copyright 1977, *Los Angeles Times.* Reprinted by permission. Earl Gustkey, "State Football Coaches Count Returns of Recruiting Drives," February 24, 1977, Part III, p. 8.
54. Copyright 1983, *Los Angeles Times.* Reprinted by permission. "Letters of Intent," February 10, 1983, Part III, p. 8.
55. Copyright 1983, *Los Angeles Times.* Reprinted by permission. Bob Cuomo, "USC Makes a Big Haul in JCs Again," February 10, 1983, Part III, p. 9.
56. *Op. cit.,* Jim Newman.
57. John C. Horgan, "Junior Comes of Age." 1977 NFL Properties, Inc. Reprinted by permission of *PRO!,* the magazine of the National Football

League. The article appeared in a 1977 Los Angeles Rams Football program.
58. Fred Baer, Director, J. C. Athletic Bureau, San Mateo, CA. "California CCs Groom 7 Brewers for a World Series Featuring 13 Ex-JC/CC Players," October 18, 1981.
59. Copyright 1983, *Los Angeles Times*. Reprinted by permission. Mark Heisler, "Rozier Recalls a Really Big Game," November 25, 1983, Part III, p. 22.
60. "Rozier 'Succeeds' All-Time Collegiate and JC Scoring Champ O. J. Simpson as Heisman Winner." reprinted by permission of Fred Baer, Director, JC Athletic Bureau, San Mateo, CA, December 1983.
61. *Op. cit.*, J. Raack.
62. Copyright 1983, United States Football League. Reprinted by permission. "USFL: United States Football League." This article appeared in *USA Today*, March 4, 1983, Section C, p. 5.
63. Tom Fears, Office of Player Personnel, Los Angeles Express, professional football team, United States Football League. Personal communication, April 22, 1983.
64. *Op. cit.*, Note No. 62 above.

Chapter Six

1. Copyright 1981, *Inglewood News*. Reprinted by permission. "Universities Losing Junior College Transfer Students," October 22, 1981, p. 1.
2. Copyright 1981, *Inglewood News*. Reprinted by permission. "JC Chancellor Asks for 'Structured Program,' " October 22, 1981, p. 1.

APPENDIX A

Geographic Locations of Members in National Junior College Athletic Association

Permission to reprint granted by the National Junior College Athletic Association, George E. Killian, Director, Hutchinson, Kansas. Taken from: *National Junior College Athletic Association 1982-1983 Handbook and Casebook*, 1981.

GEOGRAPHIC REGIONS OF THE NJCAA

Region

I	Arizona, California, Colorado west of the Continental Divide, Nevada, and Utah
II	Arkansas and Oklahoma
III	Upper New York State
IV	Upper Illinois
V	New Mexico and West Texas
VI	Kansas
VII	Kentucky and Tennessee
VIII	Florida
IX	Colorado east of the Continental Divide, Eastern Montana, Nebraska, and Wyoming
X	North Carolina, South Carolina, Virginia, and West Virginia
XI	Iowa
XII	Indiana, Lower Michigan Peninsula, and Ohio
XIII	Minnesota, North Dakota, South Dakota, Upper Michigan Peninsula, and Wisconsin
XIV	Eastern Texas
XV	Lower New York
XVI	Missouri
XVII	Georgia
XVIII	Alaska, Idaho, Oregon, Washington, and Western Montana
XIX	Deleware, Eastern Pennsylvania and Jew Jersey
XX	District of Columbia, Maryland and Western Pennsylvania
XXI	Connecticut, Maine, Massachusetts, New Hampshire, Rhode Island, and Vermont
XXII	Alabama
XXIII	Mississippi and Louisiana
XXIV	Lower Illinois

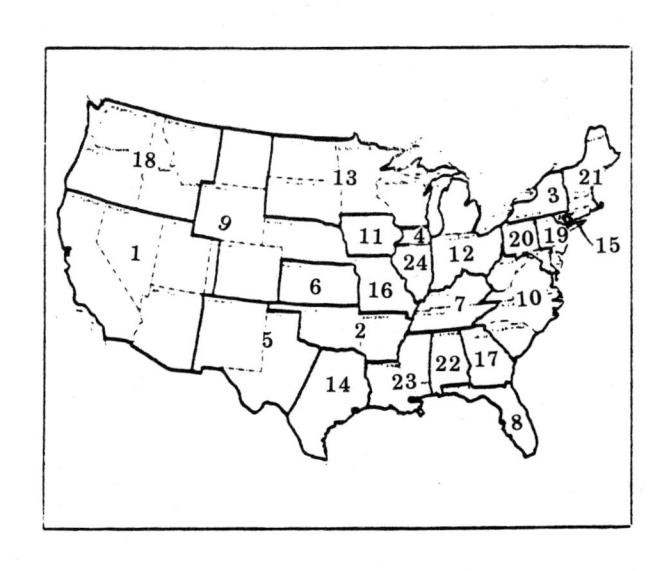

A-2

MEMBERSHIP IN NJCAA
MEN'S DIVISION

Total Members

NJCAA Regions	1964-65	1967-68	1968-69	1969-70	1970-71	1971-72	1972-73	1973-74	1974-75	1975-76	1976-77	1977-78	1978-79	1979-80	1980-81	1981-82
I	34	38	15	16	17	18	16	16	20	19	20	17	20	20	20	21
II	11	17	16	17	18	18	18	19	22	24	23	22	23	25	25	24
III	22	32	34	37	37	43	50	29	29	28	28	29	30	32	31	32
IV	24	33	40	43	47	49	44	45	44	45	45	45	46	46	45	45
V	13	16	17	18	16	18	18	20	21	20	21	21	20	29	20	20
VI	15	18	21	23	24	23	23	23	23	23	23	23	23	23	22	22
VII	15	22	22	29	34	33	38	40	38	41	40	41	45	43	41	40
VIII	35	55	28	27	27	28	28	29	29	29	29	30	30	30	28	28
IX	9	10	10	10	18	18	17	20	19	20	21	20	21	22	23	22
X	19	21	20	19	24	26	27	23	23	31	32	32	32	27	29	27
XI	20	21	21	24	19	19	20	20	21	21	19	19	19	17	17	17
XII	12	24	26	28	29	31	30	32	32	32	32	33	32	30	29	31
XIII	22	29	32	31	31	30	37	37	35	38	39	39	38	38	38	38
XIV	20	18	20	21	19	21	21	23	22	26	28	26	26	25	25	23
XV	39	48	25	22	21	23	23	22	20	19	17	16	16	16	19	19
XVI	19	17	17	16	17	17	18	16	16	17	18	18	18	17	19	19
XVII	--	--	31	32	35	33	38	43	43	50	18	17	17	17	17	16
XVIII	--	--	22	19	23	17	15	14	15	14	14	14	16	16	15	14
XIX	--	--	37	41	44	17	52	24	28	28	26	24	25	23	22	23
XX	--	--	--	--	--	--	--	26	30	28	24	23	23	23	22	23
XXI	--	--	--	--	--	--	25	24	31	33	28	27	27	26	26
XXII	--	--	--	--	--	--	--	--	--	--	29	27	27	27	27	26
Totals	329	419	454	473	500	512	533	547	563	585	579	564	574	564	559	556

NJCAA MEN'S DIVISION
1981-82 Recognized Sports Participated in by Member Colleges

Region	Membership	Baseball	Basketball	Bowling	Cross Country	Fencing	Football	Golf	Gymnastics	Ice Hockey	Judo	Lacrosse	Rifle	Skiing	Soccer	Swimming & Diving	Tennis	Track & Field (Out.)	Track & Field (Ind.)	Volleyball	Wrestling
I	21	16	17	0	7	9	8	3	0	0	0	0	0	0	0	0	10	10	0	0	8
II	24	13	24	0	1	1	5	1	0	0	0	0	0	1	0	7	2	2	0	3
III	32	16	30	12	14	1	13	0	4	0	6	0	1	7	19	4	9	12	2	0	15
IV	45	38	44	0	20	8	33	0	1	0	0	0	0	0	10	5	36	15	1	0	17
V	20	4	20	0	4	3	12	1	0	2	0	0	0	0	2	0	10	5	2	0	0
VI	22	22	21	0	9	11	16	0	0	0	0	0	0	0	4	0	17	18	1	0	6
VII	40	34	39	1	0	13	12	0	0	0	0	0	0	0	0	0	20	10	0	0	0
VIII	28	24	26	0	4	0	19	0	0	0	0	0	0	0	3	4	21	4	2	0	1
IX	22	4	22	0	2	0	16	0	0	0	0	0	0	0	1	0	11	5	3	12	3
X	27	11	25	0	3	3	15	0	0	0	0	0	1	3	0	24	2	0	0	1
XI	17	17	16	0	0	5	10	0	0	0	0	0	0	0	0	0	7	2	0	0	4
XII	31	19	30	3	9	1	16	1	0	0	0	2	0	0	6	4	10	4	5	0	5
XIII	38	24	37	0	9	21	23	0	7	0	0	0	0	0	4	0	23	14	7	2	15
XIV	23	11	19	0	0	6	11	0	0	0	0	0	0	0	1	15	4	0	0	0
XV	19	17	19	5	5	2	9	1	1	0	3	0	0	1	15	2	12	6	3	0	6
XVI	19	16	17	2	2	0	7	0	0	0	0	0	1	0	4	3	11	2	1	0	2
XVII	16	8	10	0	0	0	6	0	0	0	0	0	0	0	5	0	11	0	0	0	0
XVIII	14	10	12	0	11	2	6	0	0	0	0	0	0	0	2	0	11	12	8	9	11
XIX	23	17	21	0	13	1	14	0	3	0	0	0	0	2	16	5	17	6	2	10	9
XX	23	19	22	6	8	4	9	2	0	0	4	0	0	0	17	7	19	10	4	0	4
XXI	26	21	24	0	4	2	10	0	1	0	1	0	0	2	13	0	13	0	0	1	0
XXII	26	16	25	0	0	1	5	0	0	0	0	0	0	0	0	0	8	2	2	0	0
Totals	556	377	520	29	125	94	275	9	17	2	14	2	2	13	125	35	322	145	68	34	110

A-3

MEMBERSHIP IN NJCAA WOMEN'S DIVISION

NJCAA Regions	1975-76	1976-77	1977-78	1978-79	1979-80	1980-81	1981-82
I	2	2	15	16	16	16	16
II	14	18	19	21	24	24	22
III	18	18	25	28	30	30	30
IV	22	26	41	42	42	42	44
V	13	17	18	20	19	19	19
VI	21	23	23	22	22	22	22
VII	22	27	29	34	36	36	34
VIII	4	7	24	28	27	27	26
IX	17	19	19	20	19	19	21
X	7	6	10	12	14	13	10
XI	11	11	14	15	14	14	15
XII	20	22	23	24	26	26	25
XIII	6	14	28	29	32	32	32
XIV	18	21	21	23	24	24	20
XV	3	4	15	15	15	15	17
XVI	13	14	14	15	14	14	15
XVII	18	12	12	13	14	14	14
XVIII	3	8	13	14	16	16	15
XIX	20	22	21	23	23	23	21
XX	23	21	19	19	20	20	21
XXI	19	22	21	23	24	24	21
XXII	--	10	10	15	17	17	18
Totals	294	334	434	471	489	487	478

NJCAA WOMEN'S DIVISION
1981-82 Recognized Sports Participated in by Member Colleges

Region	Membership	Basketball	Bowling	Cross Country	Fencing	Field Hockey	Golf	Gymnastics	Lacrosse	Skiing	Soccer	Softball	Swimming & Diving	Tennis	Track & Field (Out.)	Track & Field (Ind.)	Volleyball
I	16	15	0	5	0	0	4	1	0	0	0	13	0	6	6	1	14
II	23	21	0	2	0	0	1	1	0	0	0	3	0	8	3	2	1
III	30	25	9	11	0	6	0	0	7	5	28	5	11	10	2	26
IV	44	39	0	15	0	0	0	0	0	0	0	39	6	23	12	10	40
V	19	16	0	0	0	0	1	1	0	0	0	0	0	9	1	0	0
VI	22	22	0	8	0	0	0	0	0	0	0	12	0	17	18	13	22
VII	34	34	1	0	0	1	3	0	0	0	0	7	0	11	0	0	0
VIII	26	16	0	3	0	0	3	0	0	0	0	20	5	17	5	2	19
IX	20	20	0	0	0	0	1	2	0	0	0	0	0	8	2	0	16
X	10	10	0	0	0	0	0	0	1	0	4	0	4	0	0	4
XI	16	16	14	0	0	0	5	0	0	0	0	13	0	8	1	0	6
XII	25	25	2	6	0	0	1	0	0	0	0	13	2	8	3	0	16
XIII	31	31	2	8	0	0	2	0	0	0	0	23	0	17	14	6	29
XIV	20	12	0	0	0	0	3	0	0	0	0	0	1	13	2	0	9
XV	17	13	5	4	0	0	0	2	0	1	0	16	2	11	3	1	14
XVI	15	11	3	1	1	0	0	0	0	0	0	10	3	3	1	1	12
XVII	14	9	0	0	0	0	0	0	0	0	0	0	0	7	0	0	0
XVIII	15	14	0	10	0	0	0	1	0	0	0	0	0	9	13	3	11
XIX	21	16	0	10	0	7	7	0	0	1	0	15	3	18	6	0	10
XX	21	18	5	7	0	5	3	0	2	0	0	12	4	14	8	5	17
XXI	22	18	0	1	0	3	0	0	0	1	0	21	0	6	0	0	12
XXII	18	16	0	0	0	0	0	1	0	0	0	2	0	5	0	0	0
Totals	479	417	41	91	1	22	34	9	2	11	5	251	31	233	108	46	278

A-4

APPENDIX B

National Junior College Athletic Association History and Champions

Permission to reprint the introduction, and the history which precedes some of the activities was granted by Ray Franks Publishing Ranch, Amarillo, Texas. Taken from: *The 1981-82 National Directory of College Athletics (Men's Edition)*, 1981.

Permission to reprint the record and results was granted by the National Junior College Athletic Association, George E. Killian, Director, Hutchinson, Kansas. Taken from: *National Junior College Athletic Association 1982-1983 Handbook and Casebook*, 1981.

THE NATIONAL JUNIOR COLLEGE ATHLETIC ASSOCIATION
HISTORY, RECORDS, RESULTS

Conceived in 1937, the NJCAA is dedicated to promote and supervise a national program of junior college sports and activities. Growth of this organization has been phenomenal.

A handful of Jaycee representatives in Fresno, Calif., joined together for the first meeting from which the NJCAA evolved. Thirteen California colleges were charter members of the organization.

The first activity sponsored by the young association was a national track meet in 1939. While founded by California men, they had no intentions of keeping it just a regional organization. In 1941, Trinidad College was selected to host the annual track meet at Denver, signalling the NJCAA's development into a national association.

After four years of inactivity during World War II, the organization gave its blessing to an invitational basketball tournament at Compton College (Calif.) in 1945. Two years later, the nation was divided into eight regions and plans were made to hold the first national cage tourney in Springfield, Mo., in 1948. National tournaments were also authorized in boxing, golf, gymnastics, swimming, tennis, track and field, but some of these fell by the wayside because of finances and lack of interest.

Other sports have been added since then, some of which are strictly on an invitational basis. In 1949, the association was expanded to 16 regions, and only recently was enlarged once again to include 22.

NJCAA CHAMPIONS
BASEBALL

The first baseball tournament endorsed by the NJCAA was an invitational affair at Northeastern Oklahoma A&M in 1958, and won by Cameron State.

Baseball interest was so great that the Legislative Assembly approved a National Championship Tournament and the first one was staged in 1959.

Year	Champion
1958*	Cameron State Agricultural College - Lawton, Oklahoma
1959	Paris Junior College - Paris, Texas
1960	Phoenix Junior College - Phoenix, Arizona
1961	Wilmington College - Wilmington, North Carolina
1962	Phoenix College - Phoenix, Arizona
1963	Wilmington College - Wilmington, North Carolina
1964	Dade County Junior College - Miami, Florida
1965	Phoenix College - Phoenix, Arizona
1966	Nassau Community College - Garden City, New York
1967	Bacone College - Muskogee, Oklahoma
1968	Glendale Community College - Glendale, Arizona
1969	Panola Junior College - Carthage, Texas
1970	Mesa Community College - Mesa, Arizona
1971	Mesa Community College - Mesa, Arizona
1972	Mesa Community College - Mesa, Arizona
1973	Ranger Community College - Ranger, Texas
1974	Meramec Community College - St. Louis, Missouri
1975	Yavapai College - Prescott, Arizona
1976	Central Arizona College - Coolidge, Arizona
1977	Yavapai College - Prescott, Arizona
1978	Ranger College - Ranger, Texas
1979	MIddle Georgia College - Cochran, Georgia
1980	Middle Georgia College - Cochran, Georgia
1981	Miami Dade Dade Comm. College South - Miami, Florida
1982	Middle Georgia College - Cochran, Georgia

*Invitational Meets or Tournaments

BASKETBALL — MEN

After thriving theee years as an invitational tournament at Compton, Calif., the first National Basketball Tournament was staged in Springfield, Mo., in 1948. Marin College, a California school, won the first championship.

After many years of hosting the tournament, Lysle Rishel Post 68 of the American Legion in Hutchinson, Kan., was given a 10-year contract in 1966 to continue staging the annual affair. It still is played there.

Year	Champion
1945*	Pasadena City College - Pasadena, California
1946*	Sacramento Junior College - Sacramento, California
1947*	Compton College - Compton, California
1948	Marin College - Kentfield, California
1949	Tyler Junior College - Tyler, Texas
1950	Los Angeles City College - Los Angeles, California
1951	Tyler Junior College - Tyler, Texas
1952	Wharton County Junior College - Wharton, Texas
1953	El Dorado Junior College - El Dorado, Kansas
1954	Moberly Junior College - Moberly Missouri
1955	Moberly Junior College - Moberly Missouri
1956	Kilgore Junior College - Kilgore, Texas
1957	San Angelo College - San Angelo, Texas
1958	Kilgore Junior College - Kilgore, Texas
1959	Weber College - Ogden, Utah
1960	Parsons Junior College - Parsons, Kansas
1961	Pueblo Junior College - Pueblo, Colorado
1962	Coffeyville College - Coffeyville, Kansas
1963	Independence Community College - Independence, Kansas
1964	Dodge City College - Dodge City, Kansas
1965	Vincennes University Junior College - Vincennes, Indiana
1966	Moberly Junior College - Moberly, Missouri
1967	Moberly Junior College - Moberly, Missouri
1968	San Jacinto College - Pasadena, Texas
1969	Paducah Junior College - Paducah, Kentucky
1970	Vincennes University Junior College - Vincennes, Indiana
1971	Ellsworth Junior College - Iowa Falls, Iowa
1972	Vincennes University Junior College - Vincennes, Indiana
1973	Mercer County Community College - Trenton, New Jersey
1974	Mercer County Community College - Trenton, New Jersey
1975	Western Texas College - Snyder, Texas
1976	College of Southern Idaho - Twin Falls, Idaho
1977	Independence Community College - Independence, Kansas
1978	Independence Community College - Independence, Kansas
1979	Three Rivers Community College - Poplar Bluff, Missouri
1980	Western Texas College - Snyder, Texas
1981	Westark Community College - Ft. Smith, Arkansas
1982	Midland College - Midland, Texas

BASKETBALL — WOMEN

Year	Champion
1975*	Temple Junior College - Temple, Texas
1976	Seminole Junior College - Seminole, Oklahoma
1977	Panola Junior College - Carthage, Texas
1978	Panola Junior College - Carthage, Texas
1979	Northern Oklahoma College - Tonkawa, Oklahoma
1980	Truett-McConnell College - Cleveland, Georgia
1981	Louisburg College - Louisburg, North Carolina
1982	Moberly Junior College - Moberly, Missouri

BOWLING — MEN

Bowling was added as an invitational sport in 1971, and Genesee Community College was the first winner.

1971*	Genesee Community College - Batavia, New York
1972*	Nassau Community College - Garden City, New York
1973*	Nassau Community College - Garden City, New York
1974*	Erie Community College-North - Buffalo, New York
1975*	Erie Community College-North - Buffalo, New York
1976*	Niagara County Community College - Sanborn, New York
1977*	Erie Community College-North - Buffalo, New York
1978*	Erie Community College-North - Buffalo, New York
1979*	Niagara County Community College - Sanborn, New York
1980*	Vincennes University - Vincennes, Indiana
1981	Sinclair Community College - Dayton, Ohio
1982	Erie Community College-North - Buffalo, New York

BOWLING — WOMEN

1977*	Hillsborough Community College - Tampa, Florida
1978*	Erie Community College-North - Buffalo, New York
1979*	Erie Community College-North - Buffalo, New York
1980*	Suffolk Community College - Selden, New York
1981	Erie Community College-North - Buffalo, New York
1982	Erie Community College-North - Buffalo, New York

BOXING[†]

1949*	Pasadena City College - Pasadena, California
1950*	Compton College - Compton, California

CROSS COUNTRY — MEN

In 1959, authorization was granted to conduct a National Invitational Run in cross country, and Alfred, N.Y., was the site of the first meet. Cobleskill Agricultural and Technical Institute of New York was the first team champion.

1959*	Cobleskill Agr. & Tech. Institute - Cobleskill, New York
1960*	Coffeyville College - Coffeyville, Kansas
1961*	Flint Community College - Flint, Michigan
1962*	Cobleskill Agr. & Tech. Institute - Cobleskill, New York
1963*	Muskegon Community College - Muskegon, Michigan
1964*	Muskegon Community College - Muskegon, Michigan
1965*	Ricks College - Rexburg, Idaho
1966*	Ricks College - Rexburg, Idaho
1967*	Glendale Community College - Glendale, Arizona
1968	State U. of New York Agr. & Tech. College - Cobleskill, New York
1969	Vincennes University Junior College - Vincennes, Indiana
1970	Butler County Community Junior College - El Dorado, Kansas
1971	Vincennes University Junior College - Vincennes, Indiana
1972	Lane Community College - Eugene, Oregon
1973	Tie — Southwestern Michigan College - Dowagiac, Michigan / Allegheny Community College - Pittsburgh, Pennsylvania
1974	Southwestern Michigan College - Dowagiac, Michigan
1975	Southwestern Michigan College - Dowagiac, Michigan
1976	CCAC, Allegheny Campus - Pittsburgh, Pennsylvania
1977	CCAC, Allegheny Campus - Pittsburgh, Pennsylvania
1978*	Southwestern Michigan College - Dowagiac, Michigan
1979	New Mexico Junior College - Hobbs, New Mexico
1980	Pima Community College - Tucson, Arizona
1981	Southwestern Michigan College - Dowagiac, Michigan

†National competition no longer sponsored in the activities

CROSS COUNTRY — WOMEN

1976*	CCAC, Allegheny Campus - Pittsburgh, Pennsylvania
1977*	Clackamas Community College - Oregon City, Oregon
1978*	Dodge City Community College - Dodge City, Kansas
1979*	Lane Community College - Eugene, Oregon
1980	Lane Community College - Eugene, Oregon
1981	Golden Valley Luthern College - Minneapolis, Minnesota

DECATHLON

Decathlon was adopted as an invitational championship in 1973 with Mike Kelly of Montgomery Jr. College, Rockville, Md., the winner of the first meet.

1973*	Mike Kelly, Montgomery JC, Rockville, Maryland
1974*	Mike Anderson, Brevard College, Brevard, North Carolina
1975*	John Cecil, Brevard College, Brevard, North Carolina
1976*	Dennis Miller, Northeastern JC, Sterling, Colorado
1977*	Joel Johnson, Lane CC, Eugene, Oregon
1978*	Mike Gardner, Ricks College, Rexburg, Idaho
1979*	Jeff Montpas, Mesa Community College, Mesa, Arizona
1980*	Craig Branham, Pima CC, Tucson, Arizona
1981	Conny Silfver, Ricks College, Rexburg, Idaho
1982	Conny Silfver, Ricks College, Rexburg, Idaho

FIELD HOCKEY — WOMEN

1975*	Bucks County Community College - Newtown, Pennsylvania
1976*	Bucks County Community College - Newtown, Pennsylvania
1977*	Essex Community College - Baltimore County, Maryland
1978*	Essex Community College - Baltimore County, Maryland
1979*	Mitchell College - New London, Connecticut
1980	Essex Community College - Baltimore County, Maryland
1981	Mitchell College - New London, Connecticut

FOOTBALL

Policies were adopted for determining a national football champion of the NJCAA in 1956, and the first game was staged in the Los Angeles Coliseum. Coffeyville College of Kansas defeated Grand Rapids, Mich., for the first title.

1956	Coffeyville College - Coffeyville, Kansas
1957	Texarkana College - Texarkana, Texas
1958	Boise Junior College - Boise Idaho
1959	Northeastern Oklahoma A&M College - Miami, Oklahoma
1960	Tie — Tyler Junior College - Tyler, Texas
	Cameron State Agr. College - Lawton, Oklahoma
1964	Phoenix College, Phoenix, Arizona
1965	Ferrum Junior College - Ferrum, Virginia
1966	Kilgore Junior College - Kilgore, Texas
1967	Northeastern Oklahoma A&M College - Miami, Oklahoma
1968	Ferrum Junior College - Ferrum, Virginia
1969	Northeastern Oklahoma A&M College - Miami, Oklahoma
1970	Fort Scott Community Junior College - Fort Scott, Kansas
1971	Mississippi Gulf Coast JC - Perkinston, Mississippi
1972	Arizona Western College - Yuma, Arizona
1973	Mesa Community College - Mesa, Arizona
1974	Ferrum College - Ferrum, Virginia
1975	Mesa Community College - Mesa, Arizona
1976	Ellsworth Community College - Iowa Falls, Iowa
1977	Ferrum College - Ferrum, Virginia
1978	Iowa Central Community College - Ft. Dodge, Iowa
1979	Ranger Junior College - Ranger, Texas
1980	Northeastern Oklahoma A&M College - Miami, Oklahoma
1981	Butler County Community College - El Dorado, Kansas

GOLF — MEN

Golf became a part of the NJCAA national program in 1959, when the first invitational tournament was conducted at Odessa, Tex., with Odessa Jr. College serving as host. Odessa marched to the first five titles and six of the first seven in this event.

1959*	Odessa College - Odessa, Texas
1960*	Odessa College - Odessa, Texas
1961*	Odessa College - Odessa, Texas
1962*	Odessa College - Odessa, Texas
1963*	Odessa College - Odessa, Texas
1964*	Phoenix College - Phoenix, Arizona
1965*	Odessa College - Odessa, Texas
1966*	Miami-Dade Junior College - Miami, Florida
1967*	Chipola Junior College - Marianna, Florida
1968	St. Petersburg Community College - St. Petersburg, Florida
1969	St. Petersburg Community College - St. Petersburg, Florida
1970	Miami-Dade Junior College-North - Miami, Florida
1971	Brevard Junior College, Cocoa, Florida
1972	Miami-Dade Junior College-North - Miami, Florida
1973	Miami-Dade Junior College-North - Miami, Florida
1974	Broward CC - Ft. Lauderdale, Florida
1975	Miami-Dade Junior College-North - Miami, Florida
1976	Brevard Junior College - Cocoa, Florida
1977	Brevard Junior College - Cocoa, Florida
1978	Brevard Junior College - Cocoa, Florida
1979	Broward Community College - Ft. Lauderdale, Florida
1980	Miami-Dade Junior College-North - Miami, Florida
1981	Chattahootchee Valley St. Comm. College - Phenix City, Al.
1982	Scottsdale Community College - Scottsdale, Arizona

GOLF — WOMEN

1976*	Temple Junior College - Temple, Texas
1977*	Broward Central Community College - Ft. Lauderdale, Florida
1978*	Miami-Dade Junior College-North - Miami, Florida
1979*	Palm Beach Junior College - Palm Beach, Florida
1980	Miami-Dade Junior College-North - Miami, Florida
1981	Miami-Dade Junior College-North - Miami, Florida
1982	Midland College - Midland, Texas

GYMNASTICS — MEN

Gymnastics was adopted as an invitational championship in 1969 with Miami-Dade (North) hosting and winning the first meet.

1949	Los Angeles City College - Los Angeles, California
1950	Los Angeles City College - Los Angeles, California
1969*	Miami-Dade Junior College (North) - Miami, Florida
1970*	Odessa College - Odessa, Texas
1971*	Odessa College - Odessa, Texas
1972*	Odessa College - Odessa, Texas
1973*	Odessa College - Odessa, Texas
1974*	Odessa College - Odessa, Texas
1975*	Odessa College - Odessa, Texas
1976*	Long Beach City College - Long Beach, California
1977*	Odessa College - Odessa, Texas
1978*	Long Beach City College - Long Beach California
1979*	Odessa College - Odessa, Texas
1980*	Long Beach City College - Long Beach, California
1981	Odessa College - Odessa, Texas
1982	Long Beach City College - Long Beach, California

GYMNASTICS — WOMEN

1976*	Linn-Benton Community College - Albany, Oregon
1977*	Jefferson State Community College - Birmingham, Alabama
1978*	Jefferson State Community College - Birmingham, Alabama
1979	Odessa College - Odessa, Texas
1980	Spokane Community College - Spokane, Washington
1981	Spokane Community College - Spokane, Washington
1982	Spokane Community College - Spokane, Washington

ICE HOCKEY

Ice Hockey was adopted as an invitational championship in 1972 with Rainy River hosting the first meet. Itasca State Jr. College was the first champion.

1972*	Itasca State Junior College - Grand Rapids, Minnesota
1973*	Canton Ag. & Tech. College - Canton, New York
1974*	Canton Ag. & Tech. College - Canton, New York
1975*	Canton Ag. & Tech. College - Canton, New York
1976	Canton Ag. & Tech. College - Canton, New York
1977	Rainy River Community College - International Falls, Minn.
1978	Canton Ag. & Tech. College - Canton, New York
1979	Canton Ag. & Tech. College - Canton, New York
1980	College of DuPage - Glen Ellyn, Illinois
1981	Canton Ag. & Tech. College - Canton, New York
1981	Canton Ag. & Tech. College - Canton, New York

JUDO

Judo was adopted as an invitational championship in 1972 with Jackson Community College playing host to the first meet. The first champion was Forest Park Community College.

1972*	Forest Park Community College - St. Louis, Missouri
1973*	Forest Park Community College - St. Louis, Missouri
1974*	Forest Park Community College - St. Louis, Missouri
1975*	Forest Park Community College - St. Louis, Missouri
1976*	Forest Park Community College - St. Louis, Missouri
1977*	Miami-Dade North CC - Miami, Florida
1978*	Miami-Dade North CC - Miami, Florida
1979*	Glendale Community College - Glendale, California
1980	No Tournament
1981	No Tournament

LACROSSE

Lacrosse was added as an invitational championship event in 1969. Nassau Community College of Garden City, N.Y., won the first NJCAA crown.

1970*	Nassau Community College - Garden City, New York
1971*	Nassau Community College - Garden City, New York
1972*	Nassau Community College - Garden City, New York
1973*	Nassau Community College - Garden City, New York
1974*	Nassau Community College - Garden City, New York
1975*	Nassau Community College - Garden City, New York
1976*	Nassau Community College - Garden City, New York
1977*	SUNY at Farmingdale - Farmingdale, New York
1978*	Nassau Community College - Garden City, New York
1979*	Suffolk County Community College - Loch Sheldrake, New York
1980*	Nassau Community College - Garden City, New York
1981	SUNY at Farmingdale - Farmingdale, New York
1982	Nassau Community College - Garden City, New York

MARATHON

1974*	Terry Baker, Hagerstown JC - Hagerstown, Maryland
1975*	John Roscoe, Southwestern Michigan College - Dowagiac, Mich.
1976*	Tim Frye & Robin Holland, Allegheny CCAC - Pittsburgh, Pa.
1977*	Wayne Coffman, Allegheny CCAC - Pittsburgh, Pa.
1978	Malcolm East, Allegheny CCAC - Pittsburgh, Pa.
1979	Dave Magness, Lane CC - Eugene, Oregon
1980	Joe Broze - Golden Valley Lutheran College - Minneapolis, MN
1981	Mark Wazniak - Southwestern Mich. College - Dowagiac, Mich.
1982	Mike Peveto, Brevard College - Brevard, North Carolina

MARATHON — WOMEN

1978	Nina Crampe, Allegheny C.C. - Pittsburgh, PA, Time 3:08.11
1979	Kelly Bowdy, Corning C.C. - Corning, NY, Time 2:59.30
1980	Kelly Bowdy, Corning C.C. - Corning, NY, Time 2:47.28
1981	Mickey Doane, Golden Valley Lutheran - Minneapolis, MN, Time 2:54.58
1982	Mickey Doane, Golden Valley Lutheran - Minneapolis, MN, Time 2:47.22

MARATHON — MEN — TEAM STANDINGS

1976	Allegheny C.C. - Pittsburgh, PA, Team Score 7
1977	Allegheny C.C. - Pittsburgh, PA, Team Score 7
1978	Allegheny C.C. - Pittsburgh, PA, Team Score 9
1979	Southwestern Michigan - Dowagiac, MI, Team Score 8
1980	Golden Valley Lutheran - Minneapolis, MN, Team Score 8
1981	Golden Valley Lutheran - Minneapolis, MN, Team Score 9
1982	Brevard College - Brevard, NC, Team Score 8

RIFLE (POSTAL)

1961*	Cameron State Agricultural College - Lawton, Oklahoma
1962*	Marion Institute - Marion, Alabama
1963*	Alfred Ag. & Tech. Institute - Alfred, New York
1964*	Alfred Ag. & Tech. Institute - Alfred, New York
1965*	Marion Institute - Marion, Alabama
1966*	No Tournament
1967*	Alfred Ag. & Tech. Institute - Alfred, New York
1968*	Miami-Dade Junior College (South) - Miami, Florida
1969*	Marion Institute - Marion, Alabama
1970*	Kemper Military College - Boonville, Missouri
1971*	Kemper Military College - Boonville, Missouri
1972*	Kemper Military College - Boonville, Missouri
1973*	Marion Institute - Marion, Alabama
1974-79*	No Tournament
1980	New Mexico Military Institute - Roswell, New Mexico
1981†	No Tournament

SKIING, ALPINE — MEN

Legislation was enacted in 1969 for the first invitational skiing competition.

1970*	Lees-McRae College - Banner Elk, North Carolina
1971*	SUNY Ag. & Tech. College at Alfred - Alfred, New York
1972*	SUNY Ag. & Tech. College at Alfred - Alfred, New York
1973*	Vermont Technical College - Randolph Center, Vermont
1974*	SUNY Ag. & Tech. College at Alfred - Alfred, New York
1975*	Champlain College - Burlington, Vermont
1976*	Central Oregon Community College - Bend, Oregon
1977*	Paul Smith's College - Paul Smith's, New York
1978*	North Country Community College - Saranac Lake, New York
1979*	Champlain College - Burlington, Vermont
1980*	Vermont Tech. Community College - Randolph Center, Vermont
1981	North Country Community College - Saranac Lake, New York
1982	Champlain College - Burlington, Vermont

SKIING, NORDIC — MEN

1975*	Fulton-Montgomery C.C. - Johnstown, New York
1976*	Central Oregon Community College - Bend, Oregon
1977*	Paul Smith's College - Paul Smith's, New York
1978*	SUNY Ag. & Tech. College at Cobleskill - Cobleskill, New York
1979*	Vermont Tech. College - Randolph Center, Vermont
1980*	SUNY Ag. & Tech. College at Morrisville - Morrisville, New York
1981	Paul Smith's College - Paul Smith's, New York
1982	Vermont Tech. Community College - Randolph Center, Vermont

SKIING, COMBINED — MEN

1978*	SUNY Ag. & Tech. College at Morrisville - Morrisville, New York
1979*	Vermont Tech. College - Randolph Center, Vermont
1980*	Vermont Tech. College - Randolph Center, Vermont
1981	Paul Smith's College - Paul Smith's, New York
1982†	No Event

SKIING, ALPINE — WOMEN

1976*	Central Oregon Community College - Bend Oregon
1977*	Hudson Valley Community College - Troy, New York
1978*	Champlain College - Burlington, Vermont
1979*	Central Oregon Community College - Bend, Oregon
1980*	North Country Community College - Saranac Lake, New York
1981	North Country Community College - Saranac Lake, New York
1982	Tie — North Country Community College - Saranac Lake, New York Champlain College - Burlington, Vermont

SKIING, NORDIC — WOMEN

1980*	Adirondack Community College - Glens Falls, New York
1981	Vermont Technical College - Randolph Center, Vermont
1982	Adirondack Community College - Glens Falls, New York

SKIING, COMBINED — WOMEN

1978*	Champlain College - Burlington, Vermont
1979*	Central Oregon Community College - Bend, Oregon
1980*	North Country Community College - Saranac Lake, New York
1981	North Country Community College - Saranac Lake, New York
1982†	No Event

SOCCER

The first NJCAA National Invitational Soccer Tournament was held in 1961, with Middletown, N.Y., serving as the site. Dean Junior College of Massachusetts took team laurels.

1961*	Dean Junior College - Franklin, Massachusetts
1962*	Mitchell College - New London, Connecticut
1963*	Trenton Junior College - Trenton, New Jersey
1964*	Mitchell College - New London, Connecticut
1965*	Monroe Community College - Rochester, New York
1966*	Nassau Community College - Garden City, New York
1967*	Florissant Valley Community College - St. Louis, Missouri
1968	Mercer County Community College - Trenton, New Jersey
1969	Florissant Valley Community College - St. Louis, Missouri
1970	Florissant Valley Community College - St. Louis, Missouri
1971	Florissant Valley Community College - St. Louis, Missouri
1972	Meremec Community College - St. Louis, Missouri
1973	Florissant Valley Community College - St. Louis, Missouri
1974	Essex Community College - Baltimore County, Maryland
1975	Florissant Valley Community College - St. Louis, Missouri
1976	St. Louis CC at Meramec - St. Louis, Missouri

(Soccer cont'd on next page)

B-9

(Cont'd from previous page)

1977	Ulster County Community College - Stone Ridge, New York
1978	Ulster County Community College - Stone Ridge, New York
1979	Miami-Dade South Comm. College - Miami, Florida
1980	SUNY at Morrisville - Morrisville, New York
1981	Florissant Valley Community College - St. Louis, Missouri

SOFTBALL, FAST PITCH — WOMEN

1977*	Ellsworth Community College - Iowa Falls, Iowa
1978*	Golden West Community College - Huntington Beach, Calif.
1979*	Phoenix College - Pheonix, Arizona
1980*	Erie Community College - Buffalo, New York
1981	Erie Community College - Buffalo, New York
1982	Illinois Central Community College - Peoria, Illinois

SWIMMING — MEN

Swimming was approved for invitational competition at the same time rifle was adopted, 1960, and the first meet was staged in 1961. Bay City Jr. College of Michigan was the team winner. Swimming then was discontinued until 1967.

1961*	Bay City Junior College - Bay City, Michigan
1967*	Henry Ford Community College - Dearborn, Michigan
1968*	Miami-Dade Junior College (North) - Miami, Florida
1969*	Miami-Dade Junior College (North) - Miami, Florida
1970*	Henry Ford Community College - Dearborn, Michigan
1971*	SUNY Ag. & Tech. College at Alfred - Alfred, New York
1972*	SUNY Ag. & Tech. College at Alfred - Alfred, New York
1973	SUNY Ag. & Tech. College at Alfred - Alfred, New York
1974	SUNY Ag. & Tech. College at Alfred - Alfred, New York
1975	Indian River Community College - Fort Pierce, Florida
1976	Indian River Community College - Fort Pierce, Florida
1977	Indian River Community College - Fort Pierce, Florida
1978	Indian River Community College - Fort Pierce, Florida
1979	Indian River Community College - Fort Pierce, Florida
1980	Indian River Community College - Fort Pierce, Florida
1981	Indian River Community College - Fort Pierce, Florida
1982	Indian River Community College - Fort Pierce, Florida

SWIMMING — WOMEN

1976*	Indian River Community College - Fort Pierce, Florida
1977	Indian River Community College - Fort Pierce, Florida
1978	Indian River Community College - Fort Pierce, Florida
1979	Indian River Community College - Fort Pierce, Florida
1980	Daytona Beach Community College - Daytona Beach, Florida
1981	Daytona Beach Community College - Daytona Beach, Florida
1982	Daytona Beach Community College - Daytona Beach, Florida

TENNIS — MEN

Tennis got its start with the NJCAA in 1948, but it was discontinued after three years until 1959. In the first invitational meet, Long Beach City College was the team winner, and in the inaugural meet of the "second period" (1959), Pratt Junior College won top honors at Rochester, Minn.

1948*	Long Beach City College - Long Beach, California
1949*	Modesto Junior College - Modesto, California
1950*	Modesto Junior College - Modesto, California
1959*	Pratt Junior College - Pratt, Kansas
1960*	Tie — Lubbock Christian College - Lubbock, Texas
	Tarleton State College - Stephenville, Texas
1961*	Pratt Junior College - Pratt, Kansas
1962*	Schreiner Institute - Kerrville, Texas
1963*	Tie — Odessa College - Odessa, Texas
	Central Florida Junior College - Ocala, Florida
1964*	Odessa College - Odessa, Texas
1965*	Henry Ford Community College - Dearborn, Michigan
1966*	Miami-Dade Junior College (North) - Miami, Florida
1967*	Miami-Dade Junior College (North) - Miami, Florida
1968	Odessa Junior College - Odessa, Texas
1969	Miami-Dade Junior College (North) - Miami, Florida
1970	Wingate College - Wingate, North Carolina
1971	Wingate College - Wingate, North Carolina
1972	Mesa Community College - Mesa, Arizona
1973	Central Texas College - Killeen, Texas
1974	Central Texas College - Killeen, Texas
1975	Odessa College - Odessa, Texas
1976	Odessa College - Odessa, Texas
1977	Central Texas College - Killeen, Texas
1978	3-way Tie — Odessa College - Odessa, Texas
	Midland College - Midland, Texas
	New Mexico Military Institute - Roswell, NM
1979	Odessa College - Odessa, Texas
1980	Tyler Junior College - Tyler, Texas
1981	Central Florida Community College - Ocala, Florida
1982	Seminole Community College - Sanford, Florida

TENNIS — WOMEN

1975*	Midland College - Midland, Texas
1976	Midland College - Midland, Texas
1977	Odessa College - Odessa, Texas
1978	Odessa College - Odessa, Texas
1979	Odessa College - Odessa, Texas
1980	Palm Beach Junior College - Palm Beach, Florida
1981	Tie — Midland Community College - Midland, Texas
	Schreiner Junior College - Kerrville, Texas
1982	Indian River Community College - Fort Pierce, Florida

INDOOR TRACK AND FIELD — MEN

Indoor track and field was added on an invitational basis in 1973. Essex County College took honors at the first meet.

1973	Essex County College - Newark, New Jersey
1974	Mesa Community College - Mesa, Arizona
1975	Essex County College - Newark, New Jersey
1976	Essex County College - Newark, New Jersey
1977	Essex County College - Newark, New Jersey
1978	CCAC, Allegheny Campus - Pittsburgh, Pennsylvania
1979	New Mexico Junior College - Hobbs, New Mexico
1980	New Mexico Junior College - Hobbs, New Mexico
1981	Odessa College - Odessa, Texas
1982	Odessa College - Odessa, Texas

INDOOR TRACK AND FIELD — WOMEN

1980	Barton County Community College - Great Bend, Kansas
1981	Eastern Oklahoma State College - Wilburton, Oklahoma
1982	Santa Fe Community College - Gainesville, Florida

OUTDOOR TRACK AND FIELD — MEN

First event sponsored by the NJCAA was track back in 1939. It was run at Sacramento with only California schools competing. The next year, however, teams from other Western states competed, and it soon developed into a national affair.

1939	Compton College - Compton, California
1940	Los Angeles City College - Los Angeles, California
1941	Sacramento Junior College - Sacramento, California
1942	Sacramento Junior College - Sacramento, California
1943-45	World War II — No Competition
1946	Los Angeles City College - Los Angeles, California
1947	Compton College - Compton, California
1948	Los Angeles City College - Los Angeles, California
1949	Compton College - Compton, California
1950	Compton College - Compton, California
1951	Compton College - Compton, California
1952	Victoria Junior College - Victoria, Texas
1953	Victoria Junior College - Victoria, Texas
1954	Hutchinson Junior College - Hutchinson, Kansas
1955	Victoria Junior College - Victoria, Texas
1956	Victoria Junior College - Victoria, Texas
1957	Victoria Junior College - Victoria, Texas
1958	Victoria Junior College - Victoria, Texas
1959	Hutchinson Junior College - Hutchinson, Kansas
1960	Coffeyville College - Coffeyville, Kansas
1961	Howard County Junior College - Big Spring, Texas
1962	Howard County Junior College - Big Spring, Texas
1963	Howard County Junior College - Big Spring, Texas
1964	Phoenix College - Phoenix, Arizona
1965	Phoenix College - Phoenix, Arizona
1966	Phoenix College - Phoenix, Arizona
1967	Howard County Junior College - Big Spring, Texas
1968	Mesa Community College - Mesa, Arizona
1969	Mesa Community College - Mesa, Arizona
1970	Mesa Community College - Mesa, Arizona
1971	New Mexico Junior College - Hobbs, New Mexico
1972	Essex County College - Newark, New Jersey
1973	Mesa Community College - Mesa, Arizona
1974	Mesa Community College - Mesa, Arizona
1975	Mesa Community College - Mesa, Arizona
1976	Essex County College - Newark, New Jersey
1977	Essex County College - Newark, New Jersey
1978	Essex County College - Newark, New Jersey
1979	New Mexico Junior College - Hobbs, New Mexico
1980	Mesa Community College - Mesa, Arizona
1981	Odessa College - Odessa, Texas
1982	Odessa College - Odessa, Texas

OUTDOOR TRACK AND FIELD — WOMEN

1976*	Dodge City Community College - Dodge City, Kansas
1977*	Flathead Valley Community College - Kalispell, Montana
1978	Clackamas Community College - Oregon City, Oregon
1979	Mesa Community College - Mesa, Arizona
1980	Barton County Community College - Great Bend, Kansas
1981	Mt. Hood Community College - Gresham, Oregon
1982	Eastern Oklahoma State College - Wilburton, Oklahoma

VOLLEYBALL — MEN

1974*	Kellogg Community College - Battle Creek, Michigan
1975*	Kellogg Community College - Battle Creek, Michigan
1976*	Kellogg Community College - Battle Creek, Michigan
1977*	Kellogg Community College - Battle Creek, Michigan
1978-1981†	No Tournament

VOLLEYBALL — WOMEN

1974*	Alvin Junior College - Alvin, Texas
1975	San Antonio Junior College - San Antonio, Texas
1976	St. Louis CC at Florissant Valley - St. Louis, Missouri
1977	Mesa Community College - Mesa, Arizona
1978	Kellogg Community College - Battle Creek, Michigan
1979	Kellogg Community College - Battle Creek, Michigan
1980	Kellogg Community College - Battle Creek, Michigan
1981	Scottsdale Community College - Scottsdale, Arizona

WRESTLING

Wrestling was introduced to the NJCAA championship program in 1960 with Lamar Jr. College winning the first event at Farmingdale, N.Y.

1960*	Lamar Junior College - Lamar, Colorado
1961*	Lamar Junior College - Lamar, Colorado
1962*	Lamar Junior College - Lamar, Colorado
1963*	Lamar Junior College - Lamar, Colorado
1964*	Tie — Northeastern Junior College - Sterling, Colorado
	Joliet Junior College - Joliet, Illinois
1965*	Lamar Junior College - Lamar, Colorado
1966*	Northeastern Junior College - Sterling, Colorado
1967	Northeastern Junior College - Sterling, Colorado
1968	Phoenix College - Phoenix, Arizona
1969	Phoenix College - Phoenix, Arizona
1970	Muskegon Community College - Muskegon, Michigan
1971	Clackamas Community College - Oregon City, Oregon
1972	SUNY Ag. & Tech. College at Farmingdale - Farmingdale, N.Y.
1973	North Iowa Community College - Mason City, Iowa
1974	North Idaho College - Coeur d'Alene, Idaho
1975	North Idaho College - Coeur d'Alene, Idaho
1976	Cuyahoga CC, Western Campus - Parma, Ohio
1977	Triton College - River Grove, Illinois
1978	North Idaho College - Coeur d'Alene, Idaho
1979	Lakeland Community College - Mentor, Ohio
1980	Lakeland Community College - Mentor, Ohio
1981	Iowa Central Community College - Fort Dodge, Iowa
1982	North Idaho College - Coeur d'Alene, Idaho

APPENDIX C

Geographic Locations of California Community Colleges

Source: Chancellor's Office, California Community Colleges, Sacramento, California. Gerald C. Hayward, Chancellor.

C-2

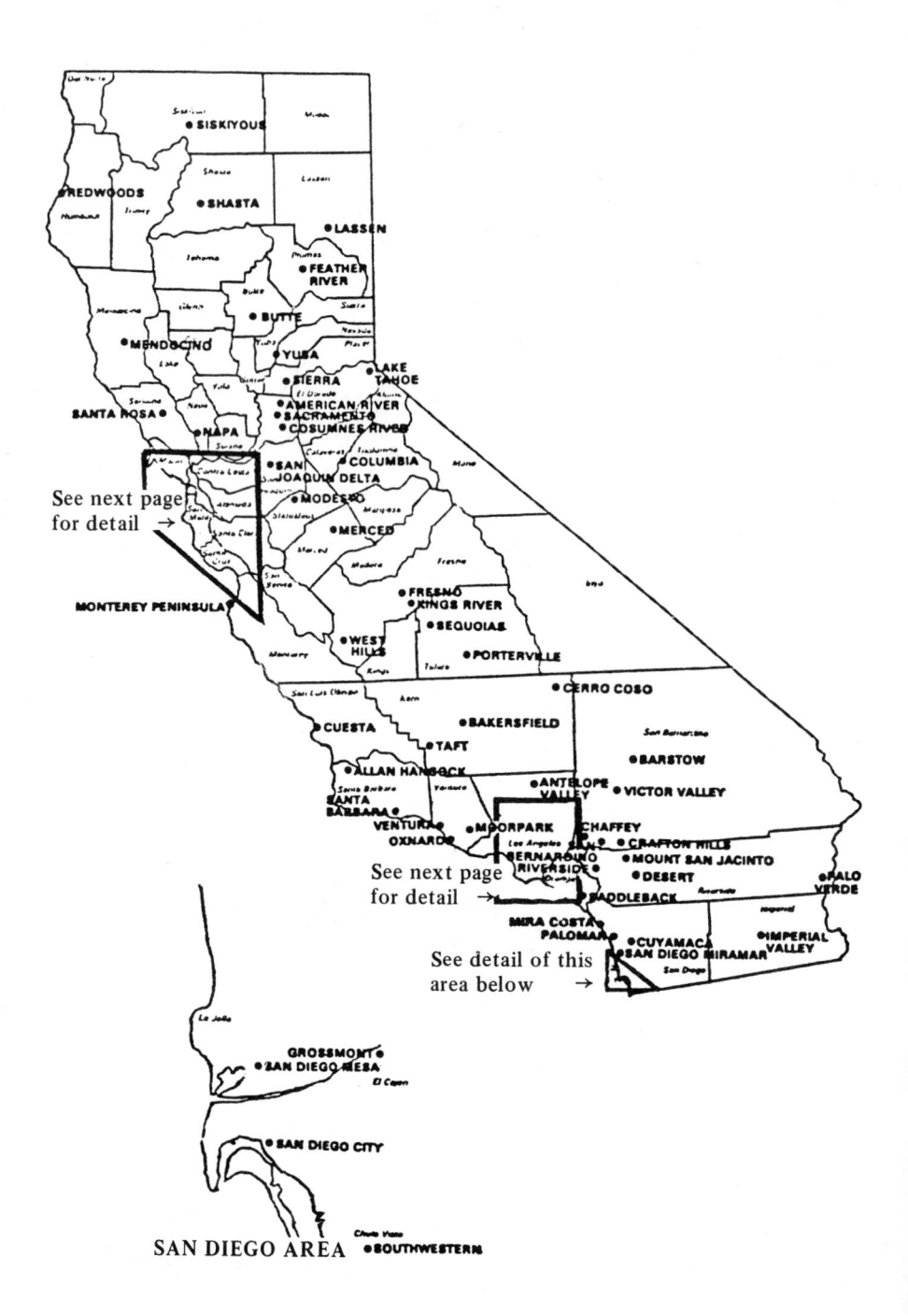

SAN FRANCISCO BAY AREA

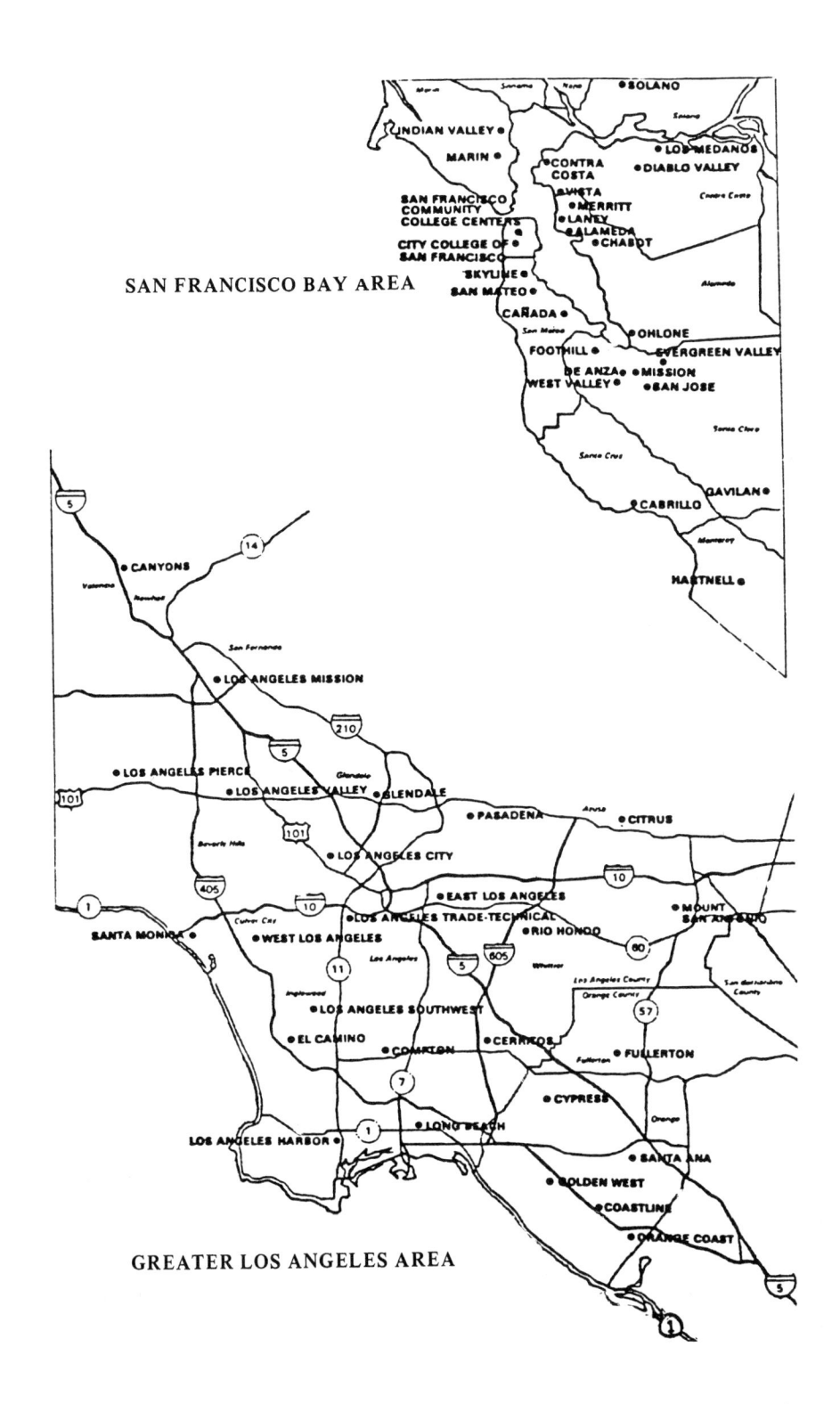

GREATER LOS ANGELES AREA

APPENDIX D

California Community College Champions

Source: California Association of Community Colleges, Walter Rilliet, Director, 15 March 1983.

BASEBALL

Year	Champion	Coach	Runner-up
1950	Pasadena	John Thurman	Santa Rosa
1951	Sacramento	Jack Warner	El Camino
1952	Santa Rosa	Bob Mastin	Santa Ana
1953	Sacramento City	Jack Warner	Long Beach City
1954	Long Beach City	Joe Hicks	West Contra Costa
1955	East Contra Costa	Gene Corr	Orange Coast
1956	Orange Coast	Wendell Pickens	Coalinga
1957	College of the Sequoias	Ron Taylor	San Diego City
1958	Coalinga	Dave Rankin	Citrus
1959	Stockton College	Larry Kentera	San Diego City
1960	Orange Coast	Wendell Pickens	Oakland College
1961	Fresno City	Len Bourdet	Cerritos
1962	Fresno City	Len Bourdet	Orange Coast
1963	Fresno City	Len Bourdet	Long Beach City
1964	Mt. San Antonio	John Arambie	Vallejo College
1965	Mt. San Antonio	Ron Squire	Allan Hancock
1966	Cerritos	Wally Kincaid	San Francisco City
1967	Pasadena	Ron Robinson	Sacramento City
1968	Long Beach City	Joe Hicks	Sacramento City
1969	Long Beach City	Joe Hicks	College of San Mateo
1970	Cerritos	Wally Kincaid	College of Sequoias
1971	Canada	Lyman Ashley	Los Angeles City
1972	Fresno City	Len Bourdet	Long Beach City
1973	Cerritos	Wally Kincaid	College of San Mateo
1974	Cerritos	Wally Kincaid	San Diego City
1975	Cerritos	Wally Kincaid	Citrus College
1976	Long Beach City	Bob Myers	Los Angeles Harbor
1977	Diablo Valley	Ernie Gecaci	Cerritos
1978	Los Angeles Harbor	Jim O'Brien	College of San Mateo
1979	Cerritos	Wally Kincaid	San Jose City
1980	Orange Coast	Mike Mayne	Los Angeles Valley
1981	College of the Canyons	Mike Gillespie	Los Angeles Harbor
1982	Los Angeles Valley*	Dave Snow	

Special Thanks to:

Bob Myers – Associate Commissioner C.C.C.B.C.A.
Vivian Myers – Ticket Director
Fred Strobel – Blair Field Director
Wally Kincaid – Athletic Director, Cerritos College
Gordy Douglas – Baseball Coach, Cerritos College
Brent Becker – Sports Information Director
Lee Stevens – C.C.J.C.A. Baseball Representative
Bakersfield College Duplicating Service
Diane Lobre – Athletic Department, Bakersfield College

*George Goff, Athletic Director, Los Angeles Valley College, 18 March 1983.

D-2

BASKETBALL — MEN

Year	Champion	Runner-up*	Tournament Site
1952	Ventura	College of the Sequoias	College of the Sequoias
1953	College of the Sequoias	Fullerton	Long Beach City College
1954	Fullerton	Grant Tech	Sacramento City College
1955	Fresno	Mt. San Antonio	Fresno City College
1956	Los Angeles Harbor	Antelope Valley	Fullerton Junior College
1957	Allan Hancock	Vallejo College	San Jose City College
1958	Long Beach City	Oakland College	Bakersfield College
1959	Long Beach City	Santa Ana	Long Beach City College
1960	San Jose City	Fullerton	San Jose City College
1961	Fullerton	San Jose	Allan Hancock
1962	San Francisco City	Citrus	Orange Coast College
1963	Fresno City	San Diego City	American River
1964	Riverside City	Allan Hancock	Mt. San Antonio
1965	Riverside City	Fresno City	College of San Mateo
1966	Riverside City	San Francisco City	Bakersfield College
1967	Pasadena	Long Beach City	Allan Hancock
1968	Cerritos	Pasadena	Cerritos
1969	Pasadena	Imperial Valley	Fresno CC (Selland Arena)
1970	Compton	Long Beach City	Long Beach City
1971	Long Beach City	Cerritos	Allan Hancock
1972	Santa Monica	Laney	Ventura College
1973	Compton	Long Beach City	Ventura College
1974*	Allan Hancock	Long Beach City	Fresno CC (Selland Arena)
1975*	Los Angeles Harbor	Cerritos	Fresno CC (Selland Arena)
1976*	Long Beach City	Compton	Fresno CC (Selland Arena)
1977*	Cypress	Santa Barbara City	Fresno CC (Selland Arena)
1978*	Bakersfield	San Francisco City	Long Beach Arena
1979*	Orange Coast	Saddleback	Fullerton State
1980*	Cypress	Chabot	Cal Poly Pomona
1981*	El Camino	San Francisco City	Fullerton State
1982*	College of the Sequoias	Compton	Santa Clara University
1983**	Cerritos	Pasadena	Santa Clara

DIVISION II

Year	Champion	Runner-up	Tournament Site
1973*	Barstow	Menlo Park	Ventura College
1974*	Menlo Park	Merced	Fresno (Selland Arena)
1975*	Butte	Skyline	Fresno (Selland Arena)
1976*	Butte	Menlo Park	Fresno (Selland Arena)
1977*	Skyline	Mt. San Jacinto	Fresno (Selland Arena)
1978*	Merced	Menlo	Long Beach Arena
1979*	Merced	Butte	Fullerton State
1980*	Barstow	Merced	Cal Poly Pomona
1981*	Barstow	Skyline	Fullerton State
1982*	Skyline	Shasta	Santa Clara University
1983**	Shasta	Marin	Santa Clara

Vokes, Lee Samuel, "A Historical Study of the California Junior College State Athletic Committee: Years 1946-1972," Ph.D. dissertation, United States International University, 1973, p. 321.
*Rilliet, Walter, Director, California Association of Community Colleges, Sacramento, California, 15 March 1983.

BASKETBALL — WOMEN

Historically, northern and southern California Women's basketball is played in different seasons. Therefore playoffs are held in each region to determine the respective champions. One state championship was held in 1978. Beginning in 1984, the seasons will be aligned and state championships will be held.

Year	Champion
1978	Fullerton College

Riley, Collen, Women's Basketball Coach, Fullerton College, Fullerton, CA, April 25, 1984.

CROSS COUNTRY — MEN

Year	Site	Champion	Score
1964	Mt. San Antonio	San Diego Mesa	57
1965	American River	Grossmont	63
1966	Pierce	Los Angeles Pierce	76
1967	Fresno	Pasadena	71
1968	Southwestern	Los Angeles Valley	50
1969	Fresno	Los Angeles Valley	39
1970	Moorpark	Los Angeles Valley	48
1971*	Sierra	Santa Ana	48 (small)
			54 (large)
1972*	College of the Canyons	Santa Ana	51 (small)
		Grossmont	46 (large)

*Divided into small and large college divisions.

Vokes, Lee Samuel, "A Historical Study of the California Junior College State Athletic Committee: Years 1946-1972," Ph.D. dissertation, United States International University, 1973, p. 331.

CROSS COUNTRY — WOMEN

Statewide competition began in 1978.

Year	State Champions
1978	West Valley
1979	West Valley
1980	Orange Coast
1981	Orange Coast
1982	Orange Coast
1983	Mira Costa

Carnett, Jim, Sports Information Director, Orange Coast College, Costa Mesa, CA, May 2, 1984.

FOOTBALL*
STATE PLAY-OFFS

Large Colleges:

1967	Fullerton	41	American River	0
1968	Fresno City	16	East Los Angeles	7
1969	Fresno City	28	Fullerton	9
1970	College of Sequoias	24	Fullerton	21
1971	El Camino	48	Santa Rosa	14
1972	Fresno City College	21	Pasadena	7

Small Colleges:

1967	Hartnell College	40	Reedley	21
1968	College of the Redwoods	51	Coalinga	28
1969	Yuba College	24	Saddleback	13
1970	College of the Redwoods	41	Reedley	28
1971	Reedley College	20	Hartnell	10
1972	College of the Redwoods	41	West Hills	21

*The bowl games are listed chronologically.

POTATO BOWL

1948	Santa Barbara	46	Willamette	7
1949	Boise	25	Taft	7
1950	Olympic	14	Bakersfield	7
1951	Boise	34	Bakersfield	14
1952	Bakersfield	25	Fresno	19
1953	Pasadena	28	West Contra Costa	13
1954	Compton	7	Boise	6
1955	Bakersfield	33	Wenatchee	6
1956	Stockton	20	Orange Coast	12
1957	Bakersfield	28	Boise	13
1958	Bakersfield	7	Riverside	0
1959	Phoenix	46	Coalinga	14
1960	Bakersfield	50	Cerritos	28
1961	Glendale	28	Riverside	14
1962	Long Beach	66	Contra Costa	8
1963	Bakersfield	48	Glendale	6
1964	Fullerton	24	Bakersfield	13
1965	Cerritos	41	Boise	12
1966	Fullerton	32	Fresno	12
1967	North All-Stars	23	South All-Stars	7
1972	Fresno	21	Pasadena	7
1973*	Fresno	10	L.A. City	10 (Tie)
1974*	East L.A.	33	San Jose	14
1975*	L.A. Valley	27	Fresno	9
1976**	Bakersfield	27	College of Sequoias	8
1977*	Pasadena	24	College of Sequoias	21
1978*	Pasadena	31	College of Sequoias	28
1979*	Bakersfield	20	Taft	9
1980*	Taft	38	Chabot	12
1981*	Bakersfield	27	Taft	13
1982*	Taft	32	Mt. San Antonio	30
1983*	Fullerton	28	Taft	7

(See following page for information about sources of the Potato Bowl games statistics and other historical data.)

D-5

Sources:
Information without asterisk —
  Copyright, 1982. Reprinted by permission.
  Vokes, Lee Samuel, "A Historical Study of the California Junior College State Athletic Committee: Years 1946-1972," Ph.D. dissertation, United States International University, 1973, pp. 313-318.
Information with single asterisks —
  Copyright, 1984. Reprinted by permission.
  Oldershaw, Gene, Co-general Chairman and Managing Director, Potato Bowl Committee, Bakersfield, CA.
**The Junior Rose Bowl was reinstated in 1976. After defeating College of the Sequoias 27-8 in the Potato Bowl, Bakersfield defeated Ellsworth (IA) 19-14 to win the Junior Rose Bowl Championship.

The annual East-West (NCAA) football game is sponsored by five Shrine Temples. Unlike that level of involvement, the Potato Bowl is sponsored by the Shriner's Club of Bakersfield, CA. The proceeds are donated as a charity for the benefit of the Shriner's Hospital for Crippled Children. Since the inception of the Potato Bowl in 1948, they have contributed in excess of one-half million dollars.

GOLD DUST BOWL

1948	San Francisco City College	20	Chaffey	7
1949	San Diego City College	32	Menlo College	14
1950	Santa Rosa	41	LaSalle-Peru (Illinois)	6
1951	Yuba College	14	Olympic Jr. College	14
1952	San Bernardino Valley	15	Vallejo	6

OLIVE BOWL

1948	Visalia	20	Fresno	0
1949	LaVerne College	33	Coalinga	0
1950	LaVerne College	38	Porterville	20
1951	College of Sequoias	19	Porterville	13
1952	College of Sequoias	37	Reedley	13
1953	College of Sequoias	27	LaVerne College	12
1954	Antelope Valley	6	College of Sequoias	0
1955	Porterville	39	Citrus	18
1956	Porterville	39	Citrus	26
1957	Stockton	33	Reedley	0
1958	Porterville	33	Shasta College	20
1959	College of Sequoias	22	Sierra College	0
1960	College of Sequoias	39	Palo Verde	12
1961	College of Sequoias	36	Oceanside-Carlsbad	0

ORANGE SHOW BOWL
(Later changed to Elks Bowl)

1953	Yuba City	34	San Bernardino Valley	13
1954	Antelope Valley	0	Mt. San Antonio	0
1955	Los Angeles Valley	20	Taft	14
1956	Antelope Valley	19	Coalinga	18
1957	Santa Ana	20	San Diego	13
1958	Stockton	19	Mt. San Antonio	12
1959	San Bernardino Valley	38	Pierce	14
1960	Hancock	12	Riverside	7
1961	Sacramento	27	Fullerton	7
1962	Orange Coast	23	Flendale	16
1963	Long Beach	21	Mt. San Antonio	14
1964	San Diego	28	Orange Coast	24
1965	Santa Ana	18	Ventura	16
1966	San Diego Mesa	12	San Bernardino Valley	0

FISH BOWL

| 1951 | San Bernardino Valley | 48 | Los Angeles Harbor | 7 |

ALFALFA BOWL

1955	Yuba City	19	Antelope Valley	6
1956	Los Angeles Valley	13	Santa Monica	12
1957	Glendale	44	Oceanside	0
1958	Long Beach	28	Antelope Valley	8
1959	Hartnell	19	Antelope Valley	0
1960	Oceanside	26	Taft	12

LUMBER BOWL

| 1956 | Everett JC (Washington) | 39 | Shasta | 6 |
| 1957 | Shasta | 20 | Olympic Jr. College | 19 |

SEQUOIA BOWL

1958	Fresno City	27	Sacramento City	19
1959	Monterey Peninsula	26	Stockton City	21
1960	Fresno City	22	Hartnell	16
1961	Hartnell	20	Santa Barbara City	16
1962	Reedley	21	Monterey Peninsula	12

LETTUCE BOWL

1961	San Francisco City	22	Monterey	14
1962	Sacramento City	44	Hartnell	6
1963	Hartnell	13	Santa Rosa	7
1964	Fresno City	22	Monterey	14
1965	Monterey Peninsula	30	Foothill	14
1966	Hartnell	30	Sierra	14

PRUNE BOWL

1961	San Mateo City	6	Hancock	0
1962	Foothill College	41	Santa Rosa	6
1965	San Francisco City	40	Long Beach City	20
1966	Laney College	35	San Francisco City	13

LIONS BOWL

1963	Coalinga College	41	Santa Barbara	19
1965	Los Angeles Harbor	41	Reedley College	16
1966	Los Angeles Harbor	47	Coalinga	13

EMPIRE BOWL

| 1965 | College of Sequoias | 22 | Shasta College | 13 |
| 1966 | Diablo Valley | 14 | Merced College | 7 |

JUNIOR ROSE BOWLS

Year	Teams and Scores		Attendance
1946	Compton (CA) – 19	Kilgore (TX) – 0	43,000
1947	Chaffey (CA) – 39	Cameron (OK) – 26	33,650
1948	Compton (CA) – 48	Duluth (MN) – 14	50,638
1949	Little Rock (AR) – 25	Santa Ana (CA) – 19	33,942
1950	Long Beach (CA) – 33	Boise (ID) – 13	37,500
1951	Pasadena (CA) – 28	Tyler (TX) – 26	41,971
1952	Bacone (OK) – 20	Hartnell (CA) – 20	35,392
1953	Bakersfield (CA) – 13	N.E. Oklahoma A&M (OK) – 6	50,358
1954	Hinds (MS) – 13	El Camino (CA) – 13	54,623
1955	Compton (CA) – 22	Jones (MS) – 13	57,123
1956	Arlington (TX) – 20	Compton (CA) – 13	37,149
1957	Arlington (TX) – 21	Cerritos (CA) – 12	36,008
1958	Santa Monica (CA) – 30	N.E. Oklahoma A&M (OK) – 12	50,797
1959	Bakersfield (CA) – 36	Del Mar (TX) – 14	46,923
1960	Long Beach (CA) – 38	Tyler (TX) – 16	38,064
1961	Cameron (OK) – 28	Bakersfield (CA) – 20	50,871
1962	Santa Ana (CA) – 20	Columbia Basin (WA) – 0	41,709
1963	Orange Coast (CA) – 21	N.E. Oklahoma A&M (OK) – 0	42,297
1964	Long Beach (CA) – 28	Cameron (OK) – 6	45,576
1965	Fullerton (CA) – 20	Henderson (TX) – 15	50,098
1966	Henderson (TX) – 40	Pasadena (CA) – 13	40,045
1967	West Texas State (TX) – 35	Valley State (CA) – 13	23,814
	DISCONTINUED BUT REESTABLISHED IN 1976		
1976*	Bakersfield (CA) – 29	Ellsworth (IA) – 14	30,000
1977	Pasadena (CA) – 38	Jones (MS) – 9	15,000+
	DISCONTINUED		

*"Junior Rose Bowl Football Classic December 10," *California Community Junior College Association News* (Sacramento), Vol. 22, No. 8, May 1977.

**Lloyd Messersmith, Past Director, California Community and Junior College Association, Sacramento, California, 3 December 1982.

GOLF — MEN

In 1950, Long Beach hosted the National Junior College Golf Tournament at Virginia Country Club. Ten schools entered four-man teams. The results were:

1. John Muir College
2. Santa Monica
3. Modesto
4. Long Beach C. C.] Tie
4. Phoenix
6. Van Port Extension Center, Portland, OR
7. San Mateo
8. Los Angeles C. C.
9. El Camino
10. Compton

Medalist: Bud Holscher, Santa Monica

In 1951, the first California State Junior College Championship was hosted at Stanford University Golf Course, with the following results:

1. Modesto
2. San Mateo
3. Santa Monica] Tie
3. John Muir
5. Long Beach C. C.
6. San Francisco
7. El Camino
8. Sacramento
9. Los Angeles C. C.
10. Hartnell
11. Menlo
12. Compton

Medalist: Dick Kayser, Contra Costa] Tie, Kayser won playoff
— Blevins, John Muir

In 1952, at Montebello, the results were:

1. San Mateo
2. Modesto
3. John Muir
4. Long Beach C. C.
5. El Camino
6. Orange Coast
7. Fullerton
8. Pasadena

Medalist: Marvin Nischan, El Camino
Ronald Miller, Santa Ana] 3-way Tie, Nischan won playoff
Ruben Solario, Modesto

Year	Results	Site
1953	1. Pasadena	Pebble Beach
	Medalist: John Tate, Long Beach C. C.	
1954	No information.	
1955	1. Modesto	Haggin Oaks and
	2. El Camino	Del Paso
	3. San Mateo	
	Medalist: John McMullin, Modesto	
1956	1. San Mateo	Bakersfield C.C.
	2. Long Beach C. C.	and Stockdale
	3. Santa Monica	
	Medalist: Tommy Jacobs, East L.A.	
1957	1. San Bernardino	Mission Valley
	2. Santa Monica	and La Jolla
	3. Menlo	
	Medalist: ---- Self, San Bernardino	
1958	1. Orange Coast	San Jose and
	2. Bakersfield	Almaden
	3. College of Sequoias	
	Medalist: ---- Wagner, Napa	
1959	1. San Mateo	Belmont and
	2. Santa Monica	-Fort Washington
	3. Santa Ana	
	Medalist: Dennis Murphy, Orange Coast	

Year	Results	Site
1960	1. San Mateo 2. College of Sequoias 3. Stockton Medalist: Felix Claveron, Stockton	Mesa Verde and Santa Ana Country Club
1961	1. San Mateo 2. Phoenix 3. San Diego Medalist: Ken Kirkpatrick, San Diego	Castlewood Country Club
1962	1. San Mateo 2. Menlo 3. Pasadena Medalist: Tom Brigham, San Mateo	Bakersfield and Stockdale
1963	1. El Camino 2. San Mateo 3. Orange Coast Medalist: Dick Lotz, San Mateo	Torrey Pines Country Club *(Start of 5-man teams)*
1964	1. L.A. Valley 2. Chabot 3. Santa Ana Medalist: Ron Carrudo, Chabot	Monterey Peninsula
1965	1. Santa Ana 2. L.A. Valley 3. Fresno Medalist: Rian McNally, Chabot	Visalia and Kings River
1966	1. College of the Desert 2. Fullerton 3. El Camino Medalist: Greg McHatton, Fullerton	Fallbrook and Pala Mesa
1967	1. College of Sequoias 2. San Mateo 3. Mira Costa Medalist: Mike Ray, San Mateo 　　　　　Jim Jensen, Foothill] 3-way Tie, Ray won playoff 　　　　　Butch Bayhouse, West Valley	Monterey Peninsula
1968	1. San Jose 2. El Camino 3. American River Medalist: Ray Arinno, American River	Santa Maria and Vandenberg Village
1969	1. El Camino 2. Fullerton 3. Menlo Medalist: Forrest Fezler, San Jose	Fallbrook and San Luis Rey
1970	1. Fullerton 2. Monterey 3. San Joaquin Medalist: Mike Reehl, Orange Coast	Rancho Canada
1971	1. Long Beach C. C. 2. Menlo 3. El Camino Medalist: Don Baker, El Camino	Mission Viejo & El Niguel *(Start of 6-man teams)*
1972	1. Long Beach 2. El Camino 3. Golden West Medalist: Mark Pfeil, El Camino	Rancho Canada
1973	1. Long Beach 2. Santa Barbara 3. San Jose Medalist: Roger Calvin, Santa Ana] Tie, Calvin won playoff 　　　　　Tom Pera, San Jose	Cottonwood

Year	Results	Site
1974	1. El Camino 2. Menlo 3. Santa Monica Medalist: ---- Johnson, Menlo	Bidwell Park and Table Mountain
1975	1. Chabot	
1976	1. Monterey	Rancho Canada
1977	1. Grossmont	Rancho Canada
1978	1. Monterey ⎤ Tie 1. Canada ⎦	Rancho Canada
1979	1. Bakersfield 2. Citrus	Bakersfield Country Club
1980	1. Menlo	De la Viega and Pasatiempo
1981	1. Moorpark 2. Cerritos 3. De Anza Medalist: Tim Thelan, DeAnza	Torrey Pines
1982	1. San Jose 2. College of Sequoias 3. Saddleback Medalist: Kerry Gritten, College of Sequoias	Rancho Canada
1983	1. Saddleback 2. Mt. San Antonio 2. Citrus 2. L.A. Mission Medalist: Andrew Whitacre, Monterye	

SWIMMING

MEN'S STATE MEET HISTORY
by Jack Flanagan
(Swimming, Waterpolo and Diving Coach, Diablo Valley College)

On April 23 and 24, 1948, the first "National Junior College Swimming and Diving Championships" were held at Compton College. Ed Holston, the swim coach at Compton since 1936, was the meet host; his team placed 8th in the meet. This first meet had 9 events and was dominated by Fullerton which scored 71 points to 2nd place Glendale's 32. During the years 1948-1950, teams from outside California were also invited to participate; thus the meet was referred to as a "national" meet.

Prior to 1948 Northern and Southern California Championships only were held. The first Northern California Championship was held in 1947 and was won by Stockton coached by Bill Antilla. His teams dominated the north until 1957. In Southern California the first sectional championship was in 1930 and was won by Long Beach City College. Fullerton started to gain power and dominated the Southern California Championships under the guidance of Jimmy Smith from 1936 to 1955.

In the first National Meet in 1948, Fullerton handily overpowered all opponents. In that first championship there were four outstanding competitors who are presently coaching swimming in the California Community Colleges. Three of them — Ernie Polte (Fullerton), Monty Nitzkowski (Long Beach), Bob Brown (Chabot) — swam on the Fullerton team; Gene Nyquist (West Valley) swam on the Stockton team (now San Joaquin Delta). According to the April 30, 1948 edition of the Fullerton Junior College newspaper, The Hornet, the lead story on the sports page was "Hornet Swimmers Capture National Title; 'Jackets' ' 71 Points Double Score of Nearest Foe." We quote from the article: "Walking away with 6 out of 9 first places, Fullerton JC Mermen made a brilliant showing in the National JC swimming championships by scoring more than twice the points of the nearest team in the meet held at Compton College last Saturday night. One of the highlighted races of the evening came when Ernest Polte, Hornet

Olympic material, took a narrow victory over Brown of Glendale. Frank Poucher reigned king in the backstroke field defeating Nyquist of Stockton JC and adding more points toward a Fullerton victory. Bob Brown, ace Fullerton free styler, bettered the field in the 200 and scored an impressive win over teammates Ed Illsley and Bill Gregg, who followed close behind. The Hornet relay squads captured both events without too much competition and received trophies in addition to medals for these races."

Ernie Polte won the 200 Breast in 2:36.1 and was the Breaststroker on the winning 300 Medley Relay (Back, Breast, Fly, Free) for Fullerton's 3:04.8. Gene Nyquist was the lead Backstroker with a 100 split of 1:04.8 for the Stockton team which placed second in that event; he was second in the 150-yard Back in 1:46.0. Bob Brown won the 200-yard Free in 2:24.0 and was also a member of the winning 400 Free Relay (3:46.2) which was close to National record time. Monty Nitzkowski was third in the 200 Breast at 2:40.3. Gene Nyquist's 150 Back race turned into a gigantic controversy because of an error in timing and judging. Nyquist, who qualified 5th for the finals and placed 2nd in an obvious two-man race between him and Fullerton's Frank Poucher, was swimming in the outside "Lane 5" where he finished 2nd. BUT no one saw him. When the results were announced, they announced only five placed with no Nyquist in the race. After much discussion and with the swimmers in the race attesting to Gene Nyquist's power, he was rightfully awarded 2nd place to Fred Poucher of Fullerton.

The events and the National Records as of 1949 were as follows:
1. 300-yard Medley Relay: Fullerton (Gass, Reed, Butts), 1940, 3:02.7.
2. 200-yard Freestyle: John Halas (Compton), 1941, 2:17.0.
3. 50-yard Freestyle: Art Blair (Compton), 1940, 23.5.
4. 100-yard Freestyle, Art Blair (Compton), 1940, 52.8.
5. 150-yard Backstroke: Fred Gass (Fullerton), 1940, 1:37.2.
6. 200-yard Breaststroke: Ralph Wright (Stockton, 1939, 2:25.7.
7. 440-yard Freestyle: John Halas (Compton), 1941, 5:01.5.
8. 400-yard Freestyle Relay: Fullerton (Holbrook, Gass, Borns, Butts), 1940, 3:44.8.
9. Springboard Diving – 1 or 3 meter: John McCormick (Glendale).

In 1949 the meet was held at Stockton with Coach Bill Antilla acting as Meet Director and Stockton College the host school. This meet concluded with Fullerton winning with 142 points and Stockton 2nd with 41 points. An elaborate Awards Banquet and Dance was held for the athletes on Saturday evening.

In 1950 the meet was originally scheduled for Coffeeville Kansas Junior College, but it was dropped because of insufficient seating capacity. The meet was then moved to Fullerton, where Fullerton emerged victorious again. In 1951 the meet became only California colleges. It was set for Kansas City Junior College in Kansas City, Missouri; however, they were unable to host. Coach Jim Smith of Fullerton managed the meet which was held at Cal Poly in San Luis Obispo. This first State Meet was won by Fullerton.

The community colleges outside of California did not organize a National Championship until 1968; thus until that time, if you were California State Community College Champion, you were, in effect, National Champion. Fullerton Community College, coached by Jimmy Smith, dominated the championships from 1948 to 1955. From 1956 to 1960-61, Long Beach City College, coached by Monty Nitzkowski, dominated the championships; and from 1961 to 1969, Foothill College, coached by Nort Thornton, dominated the meet.

Here is a listing of the previous champions [and coaches]:
1948 - 1955: Fullerton College, Jimmy Smith
1956 - 1961: Long Beach City College, Monty Nitzkowski
1962 - 1969: Foothill College, Nort Thornton
1970: Los Angeles Valley College, Mike Wiley
1971 - 1972: Pasadena City College, Ron Ballatore
1973: Diablo Valley College, Jack Flanagan
1974: Foothill College, Nort Thornton
1975: Diablo Valley College, Jack Flanagan
1976 - 1978: Pasadena City College, Ron Ballatore
1979 - 1980: Diablo Valley College, Jack Flanagan.

The California Community College aquatic program has produced some fine water polo coaches over the years, with men such as Bob Horn (Fullerton), Pete Cutino (Monterey), and Monty Nitzkowski (Fullerton) achieving national and international recognition as coaches. The California Community Colleges have some of the top swimming coaches in the world — Flip Darr, Ron Ballatore (UCLA), Don Gambrill (now at Alabama), Rick Rowland (now at Pepperdine), and Nort Thornton (now at Cal Berkeley) — all of whom have been either National coaches or Olympic coaches.

Many California community - college swimmers, both men and women, past and present, have represented their countries in Olympic, Pan American and World Games competition. Through their example community college swimming in California has grown to become one of the top areas in the country for the development of swimming talent. The list of swimmers is great and, undoubtedly, we have overlooked some swimmers. For this we apologize, but it in no way takes away from their contribution to community college swimming.

Name	Two-Year College	Team	Year
Bob Jackson	Foothill College	Olympic, USA	1976
Shirley Babashoff	Golden West College	Olympic, USA, World Games	1972-76
Suzie Atwood	Long Beach City College	Olympic, USA	1972
Ann Simmons	Long Beach City College	Olympic, USA	1972
Ralph Hutton	Foothill College	Olympic, Canada	1964-68-72
		Pan American	1967-71
Ingvar Ericsson	Foothill College	Olympic, Sweden	1964-68
Ken Campbell	Foothill College	Olympic, Canada	1972
Jorge Delgado	Pasadena City College	Olympic, Equador	1976
Ken Merten	L.A. Valley College	Olympic, USA	1968
Ray Rivero	West Valley College	Olympic, USA	1968
Peter Feil	Foothill College	Olympic, Sweden	1968
Gary Ilman	Foothill College	Olympic, USA	1964
		Pan American	1963
Monte Nitzkowski	Fullerton Jr. College	Olympic, USA	1952
John Gilchrist	Fullerton Jr. College	Olympic, Canada	1952
Bob Webster	Santa Ana College	Olympic, USA	1956

The quality of athletes now performing ... is the finest to be found anywhere in the nation. Over the past years the team winner of the California Community College State Championship could well have won the University Division II and III titles and placed in Division I competition.

The meet is rich in aquatic tradition of developing athletic potential and consistently producing fine athletes who continue to swim well after they matriculate to four-year colleges.

SWIMMING — MEN

Year	Team	Coach*	Site
1948*	Fullerton	James "Jimmie" Smith	Compton College
1949*	Fullerton	James "Jimmie" Smith	Stockton College
1950*	Fullerton	James "Jimmie" Smith	
1951*	Fullerton	James "Jimmie" Smith	
1952*	Fullerton	James "Jimmie" Smith	
1953*	Fullerton	James "Jimmie" Smith	
1954*	Fullerton	James "Jimmie" Smith	
1955*	Fullerton	James "Jimmie" Smith	
1956*	Long Beach	Monte Nitzkowski	
1957	Long Beach	Monte Nitzkowski	Fullerton
1958*	Long Beach	Monte Nitzkowski	
1959*	Long Beach	Monte Nitzkowski	
1960*	Long Beach	Monte Nitzkowski	
1961*	Long Beach	Monte Nitzkowski	

(continued on next page)

D-13

Swimming (continued)

Year	Team	Coach*	Site
1962	Foothill	Nort Thornton	El Camino College
1963	Foothill	Nort Thornton	Foothill College
1964	Foothill	Nort Thornton	Bakersfield College
1965	Foothill	Nort Thornton	Orange Coast
1966	Foothill	Nort Thornton	Foothill College
1967	Foothill	Nort Thornton	Bakersfield College
1968	Foothill	Nort Thornton	Santa Monica College
1969	Foothill	Nort Thornton	De Anza College
1970	L. A. Valley	Mike Wiley	Orange Coast College
1971	Pasadena	Ron Ballatore	DeAnza College
1972	Pasadena	Ron Ballatore	Golden West College
1973	Diablo Valley	Jack Flanagan	Foothill College
1974*	Foothill	Nort Thornton	
1975	Diablo Valley	Jack Flanagan	Diablo Valley
1976	Pasadena	Ron Ballatore	Cypress College
1977	Pasadena	Ron Ballatore	West Valley College
1978	Pasadena	Ron Ballatore	Hartnell College
1979	Diablo Valley	Jack Flanagan	Diablo Valley
1980**	Diablo Valley	Jack Flanagan	(Southern California)
1981**	Diablo Valley	Jack Flanagan	Diablo Valley
1982	West Valley	Bruce Watson	Cerritos College
1983	West Valley	Bruce Watson	Hartnell College
1984	Fullerton	Craig Brown	

Trent, Ted, Chairman, All-American Selection Teams in Swimming, Aquatics Director and Swimming Coach, Monterey Peninsula College, Monterey, CA, May 9, 1984.

*Flanagan, Jack, Swimming and Water Polo Coach, Diablo Valley College, Pleasant Hills, CA, May 16, 1984.

**See note on following page, SWIMMING – WOMEN.

SWIMMING

WOMEN'S STATE MEET HISTORY – 1978-1980
by Stu Kahn
(submitted by Jack Flanagan)

The first women's state meet was held April 31 and May 1, 1978, at Hartnell College in Salinas, California. Until that time there had been regional championships in northern and southern California, but this event marked the first year that a statewide competition was offered for women.

Since then it has been a NorCal dominated meet. Diablo Valley captured the inaugural title in 1978 and again in 1980, with rival Santa Rosa taking the crown in 1979.

All the winning times at the first meet were automatic records, and many are still the standard for this year's event. There have been many outstanding swimmers during the past three years, but some of the most talented women to compete here have been Jenny Hsu (DBC, 1978), Sandy Ferrin (DeAnza, 1978), and Caroline Hart (Grossmont, 1979-80).

Jenny Hsu, a national record-holder from the Republic of Taiwan, led DVC to its first title by winning and setting state records in the 100 fly, 100 free, 100 IM, 200 IM, 400 Medley relay and 400 free relay. Four of the records she set still stand. Sandy Ferrin

D-14

took three individual titles that first year in the 100, 200, and 500 freestyles. Her 200 (1:55.78) and 500 (5:00.87) times are still records. Most recently, Caroline Hart has been the class of the women by setting five individual records during her two-year career and capturing individual titles. She earned crowns in the 50 and 100 breaststrokes and 100 and 200 individual medleys.

From 1979 on, the meet has been combined with the men, but that initial contest at Hartnell was just a women's affair. Coach of that year's championship team, DVC's Stuart Kahn, recalls: "... The excitement and energy that weekend was unbelievable. Everything that happened was a first; nothing like it had ever been done before. There were 300 to 400 women there and maybe 20 men. It was difficult to concentrate on the contests and not the contestants. As it was, three years later I married our squad's backstroker. I'll always remember women's swimming in California."

Year	Champions	Coach
1978	Diablo Valley College	Stu Kahn
1979	Santa Rosa College	Bob Miyashiro
1980	Diablo Valley College	Jack Flanagan

SWIMMING — WOMEN

Records indicate that the first women's state championship was held in 1978.

Year	Team	Coach*	Site
1978	Diablo Valley	Jack Flanagan	Hartnell College
1979	Santa Rosa	Bob Miyashiro	Diablo Valley College
1980**	Diablo Valley	Jack Flanagan	(Southern California)
1981**	Diablo Valley	Jack Flanagan	Diablo Valley College
1982	Diablo Valley	Jack Flanagan	Cerritos College
1983	Santa Rosa	Bob Miyashiro	Hartnell College
1984	Orange Coast	Don Watson	

Trent, Ted, Chairman, All-American Selection Teams in Swimming, Aquatics Director and Swimming Coach, Monterey Peninsula College, Monterey, CA, May 9, 1984.

*Flanagan, Jack, Swimming and Water Polo Coach, Diablo Valley Collete, Pleasant Hills, CA, May 16, 1984.

**According to Jack Flanagan, no other college in the history of intercollegiate athletics has had both its men's and women's teams win back - to - back championships.

TENNIS — WOMEN

Statewide competition began in 1978-79.

Year	State Champions
1978	L.A. Pierce
1979	L.A. Pierce
1980	Golden West
1981	Pasadena
1982	L.A. Pierce
1983	Cerritos

Carnett, Jim, Sports Information Director, Orange Coast College, Costa Mesa, CA, May 2, 1984.

D-15

TRACK — MEN

Year	Champion	Points	Coach	Runner-up
1951	Los Angeles City	47¼	Wendell Smith	Glendale
1952	Los Angeles City	47 1/9	Wendell Smith	Valley
1953	Los Angeles Valley	55	Jim Slosson	Santa Ana
1954	Compton	55¾	Herschel Smith	Modesto
1955	Santa Ana	55	John Ward	Compton
1956	Compton	81	Herschel Smith	Mt. San Antonio
1957	Mt. San Antonio	68	Hilmer Lodge	L.A. City
1958	San Francisco	70	Lou Vasquez	Bakersfield
1959	Glendale College	56	Ed Tucker	Sequoias
1960	Los Angeles City	73½	Wendell Smith	Bakersfield
1961	Fullerton	54	Jim Bush	Long Beach
1962	Mt. San Antonio	35½	Hilmer Lodge	Long Beach
1963	Long Beach	61	Joe Lanning	Sequoias
1964	Santa Ana	48	John Ward	San Bernardino
1965	Santa Ana	57	John Ward	Fresno
1966	Hancock	41	Jack Cook	Long Beach
1967	Hancock	100	Jack Cook	Fullerton
1968	East Los Angeles	49	Ray Smith	Laney
1969	Merritt	54	Roy Caldwell	Sacramento
1970	Merritt	72	Roy Caldwell	Fresno
1971	Bakersfield	39	Bob Covey	Merritt
1972	Bakersfield	74	Bob Covey	L.A. City
1973*	San Francisco	45	Lou Vasquez	L.A. City
1974*	Fullerton	66	Bob Ward	L.A. Southwest
1975*	Glendale	31	John Tansley	
	San Jose	31	Bert Bonnano	
1976*	San Jose	49	Bert Bonnano	Alameda
1977*	Palomar	48	Doc Martin	Grossmont
1978*	Pasadena	64	Skip Robinson	San Jose
1979*	Long Beach City	87	Ron Allice	San Jose
1980*	Long Beach City	67	Ron Allice	Grossmont
1981*	Long Beach City	59	Ron Allice	Pasadena
1982**	Long Beach City	106	Ron Allice	Pasadena
1983***	Long Beach City		Ron Allice	

*Rilliet, Walter, California Association of Community Colleges, Sacramento, California, 15 March 1983.

**Robinson, Skip, Head Track Coach, Pasadena City College, Pasadena, California, 17 March 1983.

***Allice, Ron, Head Track Coach, Long Beach City College, Long Beach, California, 21 Feb. 1984.

VOLLEYBALL — WOMEN

Until 1977, there were no state championships. Playoffs were held to determine the southern California champions, and the northern California champions.

Year	State Champions
1977	Santa Ana
1978	Orange Coast
1979	Golden West
1980	Orange Coast
1981	El Camino
1982	Orange Coast
1983	El Camino

Hilgendorf, Jane, Women's Volleyball Coach, Orange Coast College, Costa Mesa, CA, April 25, 1984.

D-16

WATER POLO

Year	Team	Coach
1962	Foothill	Nort Thornton
1963	Long Beach	Monte Nitzkowski
1964	Foothill	Nort Thornton
1965	Foothill	Nort Thornton
1966	Cerritos	Pay Tyne
1967	Foothill	Nort Thornton
1968	Orange Coast	Jack Fullerton
1969	Fullerton	Ernie Polte
1970	Long Beach	Monte Nitzkowski
1971	De Anza	Monte Nitzkowski
1972	Orange Coast	
1973*	Fullerton College	
1974*	Fullerton College	
1975*	De Anza College	
1976*	Golden West College	
1977*	De Anza College	
1978*	Golden West College	
1979*	Golden West College	
1980*	Golden West College	
1981*	Golden West College	
1982*	Golden West College	
1983*	No state championship	

*Hermstad, Tom, Men's Water Polo, and Women's Swimming Coach, Golden West College, Huntington Beach, CA, April 24, 1984.

WRESTLING
(Team Champions)

1958	San Bernardino El Camino Mt. San Antonio	1964	El Camino Fresno San Bernardino	1970	Diablo Valley Bakersfield Cerritos
1959	San Bernardino ⎤–Tie Fresno ⎦ El Camino Modesto	1965	El Camino Diablo Valley Foothill	1971	Cerritos Fresno Bakersfield ⎤–Tie Chabot ⎦
1960	San Bernardino Cerritos Fresno	1966	El Camino Bakersfield Cerritos	1972	Chabot El Camino DeAnza
1961	San Bernardino Modesto Fresno	1967	San Bernardino Cerritos Bakersfield	1973	Chabot San Jose Bakersfield
1962	Fresno San Bernardino El Camino	1968	San Bernardino Cerritos Fresno	1974	Santa Ana Bakersfield Chabot
1963	San Bernardino El Camino San Mateo	1969	Bakersfield San Bernardino ⎤–Tie El Camino ⎦	1975	Fresno San Jose Cypress

Wrestling — Team Champions (continued)

1976 El Camino
    Cypress
    Grossmont

1977 El Camino
    Chabot
    Palomar

1978 Palomar
    Chabot
    El Camino

1979 Rio Hondo
    Palomar
    Cerritos

1980 Chabot
    College of Sequoias
    Cypress

1981 College of Sequoias
    Chabot
    Mt. San Antonio

1982 Chabot
    College of Sequoias
    Cerritos

1982 Chabot
    Cypress
    Rio Hondo

1983 Palomar
    Cypress
    College of Sequoias

Team Championships

San Bernardino 6
El Camino 5
Chabot 5
Fresno 3
Bakersfield 1
Cerritos 1
Diablo 1
Palomar 1
Rio Hondo 1
Santa Ana 1
Sequoia 1

WRESTLING
INDIVIDUAL CHAMPIONS

1958-59
115 Con Clark — San Bernardino
123 Frank Rodriguez — Fresno
130 Foster Johns — El Camino
137 Jim Moore — Fresno
147 Hank Lomax — Chaffey
157 Jerry Kirkhart — Fresno
167 Bob Moore* — Fresno
177 John Standich — San Bernardino
191 Ken Roberts — Modesto
HWT Warren Roberts — Modesto

1959-60
115 Dale Deffner — El Camino
123 Cisco Andrade* — Cerritos
130 Bob Combs — San Bernardino
137 Jim Moore — Fresno
147 Chuck Booth — Cerritos
157 Jerry Pamp — San Bernardino
167 John Bell L.A. City
177 Paul Sallinger — Cerritos
191 Allan Elliot — Modesto
HWT Aaron Oliverson — San Bernardino

1960-61
115 Roy Stuckey — Fresno
123 Larry Nehrig — Fresno
130 Eddie Davies — Fresno
137 Sam Huerta — Modesto
147 Dennis O'Connell — Modesto
157 Gary Scrivens — L.A. City
167 Errol Johansen — Fresno
177 Charles Tribble* — San Bernardino
191 Allan Elliot — Modesto
HWT Earl Corley — Bakersfield

1961-62
115 Jess Cuevas — San Mateo
123 Larry Nissen — Orange Coast
130 Aurello Andrade* — Cerritos
137 Mike Ruiz — San Mateo
147 Don Holt — El Camino
157 Bill Lung — Fresno
167 Don Nelson — Fresno
177 Claude Potts — San Bernardino
191 Will Robertson — Bakersfield
HWT Joe Aquino — Fresno

1962-63
115 Mike Remer — Chabot
123 Dave Hollinger — Fullerton
130 Larry Nissen — Orange Coast
137 Mike Ruiz — San Mateo
147 Don Holt — El Camino
157 John Snowden — El Camino
167 Bob Anderson — El Camino
177 Claude Potts* — San Bernardino
191 Charles Tribble — San Bernardino
HWT Walt Wenger — San Mateo

1963-64
115 Mike Remer — Chabot
123 Tom McCann — El Camino
130 George Schaefer — Grossmont
137 Paul Stienel — El Camino
147 George Taylor — San Bernardino
157 Dennis Albright — El Camino
167 Bob Anderson* — El Camino
177 Jim Wilson — Fullerton
191 Bob Braham — Fullerton
HWT Walt Wenger — San Mateo

1964-65
115 Rich Tamble — El Camino
123 Tom McCann — El Camino
130 Norm Dean* — El Camino
137 Tom Hook — Diablo Valley
147 Kent Wyatt — El Camino
157 Lee Ehrler — Modesto
167 Cy Lucas — Foothill
177 Ralph Orr — Chaffey
191 Bob Braham — Foothill
HWT Nick Corollo — El Camino

*Outstanding wrestler

(Individual Champions
continued on next page)

D-18

Wrestling — Individual Champions (continued)

1965-66
115	Roland Garza — Cerritos
123	Bob Hernandez — Sequoias
130	Steve Niles — Sacramento
137	Mike Brown — Bakersfield
145	Kent Wyatt — El Camino
152	Fern Arsenault — Cerritos
160	Jim Hodge — Orange Coast
167	Ben Welch — Bakersfield
177	Wayne Partee — Cerritos
191	Stan Hackett — Foothill
HWT	Nick Corollo* — El Camino

1966-67
115	Terry Hall — San Bernardino
123	Jim Galvan — Rio Hondo
130	Chuck Newman — San Bernardino
137	Steve Warren — El Camino
145	Gordon Levy — Fullerton
152	Curtis Adler — El Camino
160	Bob Hicks — Foothill
167	Pat Farner — Palomar
177	Bill Halsey — Cerritos
191	Stan Hackett* — Foothill
HWT	Jeff Smith — Cerritos

1967-68
118	Vic Gonzales* — Sequoias
123	Terry Hall — San Bernardino
130	Dan Dean — Santa Ana
137	Charles Newman — San Bernardino
145	Ron Kenworthy — Cerritos
152	Lee Torres — Fresno
160	Dan Churchill — San Bernardino
167	Joe Nigos — Bakersfield
177	Dave Reed — L.A. Pierce
191	Paul Weston — Chabot
HWT	Dan Felix — El Camino

1968-69
118	Ed Quendo — Sequoias
126	Ray Conterara — Fresno
134	John Norris — El Camino
137	Bruce Burnett — Bakersfield
145	Ron Kenworthy — Cerritos
152	Joe Smart — Bakersfield
160	Steve Dildine — San Bernardino
167	Joe Nigos — Bakersfield
177	Jim Shields* — Cypress
191	Pete Lutz — San Bernardino
HWT	Dan Felix — El Camino

1969-70
118	Ed Oquendo — San Bernardino
126	Larry Watanabe — Mt. San Antonio
134	Jim Pivera — Allen Hancock
142	Bruce Burnett* — Bakersfield
150	Pat Burris — Santa Ana
158	W. D. Martin — Santa Ana
167	Lancer Smith — Diablo Valley
177	Dave Alexander — Santa Ana
190	Jim Schleuter — Redwoods
HWT	Tim Kopitar — Diablo Valley

1970-71
118	Stacy Cody — Cerritos
126	Bob Arballo — Fresno
134	Harold Jordan — Cerritos
142	Bruce Blanchard — Foothill
150	Bruno Biocca — West Valley
158	Bill Long — Mt. San Antonio
167	Bert Dalton — Chabot
177	Dave Osterkamp* — Solano
190	Ben Ohai — Cerritos
HWT	Dave Campbell — Cerritos

1971-72
118	Ed Lee — Mt. San Antonio
126	George Palmer — Cuesta
134	Paul Strait — Cerritos
142	Charles Freeman — Fresno
150	Rodger Warner — Diablo Valley
158	Cliff Hatch — Diablo Valley
167	Brady Hall Modesto
177	John Needham — Chabot
190	Mal Alexander — San Jose
HWT	Tom Hazel* — El Camino

1972-73
118	Steve Siroy — Chabot
126	Bob Arballo — Fresno
134	Juan Pichardo — Diablo Valley
142	Grant Arnold — Modesto
150	Dennis Bradsley* — Santa Rosa
158	Dan Houchins — Modesto
167	Chris Anaya — Chabot
177	Don Wakefield — Cerritos
190	Rich Calderon — San Jose
HWT	Rudy Huerta — Imperial Valley

1973-74
118	Steve Pivac* — Mt. San Antonio
126	Mike Salcido — Cerritos
134	Frank Gonzales — Santa Ana
142	Jim Wood — Santa Ana
150	Jeff Noon — Orange Coast
158	Brad Johnson — Chabot
167	Florencio Rocha — Bakersfield
177	Rick Hale — Diablo Valley
190	Mike Bull — Bakersfield
HWT	Bob Green — Diablo Valley

1974-75
118	Mike Fleming — Fullerton
126	Butch Escalante — Ventura
134	Frank Gonzales — Santa Ana
142	Rod Balch — Fresno
150	Gordon Cox — El Camino
158	Dan Rutschke — Cypress
167	Don Schuler* — Santa Ana
177	Jeff Ramona — San Jose
190	Warren Nikulus — Palomar
HWT	Chris Wernicke — Rio Hondo

* Outstanding wrestler

(Individual Champions continued on next page)

D-19

Wrestling — Individual Champions (continued)

1975-76
118	Joe Gonzales	East L.A.
126	Butch Escalante*	Ventura
134	Franc Affentranger	Bakersfield
142	Tom Gongora	Fresno
150	Bill Cripps	El Camino
158	Mike Burgher	Palomar
167	Pete Grisafi	Grossmont
177	Craig Foster	Cypress
190	Eric Woolsey	Redwoods
HWT	Dave Shaw	Chabot

1976-77
118	David Cotti	San Jose
126	Ben Martinez	El Camino
134	Tyrone Rose	Diablo Valley
142	Joe Lopez	Bakersfield
150	Bill Cripps*	El Camino
158	Rick Worel	Palomar
167	Tony Brewer	Foothill
177	Steve Draper	Santa Ana
190	Curtis Bledsoe	Chabot
HWT	Ken Harbuck	American River

1977-78
118	Ed Dilbeck	Palomar
126	William Gonzalez	Bakersfield
134	Chris Cain	Palomar
142	Greg Porter*	Moorpark
150	Mario Lomas	Ohlone
158	Pinito Parra	El Camino
167	Bill Choate	Chabot
177	Wayne Christian	Ohlone
190	John Diaz	Fresno
HWT	Doug Severe	Modesto

1978-79
118	Karl Glover	Rio Hondo
126	Jim Hamilton	Palomar
134	Chris Cain	Palomar
142	Greg Porter	Moorpark
150	Perry Shea	Cerritos
158	Dan Mather*	Rio Hondo
167	Jim Thorton	El Camino
177	Mark Hall	Allan Hancock
190	Scott Speck	Cypress
HWT	Ernie Velton	Palomar

1979-80
118	Al Gutierrez	Sequoias
126	Tony Ovalle	Rio Hondo
134	Mike Matsuoka	El Camino
142	Steve Nickell	Bakersfield
150	Bill Weiskopf	Cypress
158	Dan Mather	Rio Hondo
167	Chris Fuertsch	Cerritos
177	Mike Robinson	Chabot
190	Mark Loomis*	Sacramento
HWT	Matt Clark	Cypress

1980-81
118	Al Gutierrez*	Sequoias
126	Keith Jardine	Diablo Valley
134	Victor Lizama	Mt. San Antonio
142	Steve Markey	Chabot
150	Ray Hammond	Rio Hondo
158	Lance Anzivine	Diablo Valley
167	Scott Teuscher	Sacramento
177	Steve Bailey	San Jose
190	Mike Porcelli	San Diego
HWT	Joshua Washington	Sequoias

1981-82
118	Jeff Chedester	Sequoias
126	Don Hopkins	Santa Ana
134	John Vega	Cerritos
142	Dave Wood*	Chabot
150	Chuck Justice	Chabot
158	Don Dodds	West Valley
167	Sylvester Carver	Chabot
177	Phil Dunford	Cerritos
190	Garen McDonald	Chabot
HWT	Tim Reilly	Golden West

1982
118	Steve Martinez	Cypress
126	Ram Bryant	Cypress
134	Dondi Teran*	Rio Hondo
142	Dave Wood	Chabot
150	Mitch Pagano	Rio Hondo
158	Fred Little	Bakersfield
167	Chris Duran	Cerritos
177	Todd Stragier	Mt. San Antonio
190	Tim Boyd	Chabot
HWT	Alonzo West	Chabot

Individual Champions By College

El Camino	30
Cerritos	23
Fresno	20
Chabot	20
San Bernardino	19
Bakersfield	16
Diablo Valley	11
Modesto	11
Santa Ana	10
Palomar	9
Rio Hondo	9
Cypress	8
Foothill	7
Sequoias	6
Mt. San Antonio	6
Fullerton	5
San Jose	5
San Mateo	5
Sacramento	3
Allan Hancock	2
Chaffey	2
Grossmont	2
L.A. City	2
Moorpark	2
Ohlone	2
Redwoods	2
Ventura	2
American River, Cuesta, East L.A., Imperial Valley, L.A. Pierce, Santa Rosa, Solano, San Diego, and Golden West	each 1

*Outstanding wrestler

WRESTLING
ACADEMIC ALL-AMERICANS
1973 - 1983

Year	Wrestler	School	Coach
1973-74	Tom Collinson	Diablo Valley	Bob Ericson
	Mario Rodriquez	Diablo Valley	Bob Ericson
	Michael Strasser	Modesto	Dean Sensenbaugh
	Ed Saules	Fullerton	Oran Breeland
	Ross Synder	L.A. Pierce	Irwin Goldbloom
	Jerry Strangis	San Jose	Sam Huerta
	Robert Swarner	American River	Bob Towers
1974-75	Jim Ainley	Cabrillo	Don Montgomery
	Michael Harr	DeAnza	Tuck Hulsey
	Jeff Ramona	San Jose	Sam Huerta
	David Rodriguez	West Valley	Jim Root
	Christopher Wernicke	Rio Hondo	Ken Bos
1975-76	Randy Alford	Modesto	Dean Sensenbaugh
	Kevin Hejnal	West Valley	Jim Root
	Joe O'Brien	Modesto	Dean Sensenbaugh
1976-77	Mario Betti	Sacramento	Bill Hickey
	Hal Dillashaw	San Joaquin Delta	Larry Jones
	Duane Fidel	Sacramento	Bill Hickey
	Lance Marcus	Moorpark	John Keever
	Gary Murphy	Moorpark	John Keever
	Dave Pacheco	Sacramento	Bill Hickey
	John Parreira	Modesto	Dean Sensenbaugh
1977-78	Mike Fredenberg	West Valley	Jim Root
	Mark Harvey	DeAnza	Tuck Hulsey
	Neal McClellen	Lassen	Dave Foster
	Thomas O'Brien	Modesto	Dean Sensenbaugh
	Craig Schoene	Skyline	Lee Allen
	Mike Wilson	Cuesta	Gary Meissner
1978-79	George Crowder	San Jose	Sam Huerta
	James Dolan	Chaffey	Paul Yaeger
	Ronald Freeman	Chabot	Zack Papacristos
	Glenn Kuhn	Modesto	Dean Sensenbaugh
	Ralph Parks	Foothill	Dan Boyett
	Robert Sole	Chaffey	Paul Yaeger
1979-80	Charles Chaney	Allan Hancock	Wayne King
	Mark Nush	Diablo Valley	Bob Ericson
	John White	Santa Ana	Frank Adleman
1980-81	Lawrence Bettencourt	Sierra	John Horrillo
	Rex Davis	Moorpark	John Keever
	Henry Gong	West Valley	Jim Root
	Steve Short	Ventura	Rick Arnold
	John Taylor	American River	Bob Towers
	Allen Thacker	Sierra	John Horrillo
1981-82	Tom Blanco	Modesto	Dean Sensenbaugh
	Tracy Cline	San Joaquin Delta	Larry Jones
	Jordon Cunning	Diablo Valley	Bob Ericson
	Don Dodds	West Valley	Jim Root
	Joe Guerrero	San Joaquin Delta	Larry Jones
	Russ Jones	Sierra	John Horrillo
	Larry Renwick	San Joaquin Delta	Larry Jones
	Dan Soden	San Joaquin Delta	Larry Jones
1982	Mike Andrews	Diablo Valley	Bob Ericson
	Craig Edling	Modesto	Dean Sensenbaugh
	Steve Glore	Golden West	Dale Deffner
	John McCarthy	Moorpark	John Keever
	Matt Vanni	West Valley	Jim Root

(continued on next page)

D-21

(continued)

Year	Wrestler	School	Coach
1983	Ron Atwell	Modesto	Dean Sensenbaugh
	Don Belletto	Modesto	Dean Sensenbaugh
	Tom Brekke	Moorpark	John Keever
	Tim Cuykendall	San Joaquin Delta	Larry Jones
	Jerry Ford	Diablo Valley	Bob Ericson
	John Gonsalves	Modesto	Dean Sensenbaugh
	Vince Gonsalves	Diablo Valley	Bob Ericson
	Gerald Johnson	Sierra	John Horrillo
	Todd Meulman	West Valley	Jim Root
	Jeff Plecg	West Valley	Jim Root
	Troy Ulmer	San Joaquin Delta	Larry Jones
	Daniel Williams	Sacramento	Dave Pacheco
	David Williams	Sacramento	Dave Pacheco

CALIFORNIA COMMUNITY COLLEGE WRESTLING ACHIEVEMENTS
N.C.A.A., A.A.U., U.S.W.F. All-Americas
Olympic, Pan American, International Team Members

Compiled by the
California Community College
Wrestling Coaches Association
Bruce Pfutzenreuter
Jim Root

N.C.A.A. DIVISION I ALL-AMERICANS

Year	Name	Community College	Four-Year Institution	Place
1963	Rahim Javamard	Fullerton	UCLA	4th
1964	Bob Janko	San Bernardino	UCLA	4th
1965	Charles Tribble	San Bernardino	Arizona State	3rd
1966	Mike Remer	Chabot	Cal Poly	4th
	Rich Whittington	Modesto	UCLA	4th
1967	Nick Carollo	El Camino	Adams State	2nd
	Lee Ehrler	Modesto	UCLA	3rd
1968	Nick Carollo	El Camino	Adams State	1st
	Jeff Smith	Cerritos	Michigan State	3rd
	Kent Wyatt	El Camino	Cal Poly	3rd
1969	Ken Bos	Cerritos	Cal Poly	4th
	Bob Buehler	Foothill	San Francisco State	3rd
	Terry Hall	San Bernardino	Cal Poly	3rd
	Jeff Smith	Cerritos	Michigan State	2nd
	Ben Welch	Bakersfield	U.S. Naval Academy	5th
1970	(no information)			
1971	Jim Shields	Cypress	Oklahoma State	3rd
	Lee Torres	Fresno	Cal Poly	3rd
1972	(no information)			
1973	Tom Hazell	El Camino	Oklahoma State	6th
	Dan Kida	Grossmont	San Jose State	5th
	Ben Ohai	Cerritos	Brigham Young	3rd

(continued on next page)

N.C.A.A. Div. I All-Americans (continued)

Year	Name	Community College	Four-Year Institution	Place
1974	Rich Calderon	San Jose City	Univ. of Washington	4th
	Tom Hazell	El Camino	Oklahoma State	6th
	Dan Kida	Grossmont	San Jose State	4th
	Ben Ohai	Cerritos	Brigham Young	2nd
	Rodger Warner	Diablo Valley	Cal Poly	6th
1975	Greg Gibson	Shasta	Univ. of Oregon	2nd
	Cliff Hatch	Diablo Valley	Cal Poly	2nd
	Rodger Warner	Diablo Valley	Cal Poly	3rd
1976	Greg Gibson	Shasta	Univ. of Oregon	2nd
1977	Franc Affentranger	Bakersfield	Cal State, Bakersfield	3rd
	Florencio Rocha	Bakersfield	Cal State, Bakersfield	4th
1978	Franc Affentranger	Bakersfield	Cal State, Bakersfield	3rd
	Don Shuler	Santa Ana	Arizona State	4th
1979	Joe Gonzales	East Los Angeles	Cal State, Bakersfield	2nd
1980	Bill Cripps	El Camino	Arizona State	3rd
	Joe Gonzales	East Los Angeles	Cal State, Bakersfield	1st
	Mike Haschak	Cabrillo	UCLA	4th
1981	Perry Shea	Cerritos	Cal State, Bakersfield	3rd
1982	Perry Shea	Cerritos	Cal State, Bakersfield	2nd
1983	Sylvester Carver	Chabot	Fresno State	5th
	Al Gutierrez	College of Sequoias	Cal Poly	8th
1984	Sylvester Carver	Chabot	Fresno State	3rd

N.C.A.A. DIVISION II ALL-AMERICANS

Year	Name	Community College	Four-Year Institution	Place
1963	Bill Fife	College of San Mateo	Cal Poly	2nd
	Roy Stuckey	Fresno City	Fresno State	3rd
	Jim Teem	Modesto	Cal Poly	4th
1964	Sam Cereceres	San Bernardino	Cal Poly	2nd
	Jim Teem	Modesto	Cal Poly	2nd
1965	Sam Cereceres	San Bernardino	Cal Poly	2nd
	Lennis Cowell	Diablo Valley	Cal Poly	3rd
	Steve Johansen	Fresno City	Fresno State	1st
	Mike Remer	Chabot	Cal Poly	4th
	Jim Teem	Modesto	Cal Poly	2nd
1966	Lennis Cowell	Diablo Valley	Cal Poly	4th
	Dennis Downing	Cerritos	Cal Poly	1st
	Steve Johansen	Fresno City	Fresno State	2nd
	Mike Remer	Chabot	Cal Poly	1st
1967	Kent Wyatt	El Camino	Cal Poly	6th
1968	Ken Bos	Cerritos	Cal Poly	3rd
	Ashlee Sherman	Merritt	San Francisco State	6th
	Kent Wyatt	El Camino	Cal Poly	1st
1969	Ken Bos	Cerritos	Cal Poly	1st
	Bob Buehler	Foothill	San Francisco State	2nd
	Art Chavez	Bakersfield	San Francisco State	5th
	Terry Hall	San Bernardino	Cal Poly	1st
	Steve Johnson	Cerritos	Cal Poly	3rd
1970	Doug Dressler	College of Marin	Chico State	4th
	Terry Hall	San Bernardino	Cal Poly	1st
	John Norris	El Camino	Chico State	3rd
	Lee Torres	Fresno City	Cal Poly	2nd

(continued on next page)

N.C.A.A. Div. II All-Americans (continued)

Year	Name	Community College	Four-Year Institution	Place
1971	Dave Alexander	Santa Ana	Northern Colorado	3rd
	Pat Farner	Palomar	Cal Poly	2nd
	Tim Kopitar	Diablo Valley	Cal Poly	1st
	Gary Maiolfi	Cerritos	Cal Poly	2nd
	Lee Torres	Fresno City	Cal Poly	3rd
1972	Dave Alexander	Santa Ana	Northern Colorado	2nd
	Ray Hernandez	College of Sequoias	San Francisco State	2nd
	Greg Maestas	San Jose City	Colorado Western	6th
	Jim Schlueter	College of Redwoods	Northern Colorado	3rd
	Doug Stone	Bakersfield	Humboldt State	3rd
1973	Frank Barnhart	Palomar	Cal Poly	3rd
	Bert Dalton	Chabot	Northern Colorado	3rd
	Greg Maestas	San Jose City	Colorado Western	2nd
	Doug Stone	Bakersfield	Humboldt State	2nd
1974	Grant Arnold	Modesto	Cal Poly	2nd
	Cliff Hatch	Diablo Valley	Cal Poly	1st
	Bill Kalivas	L. A. Pierce	Cal State, Bakersfield	5th
	Dick Molina	Bakersfield	Cal State, Bakersfield	4th
	Ruben Ramos	Diablo Valley	Chico State	4th
	Steve Tirapelle	American River	Humboldt State	5th
	Bill Van Worth	Bakersfield	Humboldt State	2nd
	Rodger Warner	Diablo Valley	Cal Poly	2nd
1975	Mike Bull	Bakersfield	Cal State, Bakersfield	4th
	Alex Gonzales	Solano	San Francisco State	1st
	Dan Houtchens	Modesto	Cal State, Bakersfield	6th
	Bill Kalivas	L. A. Pierce	Cal State, Bakersfield	5th
	Dick Molina	Bakersfield	Cal State, Bakersfield	3rd
1976	Mike Bull	Bakersfield	Cal State, Bakersfield	1st
	Alex Gonzales	Solano	San Francisco State	2nd
	Dan Houtchens	Modesto	Cal State, Bakersfield	1st
	Dick Molina	Bakersfield	Cal State, Bakersfield	3rd
	Bob Rinehart	Moorpark	Chico State	6th
	Florencio Rocha	Bakersfield	Cal State, Bakersfield	3rd
	Bill Van Worth	Bakersfield	Cal State, Bakersfield	1st
1977	Franc Affentranger	Bakersfield	Cal State, Bakersfield	1st
	Mike Anderson	Bakersfield	Cal State, Bakersfield	2nd
	Rod Balch	Fresno City	Cal State, Bakersfield	2nd
	Mike Bull	Bakersfield	Cal State, Bakersfield	2nd
	David Nelson	Solano	San Francisco State	5th
	Bob Rinehart	Moorpark	Chico State	3rd
	Florencio Rocha	Bakersfield	Cal State, Bakersfield	1st
	Ray Yocum	Antelope Valley	Cal State, Bakersfield	3rd
1978	Franc Affentranger	Bakersfield	Cal State, Bakersfield	2nd
	Rod Balch	Fresno City	Cal State, Bakersfield	5th
	Steve Draper	Santa Ana	Cal State, Bakersfield	1st
	Tom Gongora	Fresno City	Cal State, Bakersfield	4th
	Frank Gonzales	Santa Ana	Univ. of Nebraska, Omaha	1st
	Mike Johnson	Bakersfield	Cal State, Bakersfield	4th
	Dean Reichenberg	American River	Sacramento State	4th
	Andy Wilson	American River	Sacramento State	6th
1979	Steve Draper	Santa Ana	Cal State, Bakersfield	4th
	Kevin Dugan	Chabot	Cal State, Bakersfield	3rd
	Tom Gongora	Fresno City	Cal State, Bakersfield	1st
	Joe Gonzales	East Los Angeles	Cal State, Bakersfield	1st
	Joe Lopez	Bakersfield	Cal State, Bakersfield	6th
	Marty Maciel	Cerritos	Cal State, Bakersfield	4th

(continued on next page)

N.C.A.A. Div. II All-Americans (continued)

Year	Name	Community College	Four-Year Institution	Place
1980	Kevin Dugan	Chabot	Cal State, Bakersfield	2nd
	Andy Franco	San Joaquin Delta	Sacramento State	4th
	Joe Gonzales	East Los Angeles	Cal State, Bakersfield	1st
	Marty Maciel	Cerritos	Cal State, Bakersfield	3rd
	Brad Morton	El Camino	Chico State	4th
	Lee Noble	West Valley	Cal State, Bakersfield	5th
1981	Mark Loomis	Sacramento City	Cal State, Bakersfield	3rd
	Craig Schone	Skyline	Cal State, Bakersfield	3rd
	Perry Shea	Cerritos	Cal State, Bakersfield	1st
	Rich Sykes	Diablo Valley	Humboldt State	2nd
1982	Charlie Cheney	Allen Hancock	Cal State, Bakersfield	2nd
	Roger Herrera	Chabot	Cal State, Bakersfield	4th
	Bill Kropog	College of Sequoias	Chico State	6th
	Mark Loomis	Sacramento City	Cal State, Bakersfield	1st
	Garen McDonald	Chabot	Cal State, Bakersfield	5th
	Steve Nickell	Bakersfield	Cal State, Bakersfield	2nd
	Perry Shea	Cerritos	Cal State, Bakersfield	1st
	Scott Teuscher	Sacramento City	Cal State, Bakersfield	6th
1983	Roger Herrera	Chabot	Cal State, Bakersfield	4th
	Ross Jones	Sierra	Sacramento State	4th
	Mark Loomis	Sacramento City	Cal State, Bakersfield	3rd
	Jose Martinez	Mt. San Antonio	U. C. Davis	4th
1984	Jorge Acosta	Cerritos	Chico State	8th
	Don Dodds	West Valley	Humboldt State	4th
	Ross Jones	Sierra	Sacramento State	5th
	Eric Lesley	Santa Rosa	Humboldt State	6th
	Steve Markey	Chabot	Cal State, Bakersfield	1st
	Jose Martinez	Mt. San Antonio	U. C. Davis	4th

N.C.A.A. DIVISION III ALL-AMERICANS

Year	Name	Community College	Four-Year Institution	Place
1975	Dwight Miller	Foothill	Humboldt State	4th
1976	Mike Harr	DeAnza	Humboldt State	6th
	Mike Karges	Palomar	Humboldt State	6th
1977	Mike Harr	DeAnza	Humboldt State	4th
	Mike Karges	Palomar	Humboldt State	2nd
	Jim Luster	College of Canyons	Humboldt State	2nd
	Eric Woolsey	College of Redwoods	Humboldt State	1st
1978	Wayne Nickerson	Palomar	Humboldt State	2nd
	Tom Pender	San Jose City	Humboldt State	4th
	Eric Woolsey	College of Redwoods	Humboldt State	1st
1979	Mike Fredenburg	West Valley	Humboldt State	2nd
	Jon Sylvia	College of Redwoods	Humboldt State	2nd
1980	Mike Fredenburg	West Valley	Humboldt State	1st
	Mike Malkovich	Diablo Valley	Humboldt State	5th
	Rich Sykes	Diablo Valley	Humboldt State	5th
1981	Vertis Elmore	Lassen	Cal State, Stanislaus	2nd

U.S.W.F./U.S.A. WRESTLING ALL-AMERICANS

Year	Name	Community College	University/Club	Place
1970	Jeff Smith	Cerritos	Cerritos	1st-G
	Dick Vaughan	San Jose City	Unattached	3rd-F
1971	Nick Carollo	El Camino	Athletes in Action	1st-F
	Tim Kopitar	Diablo Valley	Cal Poly	1st-G

(continued on next page)

W.S.W.F./U.S.A. Wrestling All-Americans (continued)

Year	Name	Community College	University/ Club	Place
1972	Nick Carollo	El Camino	Athletes in Action	2nd-F
	Buck Deadrich	Chabot	Olympic Club	1st-F
	Mike Henry	Cypress	Unattached	6th-F
	Jeff Smith	Cerritos	Southland W.C.	1st-F
1973	Nick Carollo	El Camino	Athletes in Action	2nd-F
	Buck Deadrich	Chabot	Olympic Club	1st-F
1974	Bob Anderson	El Camino	Athletes in Action	1st-F
	Nick Carollo	El Camino	Athletes in Action	5th-F
	Tom Hazell	El Camino	Oklahoma State	3rd-F
1975	Buck Deadrich	Chabot	Olympic Club	5th-F
1976	(no information)			
1977	Rich Calderon	San Jose City	Spartan W.C.	6th-F
	Greg Gibson	Shasta	Oregon W.C.	1st-F
	Brady Hall	Modesto	Bakersfield Express	2nd-F
	Dan Lewis	Orange Coast	Southern Calif. W.C.	2nd-F
	Carlos Rodriguez	San Jose City	U. C. Berkeley	3rd-F
	Don Shuler	Santa Ana	Bakersfield Express	1st-F
1978	(no information)			
1979	(no information)			
1980	Aaron Thomas	Santa Ana	Liberty Baptist	4th-F
1981	(no information)			
1982	(no information)			
1983	Greg Gibson	Shasta	U.S. Marines	1st-F
	Joe Gonzales	East Los Angeles	Sunkist Kids	1st-F
	Dan Lewis	Orange Coast	Sunkist Kids	4th-F
1984	Don Shuler	Santa Ana	Athletes in Action	2nd-F

A.A.U. ALL-AMERICANS

Year	Name	Community College	University/ Club	Place
1960	Jim Root	Oakland City	Cal Poly	3rd-F
1961	(no information)			
1962	(no information)			
1963	Charles Tribble	San Bernardino	San Bernardino	4th-F
1964	Jerry Pamp	San Bernardino	Olympic Club	3rd-G
	Charles Tribble	San Bernardino	San Bernardino	2nd-F
1965	Nick Carollo	El Camino	El Camino	2nd-G
1966	Nick Carollo	El Camino	El Camino	3rd-F
	Jerry Pamp	San Bernardino	Olympic Club	3rd-F
1967	Buck Deadrich	Chabot	Mayor Daley	3rd-G
	Lee Ehrler	Modesto	U.C.L.A.	4th-F
	Tim Kopitar	Diablo Valley	Bay Area	4th-G
	Charles Tribble	San Bernardino	Phoenix	2nd-F
1968	Art Chavez	Bakersfield	Olympic Club	1st-F
	Buck Deadrich	Chabot	Olympic Club	3rd-F
	Lee Ehrler	Modesto	Olympic Club	4th-F
1968	Buck Deadrich	Chabot	Mayor Daley	1st-F
	Lee Ehrler	Modesto	Olympic Club	3rd-G
	Jeff Smith	Cerritos	Michigan	3rd-G
	Dick Vaughan	San Jose City	Olympic Club	3rd-F
1970	Tim Kopitar	Diablo Valley	Bay Area	3rd-F
1971	Nick Carollo	El Camino	Athletes in Action	1st-F
	Buck Deadrich	Chabot	Olympic Club	4th-F
	Tim Kopitar	Diablo Valley	Cal Poly	1st-G
	Doug Parsen	West Valley	Olympic Club	6th-F

(continued on next page)

A.A.U. All-Americans (continued)

Year	Name	Community College	University/Club	Place
1972	Buck Deadrich	Chabot	Olympic Club	1st-F
	Dick Vaughan	San Jose City	S.F. Pen. Grapplers	2nd-G
1973	Ashlee Sherman	Merritt	Unattached	5th-G
1974	(no information)			
1975	Brady Hall	Modesto	U.C.L.A.	5th-F
	Terry Hall	San Bernardino	Armed Forces	4th-F
	Tom Hazell	El Camino	Cowboy	3rd-F
1976	Rich Calderon	San Jose City	S.F. Pen. Grapplers	2nd-G
	Buck Deadrich	Chabot	Olympic Club	4th-G
	Brady Hall	Modesto	U.C.L.A.	1st-F
	Tom Hazell	El Camino	Cowboy	5th-F
	Bob McNeil	Diablo Valley	S.F. Pen. Grapplers	3rd-G
	Joe Nigos	Bakersfield	S.F. Pen. Grapplers	3rd-G
1977	Rich Calderson	San Jose City	S.F. Pen. Grapplers	4th-G
	Cliff Gosse	Chabot	S.F. Pen. Grapplers	6th-G
	Brady Hall	Modesto	Bakersfield Express	5th-F
	Tom Hazell	El Camino	Bakersfield Express	2nd-F
	Dan Kida	Grossmont	S.F. Pen. Grapplers	3rd-G
	Brendt Noon	Foothill	U. S. Army	2nd-G
	Craig Schone	Skyline	S.F. Pen. Grapplers	2nd-G
	Don Shuler	Santa Ana	Bakersfield Express	4th-F
1978	Greg Gibson	Shasta	Bakersfield Express	3rd-F
	Joe Gonzales	East Los Angeles	Sunkist Kids	6th-F
	Don Shuler	Santa Ana	Sunkist Kids	3rd-F
1979	Brady Hall	Modesto	Santa Monica	2nd-F
	Dan Kida	Grossmont	S.F. Pen. Grapplers	3rd-G
	Dan Lewis	Orange Coast	Fullerton	1st-F
	Doug Severe	Modesto	Unattached	4th-G
1980	Greg Gibson	Shasta	U.S. Marines	2nd-G
	Joe Gonzales	East Los Angeles	Sunkist Kids	1st-F
	Dan Lewis	Orange Coast	Fullerton	2nd-F
1981	Greg Gibson	Shasta	U.S. Marines	1st-F
	Joe Gonzales	East Los Angeles	Sunkist Kids	1st-F
	Dan Lewis	Orange Coast	Sunkist Kids	3rd-F
	Don Shuler	Santa Ana	Athletes in Action	6th-F
1982	Greg Gibson	Shasta	U.S. Marines	1st-F
	Karl Glover	Rio Hondo	Sunkist Kids	5th-F
	Al Gutierrez	College of Sequoias	Sunkist Kids	4th-F
	Dan Lewis	Orange Coast	Sunkist Kids	5th-F
	Josh Washington	College of Sequoias	Sunkist Kids	6th-F

OLYMPIC TEAM MEMBERS

Year	Name	Community College	University/Club	Place
1964	Charles Tribble	San Bernardino	Arizona State	FreSt
1968	Rich Tamble	El Camino	Adams State	G-R
	Bob Anderson	El Camino	Adams State	GR A1
	Terry Hall	San Bernardino	Cal Poly	GR A1
	Gab Ruz	Santa Ana	U. S. International	Mexico
	Lancer Smith	Diablo Valley	Idaho State	GR A1
1972	Buck Deadrich	Chabot	Olympic Club	G-R
1976	Rich Calderon	San Jose City	Univ. of Washington	GR A1
	Julio Gutierrez	Skyline	S.F. Pen. Grapplers	Mexico
	Bob McNeil	Diablo Valley	Univ. of California	GR A1
1980	Greg Gibson	Shasta	U.S. Marines	GR A1

D-27

PAN AMERICAN TEAM MEMBERS

Year	Name	Community College	University/Club	Place
1971	Bob Anderson	El Camino	Adams State	2nd-F
	Nick Carollo	El Camino	Adams State	1st-F
	Jeff Smith	Cerritos	Michigan State	1st-F
1977	Rich Calderon	San Jose City	Univ. of Washington	2nd-G
	Brady Hall	Modesto	U.C.L.A.	1st-F
	Tom Hazell	El Camino	Oklahoma State	1st-F
	Dan Kida	Grossmont	San Jose State	2nd-G
	Craig Schone	Skyline	Cal State, Bakersfield	1st-G
	Steve Siroy	Chabot	U.C.L.A.	1st-S
1979	Dan Lewis	Orange Coast	Fullerton W.C.	1st-F
1983	Greg Gibson	Shasta	U.S. Marines	1st-F
	Steve Siroy	Chabot	U.C.L.A.	1st-S

WORLD CHAMPIONSHIPS TEAM MEMBERS

Year	Name	Community College	University/Club	Place
1969	Buck Deadrich	Chabot	Southern Illinois	World
	Art Chavez	Bakersfield	San Francisco State	World
	Rocky Rasley	Bakersfield	Oregon State	World
1971	Buck Deadrich	Chabot	Southern Illinois	World
1981	Greg Gibson	Shasta	U.S. Marines	1nd-F
	Joe Gonzales	East Los Angeles	Cal State, Bakersfield	5th-F
	Dan Lewis	Orange Coast	Fullerton W.C.	World
1982	Greg Gibson	Shasta	U.S. Marines	3rd-F
	Joe Gonzales	East Los Angeles	Cal State, Bakersfield	3rd-F
1983	Greg Gibson	Shasta	U.S. Marines	World
	Joe Gonzales	East Los Angeles	Cal State, Bakersfield	World